Jaggernath, Awadh N., Author
From Explorations to Enlightenment / /

Issued in print and electronic formats.

ISBN: 781670440396
ASIN: B08274Q635

Imprint: Independently published
1. Jaggernath, Awadh N, -- Adult Years.
2. Jaggernath, Awadh N., --Family.
3. Trinidad and Tobago--Biography.
4. Trinidadian Canadians-- Biography.

No part of this book may be reproduced or transmitted in any form, by any means, electronic or mechanical, including photocopying and recording, information storage and retrieval systems, without permission in writing from the publisher, except by a reviewer who may quote brief passage in a review.

Copyright © 2019 Awadh N. Jaggernath

FROM EXPLORATIONS TO ENLIGHTENMENT

BY AWADH N. JAGGERNATH.

To: Jumnar, a wonderful soul. May God continue to bless + guide you throughout all the days of your life.

Love, smile + happiness always.

27 January 2020

This January, a wonderful Start.
May God continue to bless &
guide you always, as He
keeps close to...
And smile, happiness always.

27 January 2020

DEDICATED:

To my loving & supportive wife, Ambica Rani,

My beloved daughter, Anushma Nirmala

My beloved son, Ravesh Mitra

"Life is a series of natural and spontaneous changes. Don't resist them; that only creates sorrow. Let reality be reality. Let things flow naturally forward in whatever way they like."
- Lao Tzu.

"Because one believes in oneself, one doesn't have to convince others. Because one is content with oneself, one doesn't need others' approval. Because one accepts oneself, the whole world accepts him or her."
- Lao Tzu.

"Until one is committed, (there is hesitancy or the chance to draw back), there will always be ineffectiveness. Concerning all acts of initiative and creation, there is only one elementary truth, the ignorance of which kills countless ideas and splendid plans, that the moment one definitely commits oneself, then, Providence moves too. All sorts of things occur to help one that would never otherwise occurred. A whole Stream of events issue from the decision, raising in one's favour all manner of unforeseen incidents and meetings and material assistance, which no man could have dreamed it would have come his way. Whatever you can do or dream you can. Begin it. Boldness has genius, magic and power in it. Begin it now."
- Johann Wolfgang Von Goethe.

PART ONE
SERENDIPITOUS EVENTS
(1961-1966)

Being unemployed and uncertain about my future, I asked myself, "Ask not what other people can do for me, but ask instead what I can do for myself." This is the personal exhortation and determination that earned me a teaching position at Montrose Vedic School in Chaguanas. At the end of the first term of my teaching contract in 1961, I received an unexpected registered letter at the place of my employment. Being extremely excited and curious, I was tempted to open it immediately. I carefully opened it to reveal its message. The letter was elegantly written in purple-coloured ink. Having read it carefully several times, I was still unable to interpret the specific meaning of the narrative. Mrs. Sultan, Zena, wife of one of the most respected and wealthy accountants of the village had invited me to lunch with her at her home. The date and time were clearly mentioned, but no specific reason was given for the luncheon. All I had to do was to RSVP as soon as possible by phoning her at the number written at the bottom of the letter. I felt extremely privileged and honoured to be invited by Zena. After seriously contemplating possible reasons for the invitation, I decided to handle the matter most responsibly and discreetly. I promptly phoned her. On the scheduled day, I took a taxi to Mrs. Sultan's residence. On my arrival, I went directly to the front door and rang the doorbell. Mrs. Sultan (Zena) opened the door, welcomed me to her home and warmly embraced me. Having closed the door, she led me to the living room. There was no one else at home. Easy listening music was playing in the background when she offered me a non-alcoholic drink. Both of us sat down in the living room, and while drinking our refreshing drinks shared some pleasantries. A few minutes later, Zena informed me that her sister, Sheena and her family would be joining us. Her sister's husband, Eli and her two children would also be lunching with us. With a smile, I told Zena that it definitely would be a special privilege to meet her family members and share lunch with them. She only smiled. Within ten minutes, the doorbell rang. Zena answered the door. She then introduced Sheena, Eli and their son and daughter to me. It was extremely difficult for me to clearly distinguish the physical features between Zena and her sister. On noticing my confused look, Zena quickly informed me that her sister and she were identical twins. She added that her sister and she were married to two identical twin brothers. I was only able to distinguish the sisters from the colours of their clothes. A few minutes later, Zena's husband, Zahir and their son and daughter returned from the book store. Fortunately the four teenage children had distinct physical features. After we had all introduced ourselves, Zena and Sheena served tasty Trinidadian hors d'oeuvres and non-alcoholic beverages. While we were enjoying the delicious snacks, I learned that the two boys had successfully completed their first year of secondary education at Queens Royal College and the two girls had successfully completed their second year at St. Josephs Convent. I asked them about their course of studies, their teachers, class mates, their social and their extra-curricular activities. They were greatly interested in their academic studies and sporting activities. Thirty minutes later, we were served a vegetarian lunch which I enjoyed. After lunch, we all returned to the living room and sat down. I was still wondering about the purpose of the invitation. Mr. Zahir Sultan broke the ice by addressing me directly. "Awadh, I am sure you would like to know our reason for inviting you to lunch with my family and my brother and his family." With a smile I shook my head in agreement. "Awadh, two weeks ago my family had dinner with the catechist who informed us that he had had many discussions with you about education and sports." "Yes. That is very correct. The catechist is an extremely influential, intelligent and compassionate person. I greatly appreciate the work he does for the villagers." "We have invited you because the catechist had spoken favourably of you. Also, he has recommended that we invite you to inform our children on how your special study groups functioned, and how you had earned a leading role in extra-curricular sporting activities while studying at St. Philips and St. James College. We would like you to tell our children about the challenges and experiences you had while you were working your way to a leadership role in college sports." "I feel very privileged and honoured to discuss these aspects of my education with these wonderful teenagers. But before I begin to recall my academic and extra-curricular activities, I would like a glass of water. Please and thank you." Water was served to all.

I was about to explain to them how the 'Eclectican Group' and the 'Intelligentia Group' were formed and how they functioned when the children interjected and collectively said, "the catechist has taught us about the two study groups and we have already formed our own groups at our schools."

I applauded them on their achievements. After I had a sip of water, I told them the following story about the interesting cricket experiences I had while I was attending college.

Towards the end of my first year at college in 1954, I was informed by one of my classmates about the annual College Athletic Day Festival. After obtaining more details about the festival, I decided to attend it. All classes were cancelled on the afternoon of the athletic festival. All students and their teacher had to wear their blazers during these ceremonies and celebrations. Following the directions given by our teacher, we sat on red metal chairs which were previously placed on the well-groomed lawns adjacent to the Catholic Church. At the front of the seated students was a wooden platform on which were rows of green chairs. At the front of the platform were beautifully stained tables on which were placed trophies, plaques, medals and other awards which dazzled in the sunshine. Lush fruit trees draped with bunches of luscious fruits, flanked the platform. Then the dignitaries, wearing their alma mater graduation gowns, slowly ascended the platform of honour. What a colorful and inspiring spectacle! The applause was punctuated by loud whistles and howls. The principal of the college, a Scot, asked everyone to stand for the national anthem. After the singing of "God save the Queen" we sat as quietly and respectfully as possible and listened to a most inspiring speech from our principal, Mr. John Burns. He advised the students to modify old habits, eliminate poisonous relationships, avoid any dishonourable vocation and navigate towards new horizons that are exciting, beneficial, challenging and fulfilling. He emphasised that each student revise his intentions and become more holistic and synergistic, and not only be interested in academics but also in extra-curricular activities while studying at the College of St Phillip and St. James. The parish priest, Fr. Murphy, then blessed the congregation with a special prayer. The Master of Ceremonies made a few comical remarks and introduced the coach of the different athletic activity. After announcing the name of the award-winning student, either a trophy or an award was presented to him by his coach. Each recipient was greeted with cheers and applauses from the assembly. Although I did not know most of the winners I applauded all of them. After witnessing the great admiration, respect, and camaraderie the champion athletes received, I decided that I would like to be receiving an award on the stage of champions before I graduate from college.

After the ceremonies, as I worked my way through the milling students, I congratulated as many of the award-winning students. Sport reporters from both the local and the Guardian newspapers were interviewing the top athletes and photographers were busy clicking away at them. Many students in my class did receive award. However, I was not able to meet and congratulate all of them.

Before the start of classes the following morning, I met and congratulated the other classmates who had won awards. There were boys from table tennis, soccer, lawn tennis, cricket and track and field. Being extremely inspired, I resolved that I would like to get on the college cricket team. Fortunately, two champion cricketers were in my class. I could talk with them about joining the college cricket team. My friend, Faiz, had won the trophy for the best batting average on the championship cricket team. But, since the cricket season would only resume the next academic year, I decided not to ask him until a later date. Yet, my burning desire and daunting ambition to get my foot into the cricket team goaded me to approach Faiz. He was fair-skinned, tall, handsome and muscular teenager. Academically he was an average student but was never shy to ask for help from other student. I tutored him whenever he had experienced difficulties with his geometry problems. He became very popular with both teachers and students after his recognition on the Athletic Day. In spite of his fame and recognition he still maintained our regular amiable relationship.

After congratulating the other athletic heroes in my class I proceeded to offer Faiz my warmest and sincerest congratulations. He was very pleased and after I shook his hand he hugged me. I decided that I should not dilute his hour of triumph with my selfish obsession. I patiently waited for a couple of weeks before approaching him again. Then the moment had arrived for me to tell him about my intentions. At the conclusion of French class, I met him at the water fountain. After we had our drinks, I told him that I would like to talk to him about a very important issue. He gave me a very confused look and asked whether it was very urgent. I told him that it was important for me. He became very interested and wanted to learn about my problem. I told Faiz that we would discuss it at lunch time.

We met at lunch with other students who were seated on the same picnic table and who were also having lunch. Apparently these students were not aware of the accomplishments of Faiz. I proudly informed them about Faiz's athletic achievements. They were extremely excited to meet one of the celebrities of the college. The juniors expressed their belated congratulations and shook his hand.

Faiz then asked me about my question. As I did not want to directly seek his advice on how to get on the college cricket team, I decided to ask him about his personal batting prowess.

"Faiz, how did you become such a classy and fantastic batsman?"

With a big grin he responded, "Awadh. I am from a family of cricketers. My father, my brothers, my uncles and my cousins are all excellent cricketers. They all play first and second division cricket in the San Juan cricket league. Fortunately, I am privileged to practice with them regularly. They teach me all the basic skills for successful batting, bowling and fielding. What about your cricket background?"

"Faiz I am not as lucky as you. No one in my family is involved with sports. I am the only one who is actively involved in any sporting activity."

"What sporting activity?"

"I play football, table tennis and cricket."

"You play cricket!"

"Yes. I have played cricket for the Montrose Cricket Club for the past two years."

"You got to be joking. You play cricket!"

Before I could tell him my cricket story the bell rang to end the lunch period.

As we walked back to our classroom, Faiz wanted to know whether I had any other questions. I told him that I had one more question which I would ask during lunch period the next day. He smiled. After hearing Faiz's cricket experience with his families, I wondered whether he was the appropriate person to ask for help.

By chance, the catechist was in our shop that evening. I sought his advice about my special interest to join the college cricket team. First he wanted my reasons for my decision. I related my experience at the Athletic Awards Day and my burning desire to be recognized on the platform of champions. He was very pleased. He had no objections. I told him about my plans to get on the college cricket team, and what steps I had taken. I told him that one of the best cricketers for the college cricket team was in my mathematics class and I was wondering whether I should or should not ask him to recommend me the cricket coach. The catechist advised me to seek his help because his recommendations would have great weight. After hearing his words of wisdom, I met with Faiz at lunch. We sat at the same table with some students from the previous day. I had a few bites into my curried cabbage and aloo roti, and a sip of my milk when Faiz asked.

"Awadh what it is you want to ask me?"

"Faiz, with all due respect to you, I would like you to help me to get on the college cricket team next academic year."

In an instant he became very surprised and he almost choked on the morsel that he was chewing. He looked at me and continued chewing his food. After taking a few mouthfuls of his Pepsi, and after putting down the bottle, he remained silent for about a minute. Then he shouted, "Are you crazy? Do you really think that I would recommend you to my coach? I have to protect and maintain my earned reputation. I would not recommend an unknown like you." He paused and continued to eat his lunch. The students who were seated with us were stunned at his un-sports-man-like response. They looked at each other and then looked at me.

Faiz, after seeing the surprised face all around continued his tirade. "I can definitely recommend you as a volunteer to take out the equipment for cricket practices; to assist in marking the boundaries; and bringing drinks for the players during the games. I can surely do that for you but for actually playing college cricket, that will never happen."

Fiaz got up and left me at the table with the other students. As he left the table other students remarked, "Was that the champion cricketer?" I remained silently humiliated. After the students had left the table, I remained seated and gazed at the mountains in the Northern Range. When the bell rang to signal the end of lunch, I returned to my class. As I sat at my desk, my mind was completely absent from the geography lesson. Instead I became very mindful of the teachings of my grandfathers on resolving issues with toxic people. I decided to pretend that it never happened. I did not mention it to anyone. No one asked me about my embarrassing lunch–time experience with Faiz. As the days and weeks slowly elapsed, the hurt to my pride was slowly replaced by interest in other enriching and enlightening activities with the Eclecticans.

At the beginning of the next academic year and a few weeks before the commencement of the college cricket season, I made an appointment to meet with Mr. Emmanuel, the cricket coach. The coach was from Barbados. He had studied in England. It was a distinct privilege to meet such a congenial, encouraging person. He was well spoken and very analytical in his questioning. He inquired about my cricket experiences. He specifically wanted to know what special talents and skills I would be bringing to strengthen and improve the performance of the college cricket team. After my lengthy interview, he invited me to join the practice sessions scheduled to begin in two weeks. I was extremely elated and filled with energy and enthusiasm to know that I sought and obtained the opportunity to join the cricket team on my own efforts.

On the first evening of practice, fully dressed in my cricket outfit, I approached the coach who introduced me to the players who were present. There were last year's champion players, new players and volunteers. But Faiz was not present. The coach then had a private talk with me. He reiterated the information that I had given to him during our interview. According to his record, I was an opening batsman and a right-arm medium-paced off-break bowler. I confirmed his details. When most of the cricket players were present, the coach formally welcomed all the players and outlined the practice procedures. During the actual cricket practice each player would be allowed to bat, bowl and would be given fielding positions in accordance with the instructions of the coach. Also, the coach reminded the players that they were responsible for the care and safe storage of all the college cricket equipment. Furthermore, all cricketers must know and apply the rules and regulations of cricket during all cricket matches.

The practice started. I was so proud and happy to be practising with some of the best cricket players in our college. Faiz was late. He went directly to the coach and spoke with him. At first Faiz did not recognize me. But as the practice progressed, and as soon as he recognized me, he shouted, "Awadh! What are you doing on this cricket field? You are no cricketer. Get off the field." As soon as the coach heard his comment, he immediately summoned Faiz. After a brief talk, Faiz returned to his fielding position and did not harass me anymore.

The coached instructed me to get ready to bat. As I got to the batting crease, the wicket-keeper quietly said to me, "Awadh, the coach has instructed the two fastest bowlers on the team to bowl against you. I hope you could bat fast bowling! Good luck. I must go further back for these erratic and hostile bowlers." As I took my guard, I started to speak to myself. Focus on the delivery of every ball and play each according to its merit. I can do it. There is nothing to fear. I just have to be myself and put on the best batting performance.

With this self-affirmation, I soon discovered that the fast bowling attack was very similar to the ones that I was accustomed to in the other cricket league. I made my shots comfortably and I did not lose my wicket. When my batting ended, the wicket-keeper ran to me and said, "I think you can make the team."

After that my confidence and enthusiasm bloomed. I resumed my fielding position and patiently waited for my bowling spell. There was a medium-paced bowler and a slow left-arm spin bowler bowling in tandem to Faiz. He was a beautiful stroke-maker. It was a delight to watch him strike each delivery effortlessly to various parts of the field. Unexpectedly, the coach threw the ball to me to bowl to Faiz. My bowler partner did not say anything to me as he was about to bowl to Faiz. I rubbed the ball on my pants to give it a little shine. Here was my chance to prove that I deserved to be on the cricket team. My bowling action was right-arm off–spin over the wicket with a slow to medium pace. Faiz struck my first three deliveries over the boundaries. With a loud laugh he shouted, "Awadh I told you that you are no cricketer. Keep on bowling that garbage and I will hit every one for six." He did hit two of my last three deliveries for four runs. I had to redeem myself as quickly as possible. I told the coach that I would like to change my bowling action from over the wicket to around the wicket. He agreed and he told Faiz about the change in my bowling action. He struck my very first delivery for a six. Then he started his commentary, "Awadh. It doesn't matter where you bowl from, every delivery will be across the boundaries."

The coach did not intervene. My very next delivery knocked down all his stumps. He was having difficulty playing my signature 'Rat Ball'. I also bowled his stumps with my last delivery. At that instant, the coach replaced Faiz with another batsman. After the practice, the coach asked me to show him what I was doing with the ball to make it suddenly change direction, and shoot towards the wicket like a fast running rat. I told him that I really did not know. But ever since elementary school, I had that inexplicable mysterious ball that was very effective especially against left-hand batsmen. He smiled and said that I had a secret weapon which would be extremely useful during matches.

At the conclusion of the third practice session the coach declared the team for our first game. My name was second on the batting order. I felt very encouraged, knowing that I have earned a place on the college cricket team. My goal to walk on the platform of champions with a trophy appeared realistic and achievable. Our coach was always diligent, intelligent, dedicated and spent much time teaching us the psychology of winning. He believed that each player should always be respectful, disciplined, tolerant, resilient and enthusiastic on and off the playing field.

After two years the college cricket team was unable to win the championship. And I did not win any award. But the concept of 'mental toughness' as emphasized by my cricket coach over the past two years motivated me to keep on trying. His lessons on 'winning strategies and tactics' were invaluable not only in cricket but also in facing my daily life challenges.

On the first cricket practice at the commencement of my third year, I was eager to meet and greet the new recruits and my former team mates. When the coach, Mr. Emmanuel, saw the large group of cricketers, he quickly called everyone to a meeting. Each player introduced himself by stating his name, his cricket talents, skills and experiences. After hearing their stories, I strongly believed that we had the best blend of talents, skills and experiences that would help our team win the championship at the end of the season. It was a team with championship potential. I felt very confident that my dream would be fulfilled at the end of this cricket season.

Mr. Emmanuel was a life coach in disguise. He diligently conducted and executed all the necessary exercises and drills before each practice session. During the practice he always emphasised the correct techniques for batting, bowling, fielding and running between wickets. Above all, he was always courteous when interacting with the players either collectively or individually.

At the conclusion of the fourth practice and the debriefing session my coach announced the names of the players for our first official match. I was more than pleased to be included in one of the most powerfully balanced cricket sides to represent the college. Then without any fanfare, Mr. Emmanuel announced to the players that he had appointed me captain of the team. Most of the players applauded his decision. I was overwhelmed. The coach then invited me to address the players. Humbly I accepted the captaincy and thanked him for believing in my ability and capability to lead the college cricket team for the season. Then I promised my team mates that as captain that I would execute my responsibilities diligently and honestly. And that with their full cooperation both off and on the field and with each putting his best foot forward during all games, we shall bring home the cup this year. In spite of the fact that a few players were not happy with the coach's appointment of the captain, I was not perturbed.

Two days later Mr. Emmanuel met me in the hallway and told me to think about a potential vice-captain. At the same time he informed me that Faiz has decided that he would not be playing cricket for the college anymore. At the end of the day a vice-captain was chosen and was informed about his leadership role. He proved to be invaluable in all the decision-making on the field-of-play. During each competitive match, each player was fully aware of the strategies and tactics that were in effect whether we were fielding or batting. Whenever I was planning to modify the modus operandi, I would always consult the vice-captain, and the player directly involved in the pre-emptive changes.

Mid-way through the season, the coach and all the players got together in a debriefing session to analyze and discuss the performance of the team. The statistics revealed that our team was tied with the San Fernando team for first place. Although the San Fernando team had defeated us in every game we played them, we were in first place with them because St. Benedict College had always defeated them. But we had always defeated St. Benedict. That was the reason for the tied results. As our real nemesis was the San Fernando team we concentrated all our energies and talents on defeating them in the last game of the regular cricket season on their home ground. According to the latest statistics we remained two points ahead of San Fernando as result of our last victory against St. Benedict. We had to defeat San Fernando in this last game to be declared champions.

Unfortunately they outplayed us again and won handsomely. A final game was scheduled for the next weekend on our playing field.

We had five school days to prepare for this final game. After consulting Mr. Emmanuel, the vice-captain and I arranged to meet the captain and coach of the St. Benedict College team. After our consultation with them we decided to implement a few of their recommendations during our final battle against our arch-rivals.

On the day of the final match, the weather forecast suggested sunshine with intermittent showers in the afternoon. Our opponent arrived with a large entourage of supporters. We had the villagers and most of our college populous in support. The San Fernando players were extremely positive and behaved as though they had already won the game. With the mutual consent of the captains, the game started earlier than the regular scheduled time because of the weather forecast. The two umpires who were from neutral colleges asked for the list of the players who would be actively participating in the game. The vice-captain and I scanned the list and we noticed that there were three new players on their team. Our players surreptitiously found out the roles of the three new substitutions. Two new fast bowlers and a batsman were substituted. The umpires looked at their watches and informed the captains to go to the pitch and toss. They won the toss and decided to field instead of bat. I was very pleased. Having learnt that they had new fast bowlers, I decided to change the batting order. Their opening bowlers were very erratic and fast but the new batting order was able to overcome the fiery attack. I demoted myself to the middle batting order, so that when the fast bowlers return to complete their bowling spells, I would be able to at least provide some resistance and protection for the less talented batsmen on my team. At the end of the regulation forty overs we had accumulated the highest score for the season. We believed that we had a formidable total. During interval between the innings, and with confidence flowing through my team mates, Mr.

Emmanuel re-iterated the importance of 'mental toughness' and reminded us that on the playing field each player must be mindful of what specific action he must execute whenever the ball is in his hands. Every play is crucial for achieving victory. And always remember that cricket is a gentleman's game. We all acknowledged his final advice and took the field of play as soon as the umpires went to the pitch.

The new ball was given to our regular fast bowlers who requested no change in our normal opening fielding configuration. Their opening batsmen attacked our bowling and the runs came quickly. When I realised that they were handling our fast attack comfortably, I brought in my spin bowlers to replace them. Within a few deliveries, they dismissed the two opening batsmen. The new batsmen were more comfortable with the spin bowling. I replaced one of the spin bowlers with a seam bowler and we had more success. Then their batting started to crumble. After the fall of their sixth wicket the opposing captain came in to bat. He and the wicket-keeper struggled against our bowling. The weather suddenly change and it started to drizzle. I did not want to stop playing. The opposing captain appealed to the presiding umpire to stop the game because he could not see the ball clearly through the light drizzle. The umpire disallowed his appeal. On the next delivery, there was a very loud appeal for LBW (leg-before-wicket) against the captain. The umpire without any hesitation gave him out. He was furious as we ran for shelter in our school laboratories.

During the rain-delay of play, the vice-captain and I checked with scorers about the status of the match. We were informed that the San Fernando team needed forty three runs to win with two wickets (batsmen) left to bat. Having that statistics our team could smell victory. We hoped and prayed that the showers would end quickly so that our fast bowlers could demolish their bottom batting order.

Unfortunately, the unexpected happened. While we were anxiously waiting for the rain to end, the players clearly heard the captain of the opposing team, in the presence of the two official umpires, coaches, and all the players, loudly shout that he was cheated by the presiding umpire and that he was not out. As his accusatory claim reached my players and my ears, we looked at one another in utter astonishment. Although the umpires heard his claim, they looked at each other and smiled. The captain repeated his claim a few more times. When he did not get any response from either his players or anyone else, he approached me and angrily shouted, "Skipper! This is how you expect to win the championship by cheating?" I did not respond. He retreated to his team extremely annoyed. I called my players together and consulted with them. In the huddle, I sought their opinion on the accusation of the captain. There were various answers. Then I reminded them that we had to maintain and protect the integrity and the respectable reputation, not only of our team, but also of our college. It was imperative that I involved my coach on the decision that I was about to make. I told them that I strongly believed that we had the firepower and prowess to win the match. Each player had to display their best performance on the playing field. Having gained their confidence, I told my players of my decision. They were all surprised. But they had pledged their full cooperation.

As soon as the two umpires declared that play was about to be resumed, I informed them of my decision. They looked at me rather perplexed but made no comment. I expressed my sincerest apologises for over-ruling the presiding umpire's decision.

As the opposing captain was still complaining, I told him to go back and continue batting. He was surprised at my unexpected decision. I then encouraged my players unto the playing pitch. I immediately brought in my fast bowlers into the attack. Within the first two overs the captain was clean-bowled without adding to his score. My players applauded him as he walked back slowly to the pavilion with his head bent. It did not take very long to dismiss the last two batsmen. We proudly won the match and the championship.

After the match had ended and all the players had returned to the pavilion, the opposing captain came to me and apologised for his un-sportsman like behaviour. I graciously accepted his apology which I relayed to all my players. There was no champagne spraying or celebratory drinks. We shook hands with our opponents and gave them a gentleman's farewell. Since the match was played on a Saturday, I had to wait until Monday to hear the rumours that were flowing through the academic corridors of our college. The Principal congratulated me on the victory of the championship and praised the daring manner on my handling of the complaint of the opposing captain. The school newspaper had a full report on the match. Also the local newspapers reported the details about the victory. The villagers and our supporters were congratulating our players whenever and wherever they met them.

After three years, with dedicated practices and excellent coaching, I had earned the honour and privilege to walk on the platform of the athletic champions. I savoured the importance of the celebrations. In the following year, at the beginning of the cricket season, I was informed that my cricket coach, Mr. Emmanuel had taken a leave of absence. Having achieved my quest that took three years to be realized, I decided to play cricket in the Grey-Nicholls league.

After I had told the above stories to both families, there were many questions and answers. But the experience left me very exhilarated and privileged to be given an opportunity to enlighten these young teenagers about my pathways of success in academics and sports. Although there were always challenges, success could be achieved with patience and excellent coaching.

Approximately one week after my luncheon experience with the Sultan families, the catechist invited me to have dinner with him. With a strong hug and a broad smile, he welcomed me to his home. Before dinner, he told me that he was most delighted with the favourable reports he had received from the

Sultan families. He said that the Sultans' children, after they had heard about the challenges that I had to overcome before it was possible for me to walk on the athletic stage of honour, have decided to seek leadership roles in their chosen athletic activity. In turn, I thanked the catechist for recommending me to the Sultans.

After dinner, the catechist told me that I should seriously consider improving my academic qualifications so that I would be able to teach at a higher academic level. I remained silent for a few minutes. I then thanked him for his wise advice. I added that my intention was to use my present teaching job as a platform from which I would be able to elevate myself to higher educational achievements. I thanked him for an intellectually stimulating evening.

I seriously considered the catechist's advice during the remainder of my teaching contract. After the end of my first year of teaching at the elementary school, I realized that I was not enjoying the experience as much as I initially thought I would. The novelty and privilege of being an educator for eight year old students no longer stimulated me. Although, I had already gained the trust and support of the headmaster and the camaraderie and support of the other teachers, I needed to be engaged with a career that was more intellectually challenging and exciting. I expressed my concerns to Mr.Ganesh, the headmaster. He advised me to continue teaching. He assured me that after a few years, I would gradually learn to appreciate the value of teaching the young students. But if I should continue to be disenchanted then he would not be disappointed in my decision to pursue another career. On his advice I continued teaching for one more year. But, after some critical self-reflection I did not feel that teaching at that level, would bring me the fulfillment, the success and the lifestyle that I wanted to experience and enjoy. I needed a second opinion from someone outside the elementary education system. I had to be genuinely honest with my feelings. I kept asking myself. To whom could I turn? I patiently I searched for a human lighthouse to show me the way out of my rut.

❖ ❖ ❖

Then, as though someone was reading my mind, the unexpected happened. It was the beginning of the 1962 cricket season. And I was shopping for a cricket bat at the Sports and Games store in Port of Spain. While the attendant was showing me the different bats, I had noticed a well-dressed, middle-aged gentleman smiling and looking at me. After I had selected the bat and paid for it, the well-dressed gentleman inquired,

"Do you play cricket for CENTRAL INDIANS?"

"YES! Why are you asking?"

"I played against your team last year. I was with the Comet Cricket team. Your team defeated us. But I remembered you distinctly. You are the comedian. Can you wait for a moment?"

"Ok."

After he had finished his business we met at the doorway. We shook hands and introduced ourselves. I told him my name was Awadh. He told me his was Noble.

"Are you in a hurry Awadh?"

"No"

"Would you like to join me for lunch at the Emerald restaurant?"

Hesitating, I accepted his generous offer. At lunch, Noble recalled the details of that cricket match and that broke the ice for a more inspiring discussion. I inquired about his professional appearance. He informed me that he was employed by the Ministry of Education as a life-mentor and career counselor at The Donaldson Polytechnic Institute. He told me about his qualifications and his responsibilities as a career counselor. After listening carefully and hearing about how pleased he was with his accomplishments with various students, I realized that I had serendipitously discovered the person who could help me decide on a new career path. Before expressing my personal and professional issues to him, I thought it would be prudent to inform him about my background, and my present career dilemma. He listened to my problem and then he smiled. After a few minutes, he responded, "Awadh, if you would like my professional advice, I would be most willing to provide it. Here is my business card. Contact me if and only if you think that I could be of beneficial service to you."

I took his business card. I thanked him for his offer. We shook hands, and bid each other farewell. As I sat in the taxi on my way home, I seriously considered Noble's offer.

After two weeks, I telephoned Noble. We decided to meet at his well-lit and tastefully furnished office. Noble was elated to see me. First he asked me to complete a questionnaire. After I had completed the questionnaire, he evaluated it. Then with a smile he said, "Awadh! I think I can help you." He explained his programme, course outline and the timelines. I then inquired about the fee structure. I found it to be quite reasonable, and decided to proceed.

The formal lessons began the following week. After his regular classes, we met twice a week in one of his classrooms. He commenced the lessons with the following preface. "Awadh, it is evident that you are employing me to assist you to be successful in life, but I must confess that there is no guarantee that after my instructions and guidance you would achieve the goals that you have set for yourself. For you to be successful you must apply the conceptual tools that I will prescribe. No one can help you if you don't help yourself, even if you have outside help. Success starts with you and you must have the burning desire and passion to achieve excellence in your life. Whenever the opportunity arises, snatch it with both hands and take full advantage of it."

In another lecture, Noble said that on the odyssey of my life, in order to be successful I would have to appreciate the support of my parents, family and genuine friends. However, I should always be on the alert. Sometimes, they could be my most cruel and bitter critics, but I could not allow anyone to prevent me from achieving my paramount goals. I should never hide in the shadows of my fears, and must push myself out from under the dome of my comfort zone. I listened attentively and heard the voices of my grandparents.

After a pause for a drink of water, Noble continued with his words of wisdom. "Nothing succeeds like success. If you were successful in one discipline then it would be more likely that you would be successful in many others. Success breeds further success. Success just doesn't happen; you have to make it happen. Success is about living a personally meaningful life that makes you feel joyful, confident, positive, helpful, and filled with inner peace." Noble was delivering the sermon that I had needed to hear. He continued to enlighten and delight me with his recommendations. He advised that I would have to take calculated risks throughout my life's journey. And I should always imagine wonderful technicolour dreams. Noble emphasized that the most regrettable thing would be my fear to venture into anything novel and different from the norm. I should have no fear of failure and should always be willing to start over.

Although the concept of life-long learning was not coined as yet, Noble strongly emphasized the great importance of continuing to gather, learn and employ new knowledge throughout my life. He said that anyone who had stopped learning was no longer alive. But anyone who practised life-long learning would be forever young. I should commit myself to continue learning for the rest of my life because my enriched mind would be the most valuable asset that I would ever own. He also emphasized the power of my mind, and that my mind could either make me or break me.

During one of the sessions, I interjected and asked Noble to explain the role of luck in determining my success in my life's ventures and adventures. Before responding he wanted to know the reasoning behind the question. I told him that my colleagues were saying that I had to be lucky to be successful in life. And people who are unsuccessful at the game of life are just unlucky. Noble smiled, and responded that there was an old proverb that stated that "fortune favours the brave." After reciting the above proverb, he excused himself and left the lecture room.

After a few minutes he returned with a note book. He then professed that I would create my own luck through my own efforts and hard work. Good luck follows those who have the courage, wisdom and fortitude to overcome all obstacles on the path to their goal. Luck means things happen by chance rather than through your dedicated and determined efforts. Then, he opened his note book and read from it slowly. Slowly, he emphasized the following words of wisdom.

Napoleon Bonaparte said, "Ability is of little account without opportunity."

Thomas Jefferson said that whenever the opportunity to do something great presents itself, seize it. Because Jefferson believed that the harder he worked the more luck he got. Noble emphasized that I had to visualize success, taste it and smell it, and always think like a winner and become a winner. He concluded the session by saying that I should always maintain my sense of humour, keep my creativity alive and permit my intuition and gut feeling to guide me.

He started his next session with a map of the world. I did not know what to expect. But when he started to call out the names of the various countries that he had visited and places that he has planned to visit, I became very enthralled. He said, "You might be wondering why I am telling you about my private interests. But I assure you that this would be the most enriching segment of all of our discussions." I was more that delighted to listen and learn the secrets of his travels. Noble outlined in detail the advantages of travelling locally and internationally. He said that the child within him always wanted to have fun and excitement, with a burning desire to escape from the normal daily life. He often looked at the little colourful postcards that he had brought back from his travels from around the world. These postcards always brought him joyful and exciting memories.

At the end of the sessions, I thanked Noble for accepting me into his program and dedicating his private time, energy and expertise to help me progress. As I was about to leave he read Horace's, famous lines from his first book of lectors.

"Dimidium facti qui coepit habet; Sapere aude, incipe!"

The translation meant: *"He who begins is half-done. Dare to know, dare to begin."* In simple English: *"Dare to be wise."*

In 1963, after two enriching and exciting years of teaching at the Montrose Vedic School, I submitted my resignation to Mr. Ganesh, the headmaster. In my letter of resignation, I stated my reasons. Mr. Ganesh accepted my resignation with mixed emotions. But at my farewell party, he wished me continued success in all my endeavours. I continued with my correspondence courses from Wolsey Hall, and enrolled at Donaldson Polytechnic Institute for the other courses that I needed for admission to university.

A few weeks before I commenced my courses at the Donaldson Polytechnic, I received an unexpected invitation to join a cricket tour to St. Vincent as a player on the team. I told my Ajah (paternal grandfather), about it. When Ajah agreed to give me the necessary funds, I gratefully accepted the invitation. I was then invited to meet the players and to be informed about the tour. At the meeting I was warmly welcomed by the Inspector of schools, who was the co-ordinator of the cricket tour. Much to my delight, there were a few players whom I had known, and I had played against in many cricket matches over the years. They recognized me and immediately I felt comfortable as we exchanged pleasantries and shared exciting memories. Five matches were scheduled to be played against teams from various towns and villages in St. Vincent. Four days were free either to go sightseeing on the island or to take boat tours to islands in the Grenadines. We were provided with a detailed itinerary. Also accommodation arrangements were in place. I was extremely excited to travel overseas for the first time. Impatiently, I waited for the departure day to St.Vincent.

There were many friends and family members at the Piarco Airport to bid us good luck with the cricket tour. On our arrival in Kingstown, St. Vincent, we were cordially met and greeted by representatives from the various teams that had invited us for the friendly games. After all the handshakes and chatter, we were taken to the guest house reserved for the players. Having checked into our rooms, we attended the official reception party. We expressed our sincere gratitude for their generous hospitality.

Upon the departure of our hosts and hostesses the manager of the team, Mr. Khan, called a snap meeting. He told us to get dressed as quickly as possible for a cricket practice in preparation for our first match the following day at 10.00.A.M. We practised all our skills - batting, bowling, catching, throwing and running between the wickets. During the cool–down period, another meeting was held in the lobby of the guest house about the protocol for each of the matches. The executive had decided that there would be a different captain and vice-captain for each match; the team would be selected on the evening before each match based on each player's performance in his last game. However, each player was guaranteed to play at least three games. When the team for the first game was announced, I become joyful when I heard my name.

The first friendly match was played in Canaan Village. The setting for the game was in one of the valleys between rugged mountains. Both the valley and the surrounding mountains were covered with a wide range of verdant trees. The panoramic scenery was breath-taking. The atmosphere and temperature in the valley was pleasant and most comfortable for playing cricket. The setting reminded me of sceneries from the movie –The Sound of Music. Our opponents had a powerful batting line-up, and they made lots of runs. We managed, however, to snatch victory from the jaws of defeat due to their fielding errors. When the match ended, in spite of their defeat, they were hospitable and generous hosts and hostesses. We had a lavish dinner. The menus had curried goat meat, baked fish, locally grown ground provisions, breadfruit, roti filled with split-peas, salad, rice and locally baked desserts. There was a limited selection of alcoholic drinks, but a wide range of home-made soft-drinks, peanut punch, mauby, sour-soup drinks and lemonade. After the post-game celebrations we returned to our guest house. There was no cricket scheduled for the next day.

The following morning, every member of our touring team was at breakfast. The breakfast was a typical tropical colonial style menu: salted cod fish stewed with tomatoes and a mixture of local herbs; smoked herring roasted with lots of onions, garlic and hot peppers; fried bake; fried plantains; boiled and fried green bananas, yams, cassava and lots of ripened avocados. Also there was a variety of fresh tropical fruits which included papaya, mangoes and pineapples which were harvested in the countryside. The fusion of the aromas of boiling locally-grown coffee and cocoa filled the air in the breakfast area. In addition, there were fresh flowers on all the tables and around the room which greatly amplified the ambience of the breakfast setting. I also noticed that we were not the only guests at the property. There were couples, solos, and either two women or two men sitting and socializing together. After a very filling breakfast-feast, I joined the group of players who had decided to visit the capital city, Kingstown for the day. We visited the Market Place chatted with the vendors and inquired about the names and how to consume a few fruits that were exotic to us. Then, we visited the first class cricket ground where international matches were played. This was followed by a visit to the fortress on the hill in which a woman was held as a prisoner. On our way to lunch we visited the shops on the main street and a few on the side streets. I did not discover any merchandise that captured my interest. From my cursory observations, our country,

Trinidad and our sister island, Tobago, were more developed economically, socially and commercially. After a brief chat, we then had lunch at one of the restaurants which served only the local cuisine prepared by the locals with locally grown crops. The food was as delicious and as tasty as the food that we had in Caanan Village. After lunch, most of the players claimed that they felt exhausted and decided to return to the guest house. Two other players and I decided to visit the botanic garden. We were disappointed with the sad state of the flora. The flora needed lots of water and the maintenance of the garden appeared mediocre. However, we interacted with some tourists visiting from England, Europe and the United States. They were in agreement with our assessment and evaluation of the garden. Also, those who had visited Trinidad spoke very favourably about our botanic gardens in Port-of-Spain.

After we had left the gardens, we interacted with the locals on the streets. The vendors and shoppers, being unaware of the living conditions in other countries, were happy and pleased with their standard of living and their life styles. After a taste of the local flavors of the culture, dialects, culinary delights and tourist-oriented attractions, we returned to our guest house. I was exhausted. But as soon as I entered the lobby, I noticed a piece of paper pinned to the bulletin board. It was the list with the names of the players, the captain and vice-captain for the match on the following day. My endorphins kicked in instantly when I was saw my name on the team for the second match.

The second match was played in Kingstown in brilliant sunshine and with a cool sea breeze blowing across the field. There were many spectators and supporters for our opponents. These cricket players were all from the police force. Most of them were tall and well-built. There were two players on the opposing team who had played cricket for the island's cricket team. Just to intimidate me, I was made aware by one of the opponent's player that the fast bowler was the fastest bowler on the island's team. I recalled looking at his long run-up to the wicket before delivering the ball. After some self-talk, I focused on where he was pitching the ball and I mindfully played each delivery on its merit. I was pleased with my contribution to the team's score. We lost the game narrowly due to the superior performance of the policemen in all aspects of the game. There was a post-match party at the policemen club which we all attended. Then the unexpected occurred. A middle-aged gentleman of East Indian descent approached me as I was leaving the party. He introduced himself to me as Dr. Kordi. He told me that he was one of the spectators at the game and that he had played cricket for one of the teams we were scheduled to play against in the country side. He informed me that he greatly enjoyed and was delighted how I comfortably played the fast bowlers. After thanking him for his kind words, he asked me what my plans were for my cricket-free day. I told him that I didn't have any. Then he showed me his credentials and offered to take me to the guest house. I told him that I would have to speak to my coach before accepting his offer. Having no objection from my coach, I accepted his offer. On the way to his home, he invited me, whenever I had a free day, to join him, his wife and sister-in-law on their catamaran for a picnic on Bequia Island. Dr. Kordi seemed to be a genuine person. After reassuring myself of his credibility, I accepted to spend the following day with him on the trip to Bequia. He informed me about the time he would fetch me, and told me to dress casually. His family would take care of all the necessary details. After thanking him again, I went to the owner of the guest house who was at the front desk. I told her about my encounter with Dr. Kordi and his offer. She told me that I was very fortunate to be a guest of Dr. Kordi. He was one of the most respected and loved doctors on the island. I then privately informed my manager about my plans for the following day. He said, "How do you manage to meet these people?" I smiled, and requested that the given information be kept under his hat. After receiving his promise, I excused myself. I went to bed after my shower. But I could not sleep.

◆ ◆ ◆

At breakfast the following morning, I made no mention of my plans for the day to anyone. At the appointed time, Dr. Kordi arrived and we left for a day of unknown events. It was the first time that I would be a passenger on a catamaran. Its structure and shape fascinated me. Dr. Kordi had a crew that looked after the catamaran. He introduced me to his beautiful and charming wife, Sandra and his sister-in-law, Tamara. Tamara was also beautiful and charming. They were waiting on the docks for the return of Dr. Kordi. Later he introduced me to the crew who were already on board awaiting my arrival. They were all extremely welcoming and friendly. As soon as we set sail, Tamara served us refreshments. As the catamaran sailed toward Bequia, I had a lively and interesting conversation with Sandra. She wanted to know about my ancestors, early childhood, schooling, career and future plans, my belief system and how I got on the cricket team that was touring St. Vincent. Meanwhile, Tamara was reading the Holy Bible while she sipped her drink. Dr. Kordi was occupied with the crew, talking about the maintenance of the catamaran. After sailing for some time in brilliant sunshine, on the rather smooth and colourful tropical sea with the assistance of a cool breeze, the picturesque and beautiful tropical island of Bequia gradually got closer. Dr. Kordi inquired whether I had swimming trunks. I responded that I did not know that we were going to swim. He smiled and said that he had brought a pair of swim trunks for me. After the Catamaran was securely anchored, we all got into the warm clear tropical water and waded to the sandy beach. The crew brought food and drinks to the shore and placed it on a picnic table beneath the overlapping shades of a cluster of trees. We all changed into our swim outfits in the nearby bushes, and slowly entered the warm water which was exhilarating, refreshing and soothing. While we were in the water we drank refreshing rum punch and

Scotch with coconut water. After some time in the warm water, the cool breeze and a comfortable tidal flow, we retreated to the shades of the trees. After lunch, and after a rest, Tamara took out her Bible and continued to read. Dr. Kordi, noticing my loneliness, interrupted Tamara from her reading and kindly requested her to take me for a walk around the coastal sandy beach and the seashore bordering the public properties. She was happy to show me around the paradise island.

As we slowly walked, she informed me that there were several estates and mansions that were owned by wealthy families from other islands and the British Isles. She mentioned that one of the beaches, after it was visited by Princess Margaret, was named in her honour, although she vacationed on another island in the Grenadines. Then she pointed out the area which she believed was a submarine hideout for either the British or the American navy. Along the shore there were clusters of sea urchins and small turtles either crawling among the grass on the beach or struggling to get back into the water. As we walked along the shore, Tamara answered all my questions about the flora and fauna. Then she led me up a steep path to a lush idyllic valley which had fruit trees with ripened tropical fruits. She decided that we should sit under one of the trees and rest while appreciating the beauty of the landscape. As we admired the landscape, I asked her the name of the story that she was so intently reading in the Bible. She responded with a rather sad look and said, "I am re-reading the Book of Job."

"You are re-reading the Book of Job!"

"Yes!"

"Why are you reading about Job's sufferings?"

"I am trying to understand why bad things happen to good people."

"What bad things happened to you?"

She held my hand, looked into my eyes and with tears rolling down her cheeks said, "I am a widow. My husband passed away suddenly two years ago, and I am having a difficult time coping."

"Do you have supporting friends and families?"

While sobbing she managed to tell me that, the only family she had was her sister and her brother-in-law. Her husband was a generous, benevolent and spiritual man who was involved in the community helping the marginal and less fortunate people, both financially and materially. After her husband's passing, she became very annoyed at God and stopped believing in him. She stopped going to church and praying. Then one evening, the pastor paid a visit to her on the advice of friends. First, he prayed with her and related the story of Job to her. He left her with some comfort and words of encouragement. Then he strongly recommended that she should spend some time reading and re-reading the story of Job, and to pay very close attention to the roles each of the characters played in Job's life. At that point in her narration, we heard the loud blaring sound of the horn on the catamaran. That was the signal to return to the boat.

"Thank you Awadh for your empathy. I greatly appreciate your companionship and compassion. Let us return to the boat."

We re-boarded the catamaran. The crew decided that they would take us sightseeing along the coast of Bequia before heading back to the mainland. On the trip back there were hundreds of flying fish flitting along the side of the catamaran. We arrived on the mainland just before the marvellous and stunning sunset disappeared. First, Dr. Kordi took his family and me to his mansion. He instructed me to have a shower and gave me a colourful shirt. While I was showering, the sisters had quickly arranged dinner for all of us. They made me feel at home and I greatly appreciated their kindness, hospitality and generosity. In spite of all their benevolence, I wanted to return to the guest house to see if I was selected for the match on the following day. Softly, I mentioned my concerns to Dr. Kordi. He was very considerate and without any further delay he took me to the guest house. On our way there Dr. Kordi said that his family and crew enjoyed my friendly temperament and happy–go-lucky outlook on life. I thanked him again for his invitation, hospitality and generosity. When we arrived at the hotel, he accompanied me to the lobby. He gave me his business card and instructed me to contact him whenever I have a day free from cricket. He hugged me as we parted for the evening.

When I entered the lobby there were two young ladies sitting in the common room conversing in French. I picked up a bit of their conversation with the knowledge of my college French. As I perused the names of the players selected for the match on the following day, I was not on the team. Instead I was assigned the scorers duty for the match. I was not disappointed. I realized that there were other players who had paid to come on the tour and were promised to play in at least three matches. I had already participated in two matches.

After my shower I decided to introduce myself to the two beautiful young ladies who were conversing in French.

Bonsoir!

Bonsoir!

"Je m'appelle Awadh."

"Je m'appelle Chantelle"

"Je m'appelle Michelle"

"Comment allez-vous?"

"Je vais bien. Et tu?"

"Je vais bien aussi. Merci"

After my brief introduction, I said to them in my college French, "S'il te plait, parle doucement."

With a big smile, Chantelle kindly obliged and spoke to me in perfect English. I learned that they were two sisters. Chantelle was bilingual and her younger sister, Michelle, was fluent in French, could read and understand some English but did not speak it well. Michelle conversed in French. They were from the French island of Martinique and were on holidays. I informed them about our cricket tour. It was a very interesting scene to witness. During my conversation in English with Chantelle, Michelle constantly interjected in French, wanting to know what we were talking about. We were able to communicate very effectively, despite Michelle's and my language limitations. After a rather interesting conversation, I bid them "Bonne Nuit." And I left for my room. The following morning, the two sisters were at breakfast. Proudly, and to the amazement of a few of my team mates, I said to the sisters,

"Bonjour! Comment allez-vous Chantelle? Michelle?"

"Je vais bien" was their reply.

Having hugged and kissed both of them on their cheeks, Chantelle continued conversing with me in English while Michelle kept smiling and interjecting in French.

Then I joined my team for breakfast.

The manager and a few of the players who saw me greeting, hugging and kissing them asked,

"Awadh, do you know those women?"

"Yes. They are my new-found friends who are on vacation. They are from Martinique."

They did not ask any more questions as we continued to enjoy our petit dejeuner. After breakfast, as I was leaving to get dressed for the game, I waved to them, and they waved back. While we were in the van to the game, one of the players, Ameer, tapped me on the shoulder and said softly, "Awadh. I have to have a talk with you after the match." I informed him that I was the designated scorer for our team. I told him to meet me in my room after our return to the guest house. He agreed. We won the match without much opposition. Although the home team had lost they were very gracious, hospitable and accommodating hosts and hostesses.

In my room, Ameer told me that the rumour among the players was that I could speak French, and that they had overheard me conversing with the two young women in French at breakfast. With tongue in cheek, I responded in the affirmative. Then he said that he had seen the two women yesterday in the

gardens on the guest house property, and he had tried to show that he was interested in getting to know them better. But they avoided him by walking away as he was speaking to them.

"What is the problem Ameer?"

"Awadh, I am interested in the shorter woman. She is very gorgeous and I will like to get to know her better before returning to Trinidad. Can you intercede on my behalf?"

At that point in the conversation, I told Ameer that I would like to learn about his background, his job, marital status, and what his intentions were before I could attempt to intercede for him. He informed me that he was an acting vice-principal in a Government Secondary School. He was the owner of the travel agency that made all the travelling arrangements for the cricket tour. He owned his home. Above all, he was ready to get married. He continued that he would like to learn more about the woman and determine whether she could be his wife. On hearing his intentions, I suddenly realized that he had placed me in a matchmaker's role for which I was unqualified. After promising to test the waters, Ameer thanked me. After his departure, I could not fall asleep as my mind kept churning over the possible outcomes of my decision to speak to my new found acquaintances about such a delicate but serious issue.

The next day we had no match scheduled. As soon as I awoke, I phoned Dr. Kordi. I told him that I was free for the day. He told me that he would be at the guest house about eleven o'clock, and that I must be ready to accompany him on his weekly visit to his patients in the mountains in the north of the island. I accepted his plan and went for breakfast. At exactly eleven o'clock he arrived in a green land rover. He jumped out from his vehicle, and with a smile, greeted me with a hug. I joined him in the vehicle in which the motor was still running. He seemed to be in a hurry and I inquired about his great hurry. As he raced through the narrow road in the countryside, he said that he was delayed by an emergency situation. When we arrived in the village in the rugged mountains, he instructed me to stay in the vehicle until his return. While I was sitting in the vehicle, some of village people came to it, and wanted to know my reason for being in their village unaccompanied. I informed them that Dr. Kordi went to attend to his patients, and told me that as soon as he needed extra medicine he would send someone to get me with the medicine bag. On hearing my alibi they left. When Dr.Kordi returned, I reported what had occurred in his absence. In a serious tone he said that I had acted prudently and that he did not expect the village people to interrogate me. On our homeward drive he informed me that he was providing birth control tablets and condoms to the village people. Also he had to dispense medications for those suffering with gonorrhoea and syphilis. Also I wanted to know why the people were asking me for fresh water. Dr. Kordi informed me that the village people had desalinated water to use for drinking, personal hygiene and cooking. They did not like the scent and taste of the desalinated water. Some of them had containers for collecting rain water which they highly treasured. He took me to his home where we shared a meal with Sandra and Tamara. I then informed the sisters that I had to play cricket on the following day against Dr. Kordi's club. He took me in the land rover to the guest house and wished me the best of luck in tomorrow's game. I smiled and bid him farewell.

As I entered the lobby I saw the two sisters from Martinique, having a drink at the bar. They invited me to join them. I told them that I would return after a shower. They agreed to wait for me. After joining them, I suggested that we take our drinks to the patio in the beautiful garden. While we were enjoying our drinks, my team mates were periodically returning from their day trips. As they passed, they called me by name and asked me to recommend them to the girls. I assured each one who made the request that I will do my best for them. Then the younger sister, Michelle, wanted to know what my team mates were requesting. Chantelle told her that they were interested in meeting them. Michelle, to my surprise, said that she was also interested in meeting them. She would like to be friends with them. When we had finished consuming our cocktails, I invited them to join me for dinner in the restaurant across from the guest house. They looked at each other, smiled, then spoke to each other rapidly in French and then accepted. I had no idea what they communicated before their acceptance.

At the restaurant, there were many of my team mates but I did not wish to join them. Instead, we got a table away from the players. After making our dinner selections they ordered a bottle of French wine. During the dinner, Ameer entered the restaurant and joined the other players. He did not notice me with the two sisters at the corner table, but after a few minutes he came across to my table to inquire about my activities during the day. I sensed his surreptitious intentions and being aware of his interest in Michelle, I introduced him to her and her sister, Chantelle. Michelle's countenance and her eyes betrayed her innermost feelings. I got the distinct feeling that Ameer wanted me to invite him to join us, but I did not. When he left, he appeared a bit chagrined. After carefully observing Michelle's reactions to Ameer's presence, I felt that my matchmaking assignment would be relatively easy. I asked Chantelle to ask Michelle for her candid opinion and feelings for Ameer. And would she be seriously interested in dating him? Michelle ecstatically replied that she would be most interested in going out with him. I asked the sisters if I should invite Ameer to join us for dessert. They looked at each other shaking their heads in the affirmative. I took a sip of my Mouton Cadet, and slowly walked to Ameer's table. He was extremely excited to see me approaching. Instantly, he got up and came to me.

"Awadh! What's going on? Is there any favourable news?"
"Ameer, I have arranged for you to meet her."
"When!"

"Calm down Ameer. Just be yourself. Come and join us for dessert."

"Are you serious?"

"Yes Ameer. Come with me."

Ameer was very excited. He took up the bill from his friends' table and paid it. He told them not to wait for him. As we made our way to my table, I advised him to behave like a gentleman and to be very respectful to the two young women. When we arrived at the table, I directed him to sit opposite Michelle. The lovers halo enveloped both of them without delay. With the urging and prompting of Chantelle, they were able to communicate effectively. After dessert we all returned to our guest house.

The following morning, Ameer and I joined the sisters for breakfast. The other members of the team started to gossip about the newly formed relationship that was developing with the girls, Ameer and me. After breakfast, a few players asked many interesting questions about our relationship with the sisters. But we were conservative with the answers. We pleaded not guilty to all of their alleged claims. I was happy for Ameer and Michelle. As our players gathered to depart for the match against Dr. Kordi's Club, Ameer informed me that he was not selected to play. Instead he would be attending the match with the two sisters later in the day. He added that the sisters wanted to see and learn about the game of cricket. He had promised to enlighten them about the game as it was in progress. I did not comment.

On arrival at the cricket field we were warmly welcomed by the captain and players of the home team. But I did not see Dr. Kordi. I asked the captain of the team for him. He told me that the doctor was not able to participate in the match due to some unforeseen circumstances, but he and his family will be bringing all the food and beverages for the tea intermission. The umpires summoned the captains to toss the coin to decide who will bat or bowl first. My team lost the toss and had to field. Without much delay the game commenced in brilliant sunshine and a cool north–east wind. Initially, our opposition's batsmen made very good use of the batting conditions and scored effortlessly against our bowling attack. Then our captain, on realizing that his opening attack was not effective, drastically changed his strategy and tactics. His changes quickly routed our opponent's batting. As the players were walking back to the dressing room at the conclusion of the first innings, Dr. Kordi and his family arrived with all the food and non-alcoholic beverages for the tea intermission. Also at the same time Ameer and the two sisters arrived. Ameer and Michelle were holding hands when they entered the playground. When I noticed how quickly he had managed to get close to Michelle, I was happy for him. I smiled. They were invited to join the tea party, which was hosted by Dr. Kordi and his family. After tea our team went in to bat. At first we had a very difficult time against our opponent's bowling. Then slowly we recovered and managed to narrowly win the match. During the post-match party, I asked the two sisters whether Ameer had educated them about the game. They said that they were trying to understand what Ameer was describing but it was still a strange game to them. I then introduced the manager of our team, Mr. Khan and all the players to Dr. Kordi and his family. I introduced Chantelle and Michelle to Dr. Kordi and his family. Also, I introduced the two sisters to the manager and other cricketers of our team. It started to rain lightly. The light drizzle had developed into a lightning and thunder filled tropical thunderstorm. It rained continuously throughout the night. I checked the bulletin board for any information concerning the match scheduled for the next day. I was selected captain of the team. When I got in bed, the sound of the rain on the galvanised roof was very relaxing and conducive for sleeping.

When I awoke the following morning it was still raining. The manager of our team called a snap meeting with all the players. He informed us that he had received a phone call from the captain of the team we had to play our final game later that day. He continued that the match had to be cancelled because the inclement weather had flooded the cricket field. We were extremely disappointed. He then added that there would be a farewell dinner party for all the players and their guests at one of the player's home. That news was most welcomed and greatly appreciated by all the players. The two sisters were late for breakfast so they were unaware of the match cancellation. During our breakfast, Ameer and I informed the sisters about the cancellation of the match and supplied them with the reasons. They smiled and seemed rather pleased that we would have to stay put at the guest house. Then we told them about the party our players were invited to and that we would like them to join us if they were not busy. First, Chantelle spoke to Michelle in French. From their conversation I gathered that they were scheduled to leave on the following day for Martinique. They accepted our invitation with the provision to get them back to the guest house early. Ameer looked at me and we promised to honour their request. Much to our surprise, Chantelle softly inquired about our plans for returning to Trinidad. I told her that we were booked to leave Sunday afternoon. Then she said that they would like to invite us and the rest of the players to accompany them to Martinique tomorrow. In Martinique, they would take us around the tourists' areas with the assistance of her two brothers and cousins. We could spend the rest of Friday, and the entire Saturday touring around the island and experiencing the nightlife in the Martinique. We would be able to return on Sunday morning on an early flight back to St.Vincent in time for the flight to Trinidad. The entire team could be accommodated easily at any of the hotels in the capital city, Fort–de–France, at reasonable and affordable rates. In response to her suggestions, Ameer became extremely delighted and excited. Immediately, he looked at me and with glee all over his face, he said, "Awadh. All the players and the manager are still having breakfast and talking, so why don't we tell them about the invitation we have to visit Martinique for a couple of day with the sisters and her family." Ameer informed the manager about the sisters' suggestion. The manager became greatly excited about the sisters' proposal and immediately got the unanimous consent of the players. The sisters were ecstatic that the team would be holidaying with them in Martinique. Chantelle and Ameer with the assistance of the operator of the guest house made travel arrangements for all the players to leave for Martinique with the sisters the following day. Chantelle then telephoned her brothers in Martinique and informed them about us. The brothers asked for details about our team members and vouched to make all the necessary accommodations and travel arrangement for us on our arrival. After all the arrangements were finalized, we all retired to our rooms.

We went to the farewell party. As usual, the host and hostess were hospitable and generous. There was an excess of food, and both alcoholic and non-alcoholic drinks. The Latin music was very conducive for both slow and fast dancing. At the conclusion of the evening of fun and laughter, each member on our team was given a souvenir of St. Vincent by the captain of the hosting team. Each player on our team reciprocated with a gift from Trinidad, an activity we did after each game.

On the following day we boarded the aircraft for Martinique. On our arrival in Martinique, the custom officials were puzzled at the unique appearance of our cricket equipment. But Chantelle quickly explained something about cricket to them. She informed the custom officials that we were her guests until Sunday. They smiled, stamped our passports and wished us a happy vacation. As was planned, the brothers and cousins were there to warmly welcome us. We were taken by cars to a large hotel in Fort-de-France, the capital city of Martinique. After we had all checked into the hotel, our manager, on behalf of the team, graciously invited the welcoming party to lunch at the hotel.

After lunch, the brothers and cousins, who were bilingual in English and French, said that they would return later in the evening to take us around the city, the parks and the famous tourist attractions. They all returned and fulfilled their pledges beyond our expectations. It was already dark and those who were too tired to do any more sightseeing returned to the hotel.

About six of us went with the welcoming party for dinner at one of the night clubs in the brilliantly lit cityscape. After dinner, the rhythmic French music could not be resisted. We danced for quite a long time. Ameer spent most of his time dancing with Michelle. Meanwhile I danced with many women. I had a fantastic time. Before dropping us at the hotel, Chantelle told me that at 9 o'clock in the morning they would join us for breakfast at the bistro at the end of the street. We hugged and cheek–kissed as we said, "Bonsoir."

On the Saturday morning, we met at the planned rendezvous for le petit dejeuner. The breakfast was very different from what I was used to. What an interesting menu! Very strong coffee, extremely sweet chocolate drink, a variety of fruit juice, different types of bread, many types of cheese, jams, marmalade, ham, sausages and a wide variety of condiments. After breakfast, on our way a beautiful sandy beach on the coast, we stopped at a grocery to purchase food and drinks to host a picnic party on the beach. The countryside was lush and picturesque with colourful flowering trees and well- manicured fields. The weather was perfect for a beach party. It was a serene, beautiful and joyous day, not only for Michelle and Ameer, but for the entire group. The camaraderie and hilarity that existed among all of us were electric. As we were about to leave the beach, Chantelle then announced that she and her brothers, sister and cousins have planned to attend a dance in the countryside on another beach on the western side of the island later that evening, and they would be delighted to meet us at the dance. She said that she would make all the arrangements with the taxis at the front of the hotel.

After our arrival at the hotel, our manager, Mr. Khan inquired how many players wanted to go to the dance. Everyone agreed to attend the dance. Chantelle called six taxi drivers and instructed them. Ameer and I were responsible to make sure that everyone was in the taxi at the precise time to leave for the dance.

"How will we get back to the hotel after the dance Chantelle?"

"Don't worry Awadh! We will be there to bring all of you back to the hotel. Don't worry." Everyone was very excited and wished that they were already at the dance. The driver of my taxi travelled at a very high speed, and at any moment, I thought that he would crash into the fast approaching vehicle. They were driving on the right hand side of the road. What a novel but terrifying experience. We passed several villages and vast acreage of sugarcane plantations before arriving at our final destination. When the taxis left us, we were standing in a fishing village. It was early in the evening and the sun was already painting a magnificent and picturesque sunset in the clouds. Most of the boats of different colours and shapes were already moored for the evening. A few boats were still arriving with their catch. I tried unsuccessfully to speak with a few of them with my college French. We were in a French fishing village. One of the fishermen was able to understand what I was asking and showed me a long empty shed as the dance hall. An elderly woman gave me a surprised look when I mentioned the word dance. We were seventeen well-dressed Trinidadians standing at the end of a street in a fishing village in Martinique, looking at an empty shed waiting to meet our friends. I could not imagine the thoughts flashing through my team mates' minds. The sun went to sleep and the low-wattage street light came on. We were on the lowlands. At our back were hills through which narrow pathways allowed the village people to go to their homes on the other side of the hilly landscape. We looked at one another and started questioning our sanity and our trust in our new found friends. Then we heard the sounds of distant drums emanating from behind the hills. As we were standing in a cluster at the front of the shed and beneath the dim street light, a stranger, with a lighted flashlight, approached us. He was on one of the pathways between the hills. All our attention was directed to the light and we patiently waited to see who was bearing the light. A middle-aged man, wearing a hat, appeared in front of us and stopped. He turned off his flashlight and calmly said "Bonsoir my friends. What are you doing here?"

My manager answered with a frightened voice, "Good evening sir. We are here for a dance."

"A dance! Who told you there is a dance here?"

"Our friends."

"There has not been a dance here for months. No one will come here to dance since the village chain-gang murdered a woman on the dance floor. If you look very carefully you would still see faint traces of blood stains on the floor where the murder took place."

I then became petrified.

"Which country do you come from?"

"Trinidad."

"Trinidad!"

"Yes sir. We are Trinidadians."

"I did work in Trinidad, after the war, in Point-a-Pierre. But I did not feel safe. After returning to my native land, Martinique, and after several relocations, I am now settled in the serene and beautiful valley between the hills behind you. I have come to warn you about the impending danger that you are about to face. Do you hear the faint sounds of the beating drums, coming from the hills?"

After carefully listening in complete silence, we all shook our heads and responded in unison, "YES!"

"Well my friends, my neighbour overheard a few members of the chain-gang saying that there is a group of well-dressed tourists standing at the end of the fishing village. They seemed to be lost. The gang is preparing to rob them of their valuables. After hearing the unfavourable news, and being a war veteran, it became my duty to inform you, immediately."

"What could we do Sir?"

"Pray and hope your friends arrive in time to rescue you. If they do not arrive in time then you will have to defend yourselves with anything that you can lay your hands on. Do you hear the sounds of the beating drums and the banging of the chains on the asphalt-paved road on the slopes of the hill? I have to leave. Good luck. Que Dieu te proteges."

The French man left us.

Meanwhile I could distinctly hear the sound of the drums and the banging of chains on the asphalt paved road leading down the hillside. What a predicament we got ourselves into! We had to think and act quickly before the gang reached us. Having searched for stones and stick on the area surrounding around us, we did not find much that we could have used as weapons for protection. The gang had danced their way to the road leading directly to us. We decided that we were not going to retreat. We were going to stand our ground and fight to the last man. Then to our great relief we saw three pairs of automobile headlight rapidly descending the road on the hillside. We hoped that they were the headlights of our friends' vehicles. At first, the gang did not move away as the vehicles got directly behind them. But as the drivers sounded the horns they cleared the road allowing free passage to all three vehicles. The three vans pulled into the sandy beach clearance and parked in a parallel get away formation. The gang was about hundred feet away from us. We ran into the back of the open vans. The Sisters and her cousins bravely approached the gang. A confrontation developed. We could see that they were in trouble. Also, they were outnumbered. At that instant, our entire team charged the gang shouting, "We are Trinidadians and we are going to kill you bitches." I could not believe what I was witnessing. Our cricketers snatched the chains from gangsters. And they did not hesitate to beat them with their own chains. The gang dispersed. The drummers dropped their drum and they all ran away in different directions. Unfortunately, I did not get an opportunity to beat a gangster with a chain. We all returned to the vans and left for the city. In the van in which I was travelling, everyone was very silent. All I could hear was heavy breathing and beating hearts.

When we arrived back in the city, we all went to a restaurant for a late-night meal. At the dining table, Chantelle claimed that she was unaware of the murder at the dance hall and that all dances at that beachside location were cancelled. After apologizing for her innocence, she informed us about the encounter with the village chain-gang. She stated that after the vans had parked on the beach, she and Michelle approached the gang to inquire what was going on. The gangsters questioned whether they were the whores for our players. When the brothers heard the curses and insults hurled at their sisters, they ran out of their vans to defend them. At that point, the Trinidad Posse flew into action, and in a jiffy had the gang heading for the hills. After dinner we were driven back safely to our hotel. We thanked them for all their assistance. They told us that they would join us for 'petit dejeuner' at the hotel, and after breakfast they will take us to the airport. We were all packed and ready to take our flight back to St. Vincent. We eagerly waited for our friends to have breakfast. While we were waiting, the traumatic experiences at the fishing village were the main topic of discussion on our morning agenda.

After breakfast, we thanked our friend for their generosity, kindness, new formed friendships and their rescue from the village chain gang. They apologized for the unexpected traumatic incident at the fishing village. At the airport, we exchanged addresses and telephone numbers, and promised to remain friends. Privately, I asked Ameer about the status of his relationship with Michelle. He was pleased and delighted that I had connected them. He had planned to return to Martinique to meet her family, and make arrangements to get married. However, he asked me to promise not to divulge his personal affairs to anyone. I pledged to respect his wishes. Before entering the boarding area, I bid everyone farewell. But I hugged and kissed Chantelle and Michelle and thanked them again for their friendship and all the fantastic experiences we had shared.

After we arrived in St. Vincent, we went directly to the check in desk for our return flight to Trinidad. We experienced no difficulty with either immigration or customs officials at the St. Vincent airport. When we finally arrived at the airport in Trinidad, and had successfully cleared the immigration and customs officials, we were warmly and excitingly welcomed back by our friends, colleagues and our families. They were thirsty to hear about our performances in the games and about any new experiences we had to share. They were in for some real surprises from the different stories each member of the team would honestly dare to narrate. But, as I was bidding farewell to Ameer he gave me his phone number and instructed me to give him a call as soon as I had settled down with my studies. On my arrival at home, my sisters showered me with questions that I had never anticipated. My neighbours greatly surprised me with their interest in my cricket tour. At first, I did not tell anyone about my extended trip to Martinique. I did not want my Papa to know about Ameer and the French women from Martinique. After I had answered everybody's questions, I was most delighted to get into my own bed. On the following day, I slept in and spent the day at home. I organized all the information and materials that I would need for my courses scheduled to begin on the following day.

It was towards the end of 1963 when I began my advanced studies in Physics, Chemistry and Biology at the Polytechnic Institute in Port-of-Spain. After the first day of classes, I paid a courtesy visit to my mentor, Mr. Noble. He was pleased that I had not forgotten him. He inquired about the cricket tour. After I had narrated the details of the games, the new relationships developed, the adventures and the extended trip to Martinique, he became very interested in joining me on our next cricket tour. But as his telephone started to ring, I bid him farewell, and promised to keep in touch.

A few weeks into my studies, Ameer contacted me at my home to question me about my studies. I told him that I had excellent lecturers and my studies were progressing well. During our telephone conversation he invited me to spend the weekend with him at his home. I informed him that I had a few written assignments, and laboratory reports to hand at the beginning of the week. Then, he said, "I am coming for you. I must talk with you about my love life. Get all your school work together. You will complete them in my library." With that mandatory request, I organised my assignments and the essential materials that I would need. I informed my family about my plans for the weekend. Ameer arrived and I introduced him to my family. Then we went to his home. On the way, he could not stop talking about Michelle and Chantelle and their parents. I listened to his stories. But my assignments were forefront on my mind. At his home we had lunch. Then, Ameer was most excited to repeat the stories that he had narrated to me in the car. He was absolutely infected with the love virus. At that point, I teasingly asked about his written communication with Michelle. Immediately, he opened a drawer. He took out two perfumed letters that he had received from Michelle. He asked me to read them. Being surprised, I questioned, "Ameer are you serious? Do you want me to read your love letters?"

"Yes Awadh. There are many French words and phrases in them that I don't know. Please read them, and tell me if she meant what I think she meant. I wonder why she doesn't ask Chantelle to help her write her letters in English! She knows that I can neither speak nor write French."

"Maybe Michelle is trying to get you to gradually learn her language."

Then, I suggested that he should consider studying French in one of the evening classes offered at his school. He looked at me and agreed with my suggestion. I read his letters slowly and enjoyed the language Michelle used to express her love for Ameer. She was extremely infatuated with Ameer. I embellished the sentiments that she had expressed in her letters to reassure

Ameer that she was absolutely in love with him. After discussing his intense absorption in the written words of Michelle and by continuously reliving expressing his romantic and vivid memories of her, I was certain that wedding bells would soon be ringing.

Within a week, he informed me that he wanted me to accompany him to Martinique to witness his engagement to Michelle. After congratulating him, I told him that I would love to accompany him for his engagement, but I did not have the necessary finances to travel with him. He then convinced me that he would take care of all expenses, and I accompanied him to Martinique.

The Chevalier family were socialites. At the engagement, I was introduced to many of their beautiful family members. There was one of Chantelle's close female friends with whom I became infatuated. She was rhythmic and graceful as a dance partner. I thoroughly enjoyed every step I took with her as we danced to the delightful and charming French music. Coincidentally, her name was Chantelle. The engagement party was very classy. While walking around the dance floor and the garden, I renewed acquaintances with a few of the people that I had met on our first visit to Martinique. The brothers, the cousins and friends vividly recall the chain-gang incident in the fishing village to their friends and family members who had not heard of it. The exaggerated version of the incident was quite different from what had happened. I kept smiling as they thrillingly spun the yarn. At the end of the engagement celebrations, I thanked the Chevalier family, and told them my friend Ameer would be a fantastic husband for Michelle. They agreed.

On my return trip to Trinidad, Ameer informed me that he would like to get married to Michelle as soon as possible and asked me to be his best man. I told him that I felt greatly honoured that he has selected me ahead of all his other friends and family to be his best man for his wedding. He commented that if I did not speak on his behalf in St. Vincent, there would have been no relationship between Michelle and him. I smiled and thanked him for his trust in me. Realizing that he was determined to get married as soon as possible, I informed him that he should plan his wedding after my final examinations. He assured me that before setting the final date of the wedding he would consult me. After embracing, we departed from Piarco airport. Within a month, Ameer was promoted to a Principal position in another Government Secondary school. He invited me to his celebrations at his home. He proudly introduced me to his colleagues and a few interesting members of his family.

At our next meeting at a restaurant in Port of Spain, he inquired about my courses and the dates of my examinations. Towards the end of my first year of studies, Ameer was asking me to help him make marriage arrangements with which I had no experience. He told me that Michelle brought out the divine light in his heart, and that she made him feel extremely special, desirable and valuable. He firmly believed that she was his soulmate. His longing and hunger to be intimate with Michelle had resulted in many sleepless and restless nights. His performance at work was greatly affected. Also confided that he could not resist calling and speaking to her almost every day. His telephone bill was so huge that it would be less expensive for him to visit her every weekend. I interjected, "Ameer! Since you are so madly in love with her, why don't you just marry her and stop tormenting your total being." "Awadh, that's what I was waiting to hear from you." Again, he inquired whether I knew the dates of my final examinations. I informed him that I would have to confirm the dates with him over the phone. With those final words we embrace and left the restaurant. After a couple of weeks, I confirmed my examination dates with him. As soon as my examinations were completed, Ameer was at my home. In a very excited tone, Ameer said "Awadh! I have good news. Come in my car and let's go for a drive." I had no idea of our final destination as we drove towards Mount St. Benedict Church, located in the Northern Range Mountains. I had not been to that church since my college cricket days. As he drove up the winding road, I wondered whether there would be a shotgun wedding. Although he was not dressed like a bridegroom, I asked myself many rhetorical questions. Was Michelle in the church waiting for Ameer? Did he come to confess some iniquitous deed that he had committed?" But I patiently waited for the endgame. After arriving at the church, I questioned his motive for bringing me to the Catholic Church. He told me that he was a Catholic, and that he knew Father David for many years; and that he came to receive his blessings, in my presence, for the wedding plans he had made. In the front office, Fr. David's welcomed us. Eventually, Ameer declared his wedding plans to us. The wedding was scheduled to take place in two months in a Catholic Church on the beautiful tropical island of St. Lucia in the Caribbean. Ameer stated that he had come to ask Fr. David to perform the marriage ceremony. The priest had to consult his appointment book before making any decision. After consulting it, he agreed to perform the wedding ceremony. Ameer then informed the priest that he, Ameer, would look after his flights, accommodations, food and all of his expenses. Father gave us his blessings and we left.

After the end of the first year of my studies, the wedding date was around the corner. Ameer was bursting with enthusiasm. Fr. David, Ameer, his friends and relatives and I flew to St. Lucia. We were taxied to the resort on a beachfront property. Later that evening, we were welcomed and entertained by the Chevalier family. We were joined by a few of their extended family members in order to meet Ameer's family and friends. We met at a picturesque restaurant located at the end of a pier in the sea. In cages below the water level there were live lobsters and a variety of tropical fish, and each guest could select their choice of sea food. An employee with a harpoon speared the selected fish or lobster and gave it to the chefs who immediately prepared them for cooking. Before the main course was ready, French wines, oysters in shells and baked shrimps were served.

On the day before the marriage ceremony there was an evening of dancing, drinking and finger foods, fruits, and pastries. There was a quartet that played seductive and romantic dancing music. Much to my great delight and joy, I saw charming and alluring Chantelle, whom I had met at the engagement party in Martinique. She was seated at a table conversing with the people seated at the table. Without any delay, I slowly approached her from behind and covered her eyes with my hands. At first, she swore in French. But I continued to cover her eyes. Then one of her friends, seated at the table recognized me from the engagement party and spoke to her in French. Immediately she got up and called my name. I hugged her and kissed her. I was extremely excited and happy to see her. Her happiness and charm abounded. At that same moment, another enchanting piece of music started to play. Chantelle looked at me with a smile and got up. Instantly, I took her outstretched hand and joined the other lovely couples on the dance floor. I held her slim beautiful, French perfumed and delicate body closely to me, as we paraded around the dancing space. I could have danced with her all night. But she wanted to socialize with me in the garden. She informed me that she had arrived in St. Lucia only a few hours ago from Martinique. We alternated between dancing in the garden and the dance floor. But in the garden, we were able to be more intimate. Then Ameer approached me and remarked that he was watching my every move with Chantelle not only on the dance floor but when we went outside and were dancing in the garden. He commented that he could arrange for Fr. David to perform a marriage ceremony for Chantelle and me, right after his. He hinted that we could celebrate together. I declined his offer. Obviously his offer was made in jest, and I continued to remind him that marriage was not on my bucket list.

Having eliminated that option, I bid Chantelle "Bonne Nuit." Exhausted and sleepy, I went to the resort, had a shower and after giving thanks for another wonderful day, I went to bed.

The weather was most cooperative on the wedding day. What a broad spectrum of custom designed coloured dresses, shoes of patterns that I had never beheld before, matching accessories, hairdos from the French movies, and exquisite perfume scents! The French men from Martinique were fancifully dressed and their sartorial splendour greatly impressed the women. Much to my surprise, Chantelle, attired as a beauty queen, approached me. Once again, I took the opportunity to hug and kiss her. She had a body and beauty that could launch more than a thousand ships. In spite of the extreme temptation, there was no place in my bucket list for her. The marriage ceremony took place in the local Catholic Church with the full cooperation of the pastor. After the ceremony, there was an opulent reception for all the guests at the dining facilities on the resort. It was a long tiring day for me. As I was bidding Chantelle adieu, she wanted to know when I would be returning to Martinique with Ameer and Michelle to marry her. I did not respond to her question. We expressed our farewells, and I went to the resort. The next day, all the guests, families and friends had left for their homes. But I remained with Michelle and Ameer. After one day with the honeymoon couple, I felt completely out of place. I persuaded Ameer to make arrangements for my return to Trinidad, on the following day.

At the resort, however we learned that there was an English Banana Boat in Castries harbour which would be loaded at sunset by the local dock works. And they highly recommended that we should witness the actual loading of the "Green Gold" into the boat. Just before dinner, we decided to attend the loading of the bananas event. We arrived early at the loading site. Standing on wooden boxes, three of us watched the men and women workers enter the large vacant yard. Slowly they formed a line from the banana shed to the base of a short stairway ascending to the opened doorway into the ship. Although we could not see to whom the bunches of bananas were finally handed, we could only assume that the workers who had initially entered up the stairway, before the outside workers had arrived, must have organized the holding spaces below the deck to utilize the maximum cargo capacity of the ship. As soon as the sun disappeared into the ocean, and as the temperature started to decline, the chanting of the 'work song' commenced. I could not identify whether they were singing Harry Belafonte's signature lyrics of "Come mister tallyman tally me banana." The work song was directly related to the loading of the bananas. It was a wonderful and rhythmic dance and song. As the lead singers who were interspersed throughout the loading line, sang the melody "come mister tallyman tally me banana"; the other workers responded," daylight come and me want to go home." The melody and the response went as follows:

Day- o, day-ay-ay-ay- o
Daylight come an me wan'go home...

The melody and the response were repeated continuously as each bunch of bananas was passed from hand to hand and packed into the cargo hold of the ship. Just as the last bunch of bananas was in the boat, and the workers started to disperse, one of the Englishmen from the crew, who was acting as Tally man, signaled to us to wait. As the workers slowly went about their business in the dark, the English man approached us and invited us to join him for a drink with the Captain of the boat at the captain's table. We unhesitatingly accepted his kind invitation. As we climbed the staircase to the deck of the ship, we got a panoramic view of the loading area. The captain formally welcomed us. The small crew were all wearing their white uniforms and looked like high ranking officials in the British Navy. What opulence for a banana boat. Highly polished brass rails, brass fixtures and polished furniture, the colour of red-mahogany, were visible in every part of the area we were hosted. The captain, on learning that Michelle and Ameer were married a few days ago, opened a bottle of Champagne and toasted the bride, the groom and the best man. They also served us some of their British hors d'oeuvres, cheese and soda crackers, and wished the bride and groom all success in their married lives. Since they were Englishmen, I asked the question in which county did they reside. One said Yorkshire and another said Sussex. Immediately, I mentioned the topic of cricket. A very lively conversation about the status of cricket in the West Indies and England ensued. Ameer, Michelle and I thanked them for their hospitality and kindness. And after bidding them bon voyage, we left for our resort. Before returning to my studies in Trinidad, I congratulated Michelle and Ameer again. I told them that I would contact them on their return.

I resumed and maintained my social relationships with Michelle and Ameer. We attended dances, concerts, cultural and sporting events. However I had to help in the daily operations of our liquor and grocery business.

One afternoon, as I was resting on my bed, I heard a gentle knock on the door of my bedroom. "Who is it?"

Her soft and sweet voice responded.

"Ushi"

"Come in Ushi."

I got up as soon as she opened the door and turned on the ceiling light. Then, looking at me with a silly smile, she posed a question that completely bewildered me. "Did Papa give you the air mail letter?"

"What air mail letter you are talking about Ushi?"

Her countenance instantly became serious and turned pale. A surprised but calm followed. She proceeded, "Papa didn't give you the letter from overseas that he received two day ago?"

"No!"

"Yes Awadh. As soon as the mailman gave me the letters, Papa inquired whether there was any for him. I told him that all were for him except one. He wanted to know whom it was for. I informed him that it was addressed to you. He asked to see it and I gave it to him. He noticed it had an airmail sticker and became very curious. He decided he would keep it but promised he'd give it to you later. Then as he was about to open it, Tanty Seloni stopped him. She told him that it was not right to open it. She started to quarrel with him and began to fight with him for the letter. Papa reminded Tanty Seloni that he was the head of the house, and as long as Awadh was living in his house, he had the right to open the bloody letter. Instantly, Tanty Seloni got more annoyed, and reminded Papa that you were an adult, and that your privacy should be respected. Also the letter could be dealing with confidential and important information either about your educational studies or confidential matters of your friends. Papa backed down. He promised he wouldn't open it, and would give it to you when you had returned home. That was not good enough for Tanty Seloni. She asked him to give it to her so that she'd be sure that you'd get it unopened."

I became extremely worried and scared. It was true that I had met and had conversed with a wide range of people during my cricket tour to St. Vincent, my catamaran trip to Bequia, the Martinique trip with the two sisters, Ameer's engagement party in Martinique and his wedding in St.Lucia, but who could be writing me and about what!

"Ushi, was the letter from a male or female?"

"I don't know and Papa didn't say."

"Do you know what country it came from?"

"No, Awadh!"

I thanked her for the information. But after she left my room, I started to think and reflect seriously about the source of the letter. What could be the nature of the contents of this mysterious letter? Several crazy ideas and possibilities flitted and filtered through my confused mind. I then asked Tanty Seloni for Papa. She informed me that he had gone to the pharmacy. Ushi returned to my room to find out whether I had received the letter from Papa. I told her that Papa hadn't returned from the pharmacy. Then she suggested I shouldn't worry.

"Who could be writing you a negative letter?" she stated. "You haven't wronged anyone while you were away? Have you?

Have a good night sleep, and tomorrow morning ask Papa for the letter."

Hesitantly, I agreed. But she and I were quite aware that if Papa did open the letter and did read it, and if he was not pleased with the message in it, I could be in serious trouble, even though I was an adult.

Before Ushi left my bedroom, she, with a big grin remarked, "What is the worst thing could happen? He might only ask you to leave home!"

On the following morning, while we were having breakfast, in the presence of Tanty Seloni and Ushi, I told Papa that I have learned the he had a letter addressed to me.

Papa jokingly replied, "Who told you so?"

There was a dead silence at the table. Ushi and Tanty Seloni looked at each other, and then at Papa, and in unison, questioned, "What did you do with the letter Papa?"

Papa became enraged and claimed that he had destroyed it. Instantly my stepmother, Tanty Seloni, in an extremely loud and angry voice screamed at Papa, "What you mean you destroyed the letter? I do hope you're only joking because if you did destroy the letter addressed to Awadh, you and I go have it out right now!" And she jumped out of her chair and charged at him. At that instant, Papa became highly enraged. He looked at us, mumbled a few words, got up and hurried to his room. In a jiffy he returned to the table with the letter. Then in great haste he resumed his seat at the table, much to my relief. I noticed that the letter was still sealed and had an airmail sticker. Papa, in his seething anger and his blood-shot eyes opened the letter, and decided to read it to us. In a flash, Tanty Seloni got up and dashed to Papa's side of the table in a bold attempt to prevent him from reading it. I just sat there bewildered at the drama unfolding in front of me. This was not acting. It was reality in living colour. He managed to hold her at bay. But as he looked at the penmanship and scanning through the letter, he looked puzzled. He looked carefully again at the three handwritten pages, looked at me, then looked at the pages again and said, "Is this letter a practical joke? This person does not know English!"

At that point I got up and complained, "Papa, you shouldn't be reading my letter."

To which he responded in kind, "Awadh, you are absolutely right. I cannot either read or understand this strange language. I have never seen a letter like this before. Maybe you can read it for us and expose the hidden meaning within it."

Papa handed me the letter and sat down quietly in his chair. We all had a sip of tea. First I looked for the name of the person who wrote the letter on the torn envelope. Only my name and address were written on the envelope in beautiful penmanship. After rifling through the three pages, I discovered it was signed Chantelle. Which one of the Chantelle? I knew two women with the name Chantelle. At that moment, I realized that I had to read the French very carefully to decipher the true identity of the author. After the second reading, I recognised that the letter was from Chantelle Devereau. Papa wanted to know what was wrong with the letter. I replied that the letter was written in French, and I would have to read it very slowly and carefully so that I don't misunderstand the intended message. Papa challenged how could I read and understand the letter if it was written in French. Proudly, I informed him that I had studied Advanced French, Latin and English at college.

"When did you study French?"

"Papa, I was forced to study French, when you refused to allow me to accept a scholarship to study mathematics and sciences at the sister college in San Fernando."

As I slowly read the letter in my mind, I discovered that it was a blessing that it was not written in English. Because if it was written in English and Papa had read it, I would have been exposed to a very embarrassing issue.

Papa became annoyed and shouted, "Awadh stop stalling and read the blasted letter." Having understood the message in the letter, I dared not divulge the exact message to either him, Ushi or Tanty Seloni. I had to start fabricating a more palatable version of the letter as quickly as possible. But it had to be credible and logical to Papa's ears. I informed him that the letter was from Chantelle Devereau whom I had met at Ameer's engagement party in Martinique and his wedding ceremony in St. Lucia. Papa continued his interrogation.

"What does this Chantelle woman want from you?"

I continued to fabricate and told him that Chantelle was Ameer's wife sister. And that Chantelle had planned to visit her sister Michelle and Ameer in a few weeks. She wanted to know whether we would be able to meet at Ameer's home. The confused look on Papa's face told me that he was skeptical, and I could sense that he was totally in dis-belief of anything that I was narrating to him. But I continued to mask my fabrication with a serious and convincing demeanour.

"How did this woman know that you could read and understand French?"

"Papa if you could remember. On my cricket tour to St. Vincent, the team was invited to visit Martinique by two sisters with whom I used my college–based French to communicate. Also I had to communicate in French when I attended Ameer's engagement party in Martinique, and his wedding in St. Lucia."

Papa did not ask any other questions. He got up and before leaving the table, he remarked, "I don't think that was the true message in the letter. It took her three pages just to say that she would like to meet when she was holidaying in Trinidad with Ameer and his wife." I told Papa that was the key message in the letter. Chantelle also was reminiscing about the fun, laughter and adventures we had experienced in Martinique, during our cricket team brief holidaying visit, Ameer's engagement to Michelle and Ameer's wedding in St. Lucia.

He then ordered me to keep the letter handy so that the next time Mr. Du Bois was in the shop buying his groceries, he would ask him to read it. Tanty Seloni quickly came to my support again and rebuked him. They all left the table and went to open the shop. I returned to my bedroom and re-read the beautifully written letter from Chantelle. For my peace of mind, I contacted Ameer and Michelle and told them that I had a highly important and urgent matter to discuss with them. They informed me that they would be available in a few days because they were going to spend the weekend in Tobago. I told them to have a fantastic weekend in Tobago, and reminded Ameer to take Michelle to snorkel in the Bucco Reef and to swim in the Nylon Pool.

After Ameer and Michelle had returned from their weekend trip, I went to their home. He welcomed me with a cool drink. Then I inquired about Michelle. He told me that she had gone out to the shopping mall and would be back soon.

"What is the urgent and important matter you want to discuss Awadh?"

I reminded him about the scene at his wedding when I was dancing with Chantelle Devereau. He laughed aloud and could not stop joking about it, and crowned his wittiness by saying, "You two should have taken the opportunity and tied the knot, at my expense."

"Ameer that is what I want to talk about."

"What do you mean? Have you decided to discontinue your studies and get married?"

"No Ameer. The joke that you created has turned into a nightmare for me."

"What do you mean?"

"Chantelle has written me a letter notifying me of her intention of getting married to me. And she has planned to come to Trinidad to meet me and my family, and to finalize wedding arrangements."

"Are you serious Awadh?"

"I am absolutely serious Ameer. Here is the letter."

Ameer quickly opened it and tried to read it. He complained, "This letter is in French. Michelle will have to translate and interpret it."

I agreed and we decided to wait for her return. As we waited, he apologized for my predicament.

The front door opened and Michelle walked in. "Bonjour Monsieur Awadh. How are you doing?"

"Good morning Michelle and how are you doing after your weekend trip."

"Excellent. Ameer told me that you have an important and urgent problem. And you need us to help you solve it."

"Yes Michelle. I hope that both of you can help me get out of this dilemma."

So I took the letter from Ameer and handed it to her to read. While she was reading it, I could clearly discern that she was not pleased with the contents of the letter. After one year, Michelle with practice became more proficient with the English language, which greatly improved our communication. When she had finished reading the letter, she told us that she would telephone her sister Chantelle and relate the problem that her friend, Chantelle, has created. Michelle immediately phoned her sister and narrated the story in the letter. Chantelle asked to speak to me. After exchanging pleasantries, she assured me that she would talk to her friend and advise her that I have no intentions of getting married. Then she advised me to respond to her letter and explain my reasons for declining her proposal. After all the overseas communication, we had lunch and I returned home. Without delay, I phoned Chantelle Devereau, and explicitly informed her about my decision. I never heard from her again. However, I maintained my relationship with Michelle and Ameer. Also I kept in contact with Michelle's sister Chantelle and socialized with her whenever she visited Michelle and Ameer.

PART TWO

ENCOUNTER WITH ADVERSITY

After successfully completing advanced level in mathematics, chemistry and physics, I enrolled in the Faculty of Engineering at the St. Augustine Campus of the University of the West Indies. A few weeks after I had purchased my textbooks and was attending lectures, I received a letter from the Registrar's office informing me that my fees were not paid, and that I must have the fees paid by a certain date to continue my studies in Engineering. I was led to believe that the courses offered at the St. Augustine Campus were free. I consulted with fellow classmates and they enlightened me that the Faculty of Engineering was not free. I was given a three-week extension to pay the fees with a penalty. When I showed the letter to my Papa he was very surprised.

"I thought you told me University was free!"

"I thought so too Papa"

"Why the neighbours' children getting to attend University free and you have to pay?

I am not going to pay any money for you to study Engineering. There is already a surplus of engineers in this country. There are no jobs available for recently qualified engineers."

Papa tore up the letter and threw it in the garbage. Tanty Seloni, my stepmother looked at my Papa and shook her head. I took my Papa's remarks with a grain of salt, believing that he was not really serious and will pay the fees before the deadline. I decided to attend classes. After the deadline, I continued to attend classes. Then, as the Mathematics Professor was in the middle of his lecture, it was interrupted by loud knocks on the red door to our lecture hall. He opened the door and the registrar accompanied by her assistant entered. Having got the undivided attention of the students she made the following announcements:

"Good morning. I am sorry that I have to make this announcement publicly. But the following students, in spite of several reminders have failed to pay their fees."

She proceeded to call out the name of each of the delinquent student in alphabetical order. However, she was very considerate in her approach. When she had called the name of a student, she allowed him/her time to leave the lecture hall. Then she would call another name. I had hoped that Papa had changed his mind and had paid the fees. I was very tense as the students departed one by one with their heads hung low. As each one left they never looked back, being completely embarrassed. Then, she called my name. All eyes appeared to be glued to me as I stumbled my way down with my textbooks to leave my engineering class for the last time in my life. When I got outside there was nobody. Being too ashamed to walk through the main campus and through the main gate, I departed from the campus from behind the Engineering building. I slowly walked in shame, all the way to the Southern Main Road to get a taxi to take me home. When I arrived home, Tanty Seloni wanted to know whether they had cancelled classes. I told her that I had a very serious headache and did not feel well. I went into my bedroom and silently cried on my bed. I was very nauseated and vomited several times. My life was taking another unexpected direction despite all the studies I had invested my time in. When Papa came home from doing business in the city, Tanty Seloni informed him about my headache and nausea, and that I had returned home from university very early. He did not come to my room to find out what was my problem. On the following morning, when Papa noticed that I was not dressed to go to university, and with a puzzled look, he questioned,

"Awadh, are you not going to university today?"

"No Papa."

"Why! Are you still having your headaches and vomiting?"

"Yes Papa."

"Why are you feeling so sick?"

"Papa they kicked me out my class yesterday in front of all my classmates."

"Why?"

"You did not pay my fees."

"I told you that I will not pay for you to study engineering, pharmacy or law. I want you to study either medicine or how to manufacture paper. There are already too many lawyers, engineers, and pharmacists in the country."

I had no idea where Papa got his statistics. But he had full control of the family's finances and I lived in his house. If I do not comply with his wishes, there might be unbearable consequences. After a few days at home, I realized that I would have to start my studies over at an unknown institute. In addition, I would have to face all my friends who were pursuing courses that they were interested in. I became very ill. I made an appointment to see my family doctor, Dr. Mohammed at his office in Montrose. After narrating my situation, he promised to help. He gave me an injection and some tablets and told me to revisit him in seven days. On my return, he told me that I need more rest and to continue to take the prescribed medication. I did follow his instructions and within two weeks, I felt much better. Then he consulted with me about my future. He informed me that he had studied at Aberdeen University in Scotland, and he had the full support of his family while he was studying.

"Your father wants you to study medicine that's for him to say. Although you have the pre-requisite to get into medical college, do you know whether you could tolerate the sight of blood, the cadavers, the scents in the biopsy laboratories and performing post mortem," inquired my family doctor. I was not able to give him a competent and convincing answer. After seeing the puzzled look on my face, he suggested that before I begin to think about studying medicine, I should consider working in the hospital, and see whether I had the stamina to face the challenges that doctors face. In response to his logical comments, I conceded that I would be most willing to accept a position in a hospital. Then he informed me that he would speak to his contact at the General Hospital and recommend me for a job. Having thanked him for his advice and recommendation, I returned home.

Within two weeks, I received a phone call from the doctor. He notified me that he had arranged an interview for me with Mr. Mohan at the records department at the Port-of-Spain General Hospital, which I duly attended. During the interview, Mr. Mohan told me that my doctor had informed him about my relationship with my father, and the reason why I needed to work in the hospital. He had decided to help me get exposure to the different departments in the hospital compounds. Within several weeks, after reading hundreds of medical records, I was exposed to a world of medical terminologies which greatly interested me. Also, Mr. Mohan had loaned me a dictionary of medical terms which provided me with invaluable medical knowledge. I bought myself a pharmaceutical dictionary to learn about the different types of drugs, their symptom relieving function and the chemical composition of each one that I had read in the medical reports. Within a few weeks a valuable amicable relationship had developed between Mr. Mohan and me. There was another employee who was also interested in studying medicine. I had met him at the lady, who provided lunch for many of the hospital staff members at her home. He wanted to know whether I had applied to any medical colleges. When I responded negatively, he became annoyed and shouted, "What the hell are you waiting for?" I told him that I wanted to experience the hospital scene before applying. He sternly advised me to apply immediately.

Fortunately, I had studied and attained credits in Biology, Chemistry, Mathematics and Physics. Since my courses of studies and examinations were from England, I thought that I should proceed immediately to apply to universities in England, Scotland and Ireland to their Faculty of Medicine. I told my lunch mate that I had mailed my applications away as requested. After our regular working hours I would accompany him to different departments where he was friendly with the nurses. We also did statistical research in Neurology for the Faculty of Medicine in Jamaica. Eventually, I had to take the real acid test. Mohan arranged visits for me at the biopsy laboratories and the morgue. Dr. Messiah was the chief pathologist. The conditions in the biopsy laboratory were not a pleasant experience for me. When I exited the building, I vomited on the lawn. Mohan on seeing my reaction to the biopsy laboratory experience inquired whether I was prepared emotionally to visit the morgue. I told him that I would be ready after I had visited the washroom. It was a very hot and humid afternoon when I agreed to enter the morgue with Mohan. Not knowing what to expect, I became scared, and felt that morbid fear that I had always for horror movies engulfed me. As the steel door of the morgue got closer and closer to me, I could feel the adrenalin accelerating my heart rate and my pulse rate. There was no turning back, in spite of all my self-talk. I don't know whether it was imagination or my inherent fear of the dead, but as Mohan opened the door, the first thing that I saw were corpses wrapped in white cloth laying on both sides of the path we had to walk through to get to where autopsies were done. As I gingerly walked in, I could distinctly hear the steel door behind us slowly closing with a creaking sound. Then it closed with a frightening bang. Inside the morgue, a deathly silence welcomed us. Eventually, we entered the chamber with the drawers containing the corpses. Not seeing any living human present, I held Mohan by the shoulder and motioned that we should leave quietly. Instead, he shouted," Dr. M where are you?"

"We are in the autopsy room on the left," was the response from the room. When I turned to the left, through the crease between the door and the wall I could see a bloody body that was undergoing an autopsy. Mohan led the way and I followed slowly. He told Dr. M that I have decided to study medicine and that I wanted to be exposed to the various activities of doctors. Dr. M remarked that he could not welcome me properly because his hands were covered in blood. Dr. M then got me directly involved in the autopsy. He spoke to me as if I was one of his students who knew about human anatomy and physiology. In turn, I asked him to show me the different parts of the anatomy and to show me the sliced sections of the various organs that he had removed. But as I stood next to the dissected corpse, the constant spray of water on the bloody body left my white shirt sprinkled with blood. The other person in the room with him was a detective from the police force who was investigating the death of a famous cyclist of the island. Dr. M and the detective were preparing a forensic report. I did not expect such a traumatic experience on my first day at the morgue. When I returned a week later, Dr. M gave me a scalpel and showed me how to begin an autopsy on another body. He told me to cut down the Linea Alba, and instructed me what to do with the help of one of his assistants. At first, I noticed a familiarity in the face. It was the body of one of the women who did her groceries with her husband whom I knew, in our shop. I told Dr. M about it and he kindly excused me for the day. The following week, I had another traumatic experience, when I entered the morgue it was very noisy. There were discussions going on between several policemen and Dr. M assistants. When I did not see Dr. M, I inquired about him. One policeman responded that he would be in later and that I can sit and wait for him. Each one of the slab had a body. But the bench on the side of the room against the wall had people sleeping in sitting position. I sat next to them in the vacant spot at the end of the bench and wished them good morning and asked them whether they were with the police. There was no response. Then there was big laughter from the policemen. I looked at them and wondered why they were laughing. One of the assistants remarked that I was sitting with dead people. Immediately I got up, left the morgue and went directly home.

I got extremely ill and could not sleep. I was afraid to stay in my bedroom at night. I kept seeing the bodies of the people on which Dr. M and I performed autopsies on in my room and on my bed. I was extremely traumatized, and afraid to go to anywhere when it was dark. I begged my sister Ushi, to hold my hand and lie on the bed with me until I fell asleep. In the night when I woke up, I would scream and run into my sister's room. I could not eat any red meat. I had headaches, fever, and was extremely exhausted. I did not report to work. After two weeks absence from my job at the hospital, Mr. Mohan telephoned to find out the reasons for my absence. I related my story to him and he advised me to resign. After I sent my resignation to him, my family doctor visited me at my home. He made no reference to my job. He was very concerned about my physical and emotional wellbeing. After diagnosing my symptoms he prescribed medication, told me get as much rest as possible, and to give him a call anytime either at the office or his home if my health does not improve. Within three weeks, my health improved dramatically. My friends and families came to my home when they heard of my poor health. Their positivity, encouragement and laughter greatly improved my outlook on life. They assured me that they would continue to pray for my fast recovery so that I could return to living and enjoying life to the fullest.

After my full recovery, my Papa asked me whether I had any intention of furthering my studies in medicine. I responded that first I would like to talk with my family doctor, and to hear what advice he had for me concerning studying medicine. Papa became annoyed with my response and commented that I should be able to make my decision without anyone's advice. He then quoted Cicero: "Nobody can give you wiser advice than yourself." But I was determined to seek the professional advice of my family doctor and I made an appointment for a consultation with him. He assured me that I had experiences that he did not have while he was at medical college, and that I should use the hospital experiences to my advantage and further my studies in medicine. First, he advised me to get admitted to medical college. Then depending on my experiences in medical college, I would be able to make the necessary changes with the assistance of the counsellors at the faculty. Satisfied with his advice, I eagerly waited for the response from the universities to which I had applied. I received my first reply from the University of Aberdeen. I was accepted to study medicine. I immediately informed my doctor who congratulated me and wished me all success. Next, I informed my immediate family. Everyone who was at home congratulated me with embraces and light kisses. But Papa was not at home when the letter arrived. Normally, he would unseal and read my letters before giving them to me. His house rule was: as long as I was living under his roof, I was under his control. If I did not agree with his rules and way of life, I was free to leave and find my own accommodations at my own expense.

When Papa did return home after doing business at another property, the shop was very crowded. My sisters, my stepmother and I were all busy serving our customers. On noticing how busy the shop was, Papa joined in serving the other unattended customers. Although I had favourable news from the university to share with him, I preferred to wait until the business day was over and we were all at the dinner table. After dinner, my sister Ushi told Papa that I had some good news to share with him. Papa smiled and said, "What is the good news!" Proudly, I handed him the letter from Aberdeen University. After reading it a few times, he said nothing to me. He folded it and replaced it in the envelope. Then he handed it to me. He complained that he was too tired to discuss the contents of the letter and went into his room.

The following morning, Papa left earlier than usual for the city to purchase groceries and liquor for the business. I asked my stepmother about Papa's decision to send me to Scotland to study. She told me that that decision was yet to be made. Papa avoided me for a few more days. Realizing that I needed to know as soon as possible what would be his definitive verdict, I decided to ask him when our family was all together in the living room.

"Papa, you have read the letter from the university."

There was a dead silence in the room. My stepmother's head was bent, and my sisters' faces assumed an innocent look. Hesitatingly, Papa responded.

"Awadh you are a twenty-two years old adult. I can no longer look after your studies. If you wish to further your studies in Scotland or any other country, you will have to do it on your own. I have told you on several occasions that I want you to learn how to make paper. Paper and paper products will always be in demand."

"But Papa you also told me to study medicine."

"Yes. But you have learned from the experiences that you had at the hospital that you do not have the capability and stamina to do it."

"Papa, my doctor has encouraged me to accept the offer from the university. Also he informed me that my experiences in the morgue were too extreme for any beginning medical students. He advised me to go to Aberdeen and to begin the program, and if I should change my mind due to unforeseen unpleasant and incompatible events then I would have the opportunity to consult with the admission's office officials, and adjust my courses accordingly. But he was confident with my commitment and perseverance success would be mine."

At that stage of the discussion my sisters left the room. Papa continued his lecturing,

"Awadh, apparently you were not paying attention to my opening statement. I repeat, if you are determined to go to Scotland to study medicine, you will have to do it on your own. You will have to pay for all your expenses. Presently you have no money. So go find a job. And when you are confident and convinced that you have accumulated the amount of money you will need to further your studies, then you go and study whatever you want in any country of your choice. But don't look to me for any help." I was disappointed with Papa's attitude. However I bravely made the following life–changing claims: "Papa, I will like you to give me back the thousands of dollars that I gave you."

"What money are you talking about?"

"The money I gave you in the lawyer's office in San Fernando, after we had sold the inherited properties that Nana (Maternal grandfather) had given to me before he had died. Don't you remember when the lawyer handed me the large envelope with approximately twenty thousand dollars you asked me what I was going to do with all that money. And I told you that I shall deposit it in a saving account in the Barclays Bank. Then you explained to me that you will be able to invest the money in a new business venture which will yield a better return than any bank. After you made that suggestion, I looked at the lawyer and I asked him for his advice. The lawyer told me that it was my money. And if I believed that I could trust you to look after my money then I had the final decision to make. In the presence of the lawyer, I handed over the money to you, in the confident belief that when I would need it, it would be readily available. And today you are telling me that I am an adult and that if I want to further my studies that I will have to pay my way."

"Well Awadh, in the first place, that money was never yours. It's true your Nana gave you all his wealth, but if your mother was alive she would have inherited all of your Nana's wealth. And since your mother was my wife, technically all the money that you are bravely talking about belonged to me. You make your money and spend it in whatever way you wish. So please don't ever say that I have money for you."

I was absolutely shocked by his response. I looked at him and felt very betrayed and helpless. He got up and went into his room and slammed the door. My stepmother was quiet as she left for the kitchen. I went into my bedroom and wept on my pillow. My mind started to replay all the disappointments that my body, mind, and spirit had to withstand from my Papa over the years. As I mindfully rehearsed all possible options that were available, I fell asleep. The following day, I remained in bed until almost noon. Ushi knocked on my door to find out why I was still in bed. I told her that I was hungry and that whether she could prepare something for me to eat. She agreed and left for the kitchen. I got out of bed, went to the washroom, shaved, showered and got dressed to face the world as best as I could after last night's events. Ushi and I were the only ones in the kitchen dining room when she inquired about what had happened after she had gone to sleep. When she heard what Papa had told me she became sad and cried. She could not understand Papa's unwillingness to support me. And how he falsely laid claim on my inheritance. She hugged me and reassured me that everything will turn out favourably for me in the end. She wondered why Papa was always against my choices. She pointed out that this was the third time he had forced me to change my study paths. I concurred with her when she recalled the instances Papa did not allow me to further my studies in mathematics, physics and chemistry in San Fernando because he needed me to help in the shop. How he forced me to study languages at the College of St. Philip and St. James in the hometown, and how he refused to pay the fees for me to study Engineering and now he denied me the money I inherited from my maternal grandfather. Ushi wanted to know what options were open to me. I explained that in order for me to study medicine in Scotland, I would need money. Ajah was aware that Nana had given me all his wealth so he was not obligated to give me anything more.

My mind was definitely in a maelstrom. I spent a lot of my waking time reflecting on advice that my grandfathers had passed on to me during my interactions and discussions with them. I specifically recalled a conversation with my Nana about his facing up to adversity during his life, and how he and his wife prevailed. Nana had instilled in my mind that life would not always be full of joy, happiness, and free from worries. But he emphasized that if adversity should strike, and they would definitely strike at any time, then I should identify the reasons for it, analyze the causes of the adverse conditions, evaluate them, and immediately start seeking a viable solution. I should always try to convert adversity into opportunity. Also, I should be absolutely sure of my future plans so that the actions that I take would directly impact the results of my final goals. In other words, I must commit to the things that are important to me and would have positive and beneficial consequences in my life. In addition, in order to strengthen my resilience to adversities, I have to be fully involved in the situation and not only possess a passionate willingness to confront the challenge directly but also have the burning desire to control my life and influence the existing situation.

As I lay on my bed reflecting on the thoughts of Nana, the idea of no income and no financial support from my parents for me to further my studies provoked in me fears, despair, sadness, worries and failures. But I decided that I had to replace all these negative emotions with hope, curiosity and a positive attitude. I started thinking about making new connections, about seeking new adventures and about exploring new possibilities of which I may be innocently incompetent.

For a few days, I just tossed in my bed with a hollow feeling in my stomach and with little appetite. Ushi was always at my side encouraging me not to give up. When few of my friends did not see me at the bicycle stand they came into the shop and inquired about my whereabouts and wellbeing. I welcomed them to the upstairs veranda and informed them about my predicament. They offered several possible solutions by looking at the problem from different perspectives. I greatly appreciated their interest and their support which made me feel healthier and ready to start putting an action plan in place.

The next day, I telephoned Marvin one of my reliable friends, and invited him to visit me at my home. I told him it was urgent. Within an hour he picked me up and drove me to his home. I related the confrontation between my Papa and me, and the predicament I was in. Marvin belonged to a very reputable and prominent family in the neighbouring village. They were well connected to people in influential positions. His family had known me for a very long time because his father was once my teacher in elementary school. I was always welcomed at his home by his parents, brothers and sisters. Fortunately his father, who held political and social clout in the community, was at home. After getting his father's attention, he asked me to narrate the confrontation I had with my father. He decided to help me. He took out his black notebook, searched through it and after he found what he was searching for, he went to the telephone anchored on the corner wall. He dialed a number from his notebook and patiently waited for someone to answer. Someone answered after a few rings. He asked to speak to a woman and was informed that she was at a meeting. After leaving a message for her, he hung up and told me that he would do the due process and Marvin would inform me about what actions would have to be taken. I felt hopeful and a bit more confident that a solution to my problem would happen soon.

A few days later Marvin visited me at my home, and he informed me that his father had spoken to his contact, and had arranged for an interview for me at the Ministry of Education on Haig Street in Port of-Spain. Then, he outlined the various documents that I had to take, and noted the name of the person with whom I had the interview and the date and the time. Elated, I embraced him and extended my sincerest gratitude to him, and I told him that I would call his father and thank him for the efforts that he had expended on my behalf.

One week later, I was in the Ministry of Education office, waiting for my interview. At its conclusion I was offered the choice of a teaching position at either of two secondary schools. One of the schools was located in south east Port of Spain and the other was located in Belmont. She advised me to think very carefully before making my decision, and that I should contact her within four days with my final decision. On my return home, I was very exhausted from the length of time I had to sit in the taxi, as the driver struggled in the heavy traffic to get from the city of Port of Spain to Montrose Junction. Ushi was waiting for me to return from my interview. Before asking any questions, she gave me food and a cold drink that she had prepared, and was pleased to see me consume all the delicious food. When I had finished, she requested that I change into more comfortable clothes. She then inquired about the outcome of my interview. As I spoke, she became very excited and truly happy. She embraced and kissed me, and with tears in her eyes, said, "God is watching, and He will bless and guide you always."

After getting a taste of the traffic congestions on the highways between Port of Spain and Montrose, I decided that before I make a decision about the school in which to teach, I should first experience the travelling involved to each one of the schools, and take into serious consideration the travelling time, the inconveniences, the cost, and the time of departure from my home and the time of arrival for each school. Also I had to assess and evaluate the working environment both inside and around each school. It took three days to do my investigations. After I made my decision, I returned to the Ministry of Education office and waited until my interviewer was available. Again she was accommodating and congenial. I informed her that I would prefer to teach in southeast Port of Spain Government School. She inquired whether I would be interested in having an interview with the principal of the school, Dr. Aron, before the resumption of classes in a few days. Without any hesitation, I accepted her offer. She phoned the school and spoke to the principal who agreed to meet me that afternoon at two o'clock at the front gate of the school. I thanked her for all her assistance and cooperation. When I got outside of the building, I took a few deep breaths, looked into the blue sky and expressed my sincerest gratitude. I seriously contemplated walking to the school which was located in close proximity to the market and the core of the downtown. But after carefully studying the map of Port of Spain, I decided that after that long walk through the various streets in the city core, I would be too exhausted to have a relaxing interview with the principal. Instead, I took a taxi to the downtown and headed for the nearest restaurant and had a late lunch. After lunch, I walked down the main street, and did some window shopping on my way to meet the principal.

◆ ◆ ◆

When I arrived at Southeast Port of Spain School, I was warmly greeted by Dr. Aron at the front iron-gate. He addressed me as Mr. Jaggernath. He escorted me to his office on the second floor and introduced me to his secretary. Dr. Aron inquired about my qualifications, my teaching experiences and my social and educational background. After looking at my qualifications, he shook his head agreeably and announced that I was suited for English, mathematics and sciences. In a pleasant tone, he remarked that he was happy that I had chosen to teach in his school.

He added that although his school was located in a government housing area, and near the city market, the student population was composed of not only city families but also families from the outlying towns and villages. The staff members, on the other hand, were an assemblage of professionals who had received their teaching qualifications in different countries, were of different ages and were from a variety of ethnicities. Dr. Aron was confident that with my background, despite being from the country, I would quickly fit in and gain invaluable life-long experiences in all area of my life. I thanked him for having such confidence in me and for his assurance in my abilities and capabilities. After his encouraging talk, he led me on a tour of the facilities within the school and outside the school. I questioned him about the green and blue graffiti which adorned the walls on the large walls facing the yard, where the students assembled in the morning to sing the national anthem and recite the daily prayers. He avoided answering my question directly, pointing out that I would gradually learn more about the coloured graffiti during my teaching assignments. His answer reminded me of my Latin teacher who used to say, "Wisdom is knowing when and where to use your knowledge to your advantage."

The morning arrived on which I had to begin my teaching career at the secondary level in S.E. Port of Spain. I got up earlier than usual, and after performing my daily ablutions, I got dressed as a model teacher of the times: a well-ironed pair of brown cotton slacks and white cotton shirt, a slim tie and highly-polished pair of brown shoes to coordinate with my belt and socks. I had breakfast with Ushi and then I left just before seven o'clock for the taxi stand. With the help of a tout, I got a taxi to the city. The traffic was very busy and at times it came to a standstill, a situation I never anticipated to take place so early in the day. The taxi dropped me on the street behind the Cathedral of the Immaculate Conception. It was after eight o'clock, and I had to walk briskly with my white Pan-Am bag slung over my shoulder. As I approached the school, already there were hundreds of uniformed students milling around in the school yard, the corridors and alighting from a variety of vehicles. I waded bravely and confidently through the gateway and the stairway leading to the second floor to report to Dr. Aron. He was extremely welcoming. At once, he handed me my teaching time table and asked me to study it. I was very pleased and excited to get in the classroom in front of the young minds. He took me to the staff room and introduced me to the other staff members who were in the room. He assured me that before the end of the school day, I would become acquainted with the other staff members. I thanked him for his kindness and personal interest.

When I approached my first class, the students were extremely noisy but as I entered and said good morning to them, they responded and gradually the noise evaporated. The population of the classroom was similar to ones when I attended the government elementary school as a little boy. There were students of every ethnicity, colour, race and religious belief. Within a few weeks, I felt very comfortable and happy with the staff and the students that I interacted with. Towards the end of my first month of teaching at school, I received my first pay in cash. I felt very happy, hopeful and joyful. That was the money I planned to use as the seed for furthering my studies overseas. But as I exited the school premises through the iron-gate, I was approached and surrounded by four young adult men of African descent.

"Hello teach we know that today is payday. So we come for a lil piece of it. We only want a few drinks and some cutters. We don't have to go far. The rum shop is just around the corner. Come Lay we go."

I had no choice but to obey their request. They were wearing their caps reversed and had toothpicks in their mouths. I was definitely in unfamiliar territory and was in the middle of a precarious situation. In my mind, I contemplated running back to school but when I saw the seriousness on their faces and eyes, I realized that discretion was the better part of valour and accompanied them to the rum shop. It set me back about ten dollars but my life and safety was worth more.

The following morning, I reported to the teachers who were in the staff room about the incident that I experienced yesterday after school. Mrs. Kam laughed aloud and so did a few other teachers. I wanted to know what was so humorous about my complaining about the unexpected challenge I had to endure. She said that I should expect anything to happen in the seedy neighbourhood in which I was working. Mrs. Jackman piped up and said, "Jaggers have you carefully examined the mixture of the ethnicity of the staff? Don't you realize that you are the only pure East Indian teacher?"

Mrs. Kam interjected, "Jaggers. You got away very cheaply. The money that you spent on those young men was your protection money for the month. They will be at the iron-gate every pay day waiting for your protection contribution. So be happy that you have a protection shield in this community at minimum cost."

I never brought up the issue again with the staff. And every month I paid my safety premium insurance. But I did forge a cordial relationship with them, and they promised me that in the event anyone should attempt to harass or hassle me for anything, I should not hesitate to inform them at our next meeting.

As I continued to teach diligently and co-operatively, many staff members inquired about my future goals and expectations. Believing that no man is an island, I told them about my experiences with my father and my quest for any opportunity to earn cash as quickly as possible so that I could support my planned studies overseas. I was happy that I did divulge my plans to them. Not long after, the principal met me in the hallway and asked me whether I would be interested in teaching English to adult students at our school, for the extra mural department of the University of the West Indies. I immediately accepted the offer. And I started on the English assignment twice per week after regular classes had ended. The extra salary was most welcome. In addition to my regular teaching assignment at the school, and the extra-mural English assignment, I did private tutoring in the sciences on two evenings after school.

One Monday morning I arrived at school very early. Much to my surprise as I walked up the stairs to the staff room, I noticed that the asphalt in the school yard where the students assembled each morning, had rags with blood stains, empty cartridge shells and broken glass. Again, I consulted Mrs. Kam, who was one of the most experienced and senior teacher at the school, about the disgusting sight in the school yard.

"Jaggers. You see that blue and green graffiti painted on the walls."

"Yes."

"Those are the names of the two rivalling gangs in this area. Apparently the school yard is their battle arena. Every time the graffiti are painted over, they reappear again in a short time. However, the principal decided to leave them. I think the students know what they represent and just live with it."

I dared not pursue the topic any further.

◆ ◆ ◆

There was no shortage of novel, challenging and exciting experiences for me at the school. After two months I noticed that my lunch, which was prepared and packed by Ushi in my Pan-Am bag, had changed from macaroni and cheese –pie and baked chicken on Mondays, home-made soups on Tuesdays, paratha roti with vegetable fillings on Wednesdays, dhal puri and curried or stewed shrimps on Thursdays and pelau on Fridays to a variety of sandwiches on Wednesday and Thursdays. After two weeks of these surprise sandwiches instead of my favourite rotis, I complained to my sister. She appeared puzzled and asked me to explain. When I had finished my explanation, she concluded that someone was exchanging their lunch with mine on those days. She claimed that she neither made nor gave me sandwiches at any time for lunch. I did not mention this oddity to anyone in the staff room. I contrived a scheme with Ushi to catch the surreptitious swapper. Ushi suggested that she prepared two similar lunches on Wednesday and Thursday. But she would lace one with Papa's dynamite pepper sauce and one without the pepper sauce. She would mark the paper bags so that when I arrived at school, I would remove the lunch without pepper, and hide it in one of the drawers in my desk. The first day we implemented the scheme, resulted in the capture of the switcher.

At my lunch time, Mrs. Kam smiled and said, "Jaggers! What did you put in your lunch today?"

"Why are you asking?"

"Candice almost died!

"Why?"

"She could not stop drinking water after she ate your lunch. In fact Miss Chan is babysitting her class while Candice is in the washroom."

Why was she exchanging my lunches only on Wednesdays and Thursdays?"

"Jaggers. Candice is mulatto who loves roti but it is unavailable in this city where she lives."

"Why didn't she ask me to share my lunch with her?"

"That's the question that you will have to ask her."

"Thank you for the information Mrs. Kam. I will have a talk with her at the end of the day."

At the end of the day, Candice was still uncomfortable. I went to her and apologized for the unexpected pain and suffering that I had inflicted on her. She did not respond to my apology. I walked away, feeling remorseful. However, on the following Monday, Candice looking as glamourous as ever and wearing a big smile, came to me and asked me to pardon her for her misdemeanour. I did and apologized again for my silly prank. She accepted. We then made an agreement to share lunches on Wednesdays and Thursdays.

This secondary school was never short of excitement and unexpected events. One beautiful morning, immediately after the opening exercises with the students were safely in their classrooms, the principal informed me that a parent wanted to talk to me about his son in the corridor on the second floor. The principal looked rather concerned and advised me to be very careful. I walked up the concrete step to the second floor where the father and his son were waiting for me. I recognized the student who appeared to be very happy that his father wanted to talk to me. Honestly, I did not have a clue why this student's father wanted to talk to me.

"Good morning sir. Are you Mr. Jaggernath?"

"Yes!" "Do you know why I am here?"

"Not really!"

"My son tells me that you beat him frequently in math classes for no good reason."

Instantly, I realized that I had to tell the parent my reasons for using the strap on him.

"Well. Your son does not do his homework. And when I ask his reasons, he says that he has no time to do his homework because he is busy doing things."

"Did he ever tell you what he was busy doing?"

"Yes! He told me that he has to help his father carry guns over the hill."

At that point, the father became very angry at his son. He turned around, picked up his son and shouted, "You lil bitch, I go kill yu ass". The father threw his son over the railing and ran down the concrete stairwell after him. At that same moment, the son got up from the asphalt pavement on the ground floor in a flash, and ran for his life with his father in close pursuit. The father was a tall and heavy man of African descent. The noise and vibrations created by his footstep down the steps and across the yard loudly echoed through the entire building. Calmly, I stood on the second floor taken in all the action. Then slowly the doors opened on all the floors and the occupants came out to view the debris. The principal was the first to question me about the running and the loud noises. I fabricated a story which no one challenged. I told them that the father was displeased that I was strapping his son for not doing his mathematics homework, and he had come personally to give me a strapping. But as he pulled out his strap and struck his first blow, I stepped aside and let my karate and judo skills go to work. Later on in the day, the principal spoke to me privately and informed me that the father was the leader of one of the gangs in the hills. However, my version of the story travelled throughout the students' grapevine system and, I earned the respect of both staff and students as a fighter.

Unexpectedly, Dr. Aron appeared at the doorway of my science class and questioned me about the progress of the preparations for the school's annual science fair. I responded that I was collaborating with the laboratory assistant, who was quite competent and experienced in organizing science fairs. Dr. Aron then informed me that I had the responsibility to supervise the entire project, and had to take all necessary precautions to ensure the security and safety not only of the visiting parents and visiting students, but, also the Prime Minister, Dr. Eric Williams and his entourage while they were at the science fair. After assuring him that the laboratory assistant and I would do our best to prevent any mishaps, he left.

This unexpected visit by Dr. Aron and his concerns about the safety factors at the coming annual science fair immediately forced me to meet with the laboratory assistant. Meticulously, we checked all the safety features for each of the exhibits, demonstrations and displays. Also, the assistant requested that the two top performing students in science be selected to perform the chemistry demonstration that he had performed earlier in the science program. I asked him why he was selecting that particular demonstration. He said that it reminded him of the undivided interest exhibited by the students during the demonstration and the tremendous ovation he had received after the final results of the reaction. He added that that particular demonstration had always entertained both the parents and students at the science fairs at the other schools. Implicitly, I trusted his judgement to include the demonstration in the program. Afterwards, I informed the principal about the details of the activities that we had planned.

The evening of the annual science fair arrived. Many parents and uniformed students had arrived early to meet the Prime Minister and to share their scientific experiences with him. As soon as the police escort and security team assigned to the Prime Minister had arrived, the crowd was controlled to allow the Prime Minister safe and free passage to the school. Leading the welcoming party was Dr. Aron and the administrators of the school. First, the Prime Minister was given a brief tour of the three floors of the school. This was followed by a private reception for the dignitaries.

I double checked with the laboratory assistant. He informed

me that the two top science students were in the back laboratory doing their final preparation for the demonstration and explanations. Dr. Aron looked at me as he accompanied the Prime Minister to the exhibition area. Suddenly there was a loud explosion in the back laboratory. In a flash, members of the Prime Minister's security team shielded him with their bodies. Other security officers ran to the site of the explosion. The other visitors ran for safety outside the building. The Prime Minister, in full control of all his faculties inquired immediately "Who is in charge?"

Without hesitation, the principal responded, "Mr. Jaggernath!" At once he identified me. As this dialogue was taking place, two students were brought out from the back laboratory where the explosion had taken place. The security captain spoke to the Prime Minister in confidence. The Prime Minister smiled. Then the Prime Minister approached the youngsters and asked them what they were doing that caused the explosion. Although the two boys were shaken, the Prime Minister led the two youths to the front of the re-gathering parents and short-circuited our science programme. He asked the two boys to demonstrate the activity that led to the explosion. Having regained their confidence the two boys did as instructed by the Prime Minister. They received tremendous applause from every person in the room for their dynamic presentation of the reaction of a piece of pure sodium with water. In fact, the Prime Minister was laughing and told the congregation that he personally had that experience with his lab partner many years ago at Queen's Royal College.

Dr. Aron, in spite of the initial excitement, was pleased with the final outcome of the annual science fair. In the following year, I was assigned again to supervise the annual science fair. When the Prime Minister arrived at the school, the superintendent of police entered the school, and told the principal that the prime minister would like to talk with Mr. Jaggernath. I was escorted to him. "Have you planned any explosion for the evening?" "No mister Prime Minister," I promised.

"Then you lead the way."

At the beginning of my second year of teaching at S.E. Port of Spain Government Secondary, I learned that new teachers had joined the teaching staff. At the first staff meeting, Dr. Aron introduced the new staff to us. The three new teachers were on exchange programmes from Ontario, Canada. I was greatly impressed with their friendliness, professionalism, kindness, and intelligence of each of the Canadian teachers. At once, I desired to form friendly relationships with them. After the staff meeting, I introduced myself to each one of the Canadian teachers. Within the first week, I communicated and exchanged pleasantries with them. I socialized with each of them either at lunch, spares or before the commencement of classes in the morning. During our conversations, I learned that Bruner had a specialist degree in geography from McMaster University in Hamilton, Ontario. His wife Laura had accompanied him. She was a teacher-librarian on exchange at the Public Library in downtown Port of Spain. Also, they had two adult children who were employed as teachers in England. Three years before, they had been on a teacher's exchange in Yorkshire County, in England. Charlie, a mathematics graduate from McMaster University, was accompanied by his wife Nancy. Nancy was French Canadian, a graduate of McGill University, had got a position with the Alliance Francaise in Port of Spain. They resided in the city of Port of Spain. Charlie and Nancy had already experienced teacher exchanges in New Zealand.

The physical education teacher, Kennedy and his wife Sandy, an English teacher, had both graduated from the University of Toronto, and had exchanged their homes in Toronto with a teacher and his wife from Maraval. Sandy was originally from England. She had received her teaching qualifications from Cambridge University. Sandy was also on an exchange, and taught English at another secondary school in Port of Spain.

Both of them had previous experience with teacher's exchanges in Melbourne, Australia. I was extremely fortunate to be in the company of such experienced, talented, widely travelled, adventurous, and congenial educators from Ontario.

In addition to learning about their families and their teaching experiences, they strongly expressed their passionate desire to experience the social lifestyles and the diverse cultural heritage of the people of Trinidad and Tobago. In addition, they were interested in exploring the natural wonders of Trinidad and Tobago.

With cautious optimism, I then approached a few members on staff and informed them of my newly acquired knowledge of the Canadian teachers. Four of them were extremely interested in helping me fulfill the passionate desires of the visiting teachers. Each one of the volunteers was experienced educators who had studied overseas, had a wide range of talents and skills. Harriet had studied political science and sociology at the University of Belfast. She was married to a lecturer at the university. Nicholas had graduated with a degree in mathematics from U.W.I. in Jamaica. Daniella got her science degree in Germany. Yasmin did her studies in the University of Benares. Having established an orientation team, we collectively developed a tentative outline. It encompassed the cultural, social, economic, political, ecological, and geographical aspects of Trinidad and Tobago.

After we had all agreed that the programme that we designed and planned to execute was in the best interest of the exchange teachers and wives, we decided to meet with them. We met the three families at the courtyard of the restaurant situated at the entrance to the Botanical gardens, across from the famous Queen's Park Savannah in Port of Spain. While having lunch, we asked them what were they interested in seeing, in doing and in learning. Much to our delight, our scheduled activities had included all of their wishes. Then we asked them to prioritize their interests. After some serious deliberations, they presented us with their final list.

With unbridled exuberance, we snatched the opportunity to be tour guides for our Canadian guests in our country. With the full cooperation of the librarian Laura, we received the necessary information for our planned events. It was towards the end of September 1965 and the next two significant cultural Indo-Trinidadian celebrations were Ram Leela and Diwali. These celebrations took place in villages throughout the island each towards the middle of October. In order to prepare them to appreciate Indian culture in Trinidad, we organised two tours. The first tour was to the Lion House, officially named the "Anand Bhavan", which in English means "mansion of Bliss". This house is one of the architectural wonders in the western hemisphere, and is not only a symbol of but also a memorial to the indentured Indian Immigrants who came to Trinidad in 1845. The second Hindu icon was the Port of Spain Hindu Mandir, officially named the "Paschim Kaashi," which means the "Benares of the west". It was an orthodox Sanatanist Hindu Mandir located in St. James on Ethel Street. This mandir was quite unusual. It provided seating for the devotees, which made it appear like a Christian church. On the visit to the Lion House, our guests learnt about the history and the families that lived in it and the various functions it fulfilled over the years. Meanwhile, at the Paschim Kaashi, the guide, who was a Hindu pundit (priest), was very knowledgeable about Hindu mythology and the history of the temple. He was fluent in English and Hindi, and we took the liberty to find out the significance of each Hindu festival that would take place during the year. He was most enlightening and hospitable. After listening to the pundit's lecture, our guests were impatiently waiting to witness and participate in the upcoming Hindu festivals, when possible, later in the year.

Our guests were reminded about the two great Hindus festivals in October, Ram Leela (Lord Rama's play) and Divali. According to the pundit at the Mandir on Ethel street, two weeks before the festival of Divali, the story of Lord Rama and his ten-day battle against the ten-headed, Ravana, would be re-enacted in villages and savannahs, in an open-air theatre format, in various parts of Trinidad. Our guests were taken by car to Felicity grounds to see the play in the open air. The battle was fought between Lord Rama and his consorts against Ravana and his army, in Sri Lanka. Ravana had kidnapped lord Rama's wife, Sita, and had taken her back to his kingdom. After Lord Rama defeated Ravana with the invaluable support of Hanuman, and having rescued his wife, the story culminated with the burning of an effigy of Ravana.

Being very ecstatic and charmed by the acting and the presentation of Lord Rama's play, our guests were more than anxious to witness and participate in the festival of lights. On our way to see the festival of lights at the Mandir, the librarian was relating the story to her colleagues. She said that the festival of lights was celebrated in honour of Lakshmi, the goddess of wealth and prosperity. In response, Charlie recalled that the pundit said that the festival of lights was to commemorate the return of Lord Rama to his home town of Ayodha, after being exiled for fourteen years. I reassured them that according to Hindus they were both correct. What was most appreciated was their openness to dialogue with the Hindus in the crowds as they wondered at the fantastic configurations of thousands of lighted diyas (very tiny crucible-shaped clay pots) on top of the walls encircling the Mandir. On the inside of the mandir, the marble statues of the Hindu gods and goddesses were decorated with lighted diyas. Also, on the surrounding grounds, thousands of lighted diyas were arranged in different patterns on bamboo structures. This spectacular light fantasy was accompanied by lilting and rhythmic music and songs of Indian heritage. Our guests did not hesitate to mingle with the people in the crowd. On account of our guests' curiosity to learn more about the Divali celebrations, a woman invited them to her family home for savouries and Indian sweets. But before we went to the family's residence on Patna Street, we drove around the streets of St. James to see the homes decorated with lighted diyas. Many of the streets had the same name as those in Uttar Pradesh in India. Our guests commented that the spectacle of lights reminded them of Christmas lights in Canada.

On one of the regular school days in November 1965, few students requested a field trip to the library to do research for their English project. It was a request that captured my interest. I told the students that I greatly valued their suggestion, and I would give it some serious consideration.

At the end of the class I phoned Laura, and told her about the request of my students. She told me to call back at the end of the day. Before I could take my students on a field trip to the public library, I needed the approval of Dr. Aron. With his permission, I decided to visit Laura at the library instead of phoning her. Since the library was only a few streets away I took a brisk walk to it at the end of the school day. When I arrived at the library, Laura was attending to a young, beautiful and charming young woman. I was fascinated with her mannerism and enthusiasm for whatever she had researched. As she left and had returned to her cubicle, Laura commented, "What a wonderful person!"

"Who is she Laura?

"Why don't you find out Awadh?"

With that idea planted in my head, I decided that after I had completed my field trip arrangements for my two English classes, I would attempt to break the ice with the young woman. Fortunately, after Laura had made the reservation for my classes, the woman was reading. As I cautiously approached her cubicle and peered over her shoulder, I noticed that she was reading the play written by Goldsmith - She Stoops to Conquer.

"Hello! My name is Awadh. I hope that I'm not disturbing you from your studies!"

"No! In fact, I was just about to call it a day. My name is Ambica."

"OK Ambica. I can help you pack your bag."

"That's OK. I will do it faster. I know where everything goes."

"I hope that I'm not rude by offering to help?"

"No. You are not."

She took her bag, said "nice to meet you" and started to walk away from me. At that moment, I thought that she was not interested in me, but I was interested in her. I followed her out the library and asked her to slow down. She did not answer. She walked too fast for me and I had to hurry after her through the crowded streets. I then caught up with her and asked her to slow down. Out of breath, I warned her that I was going to follow her wherever she went. She stopped, looked at me and said, "Why are you harassing me?"

I told her that I was interested in her, and would like to know more about her. Also, I would like to share a cold drink with her. She disregarded my request and continued to walk away. Finally, I was beside her and told her that I liked her and that she was beautiful. I wanted to call her by name. But I had forgotten it. I pleaded with her to stop. I had to repeat it several times. Then she stopped, looked at me and inquired. "Are you a teacher?"

"What made you ask that question?"

"The way you are dressed. Also, I heard you talking to the librarian about your English classes."

"Yes. I am a teacher at the secondary school located a few streets from the library. Will you have a cold drink or a tea with me before you go home?"

She hesitated and with a smile agreed to have a cold drink with me. I told her to decide where we should go. She led the way and I followed her to a restaurant on Frederick Street.

At the restaurant, I asked her to repeat her name. She looked at me in disgust and said, "Already you have forgotten my name! And you claimed that you like me and want to know me better!"

I did not reply to her caustic tone. Instead, I apologised and kindly ask her to repeat her name. She repeated it. Then, she told me that I could call her Rani.

I told had that I was hungry, and I had a long tiring day in the classroom teaching. While they were preparing milk shakes for both of us, I looked through the menu and selected my dinner. Then I passed the menu to her and told her to order whatever she wished to have for dinner. She said that she was not hungry. I insisted. And after much fussing, she did place an order. During dinner I asked about her family, her address and her phone number. She refused to give me either her address or her phone number. Being a bit enlightened about her family and her lineage, I realized that she was from one of the most prominent Hindu families in Trinidad and Tobago. Since she did not inquire about my family I did not say anything.

After dinner, Rani thanked me for dinner and my interest in her. Since it was very dark outside, I volunteered to accompany her to her home across the city. She declined the offer and started to walk away. I was not going to let her walk alone in the dark. I liked her and was truly interested. I was determined to know her place of residence, and I boldly accompanied her on her homeward walk. The walk was more than I had bargained for, but in the long-run it was worth my time and effort. Before I said farewell at the gate in front of her home, I told her that I would like to meet her again at the library. After giving her my school's phone number, I said good night.

I met her at the library a few times and did share cold drinks and food with her. Our relationship gradually strengthened and I started dating her. She was adorable and vibrant, qualities that I greatly admired and appreciated. We went to movies, dances, concerts, and on beach picnics. Then, one evening I borrowed my Papa's car to take her to the drive-in cinema in Diego Martin. We did have a lot of fun at the drive-in. I recalled it was the movie, "Gigi", with Maurice Chevalier, Leslie Caron and Louis Jordan. Two days later, my Papa, with a big grin questioned me in the presence of my sisters and stepmother while we were in the living room.

"Who was the beautiful, dainty and well-groomed young

lady you had at the drive-in cinema in Diego Martin the other night?"

Papa's question completely stunned me. How could Papa know that I went to the drive-in cinema in Diego Martin! Was he stalking me? Did he hire a private eye to follow me? All these ideas swirled in my brain before I was able to give a cogent answer. His question sparked everyone's keen interest. At first, I felt embarrassed that Papa found about my secret love affair from an outside source. While I was narrating the story about Rani, I was interrupted several times by my sisters, my stepmother and my Papa, as they all wanted more details. It was like a courthouse cross examination. They were very excited when they heard about her family background and that she was studying. But I did not anticipate the long-term consequences of my confession. My family requested that I introduced her to them as soon as possible. In fact my Papa told me that he would like to meet Rani's family on the weekend. I did not encourage his suggestion. They were all excited and kept on repeating that they loved the name Rani. Papa with a smile said, "We will have Rani in the house."

It was only when I was in bed that I realized that Papa would want me to marry her and settle down, open a business place and not to think about furthering my studies.

The following morning, at breakfast, Papa decided to explain to me how he learned about my night at the drive-in cinema, and the details about the movie that I saw. He informed me that his car was well known to the business merchants and their support staff in the commercial district of Port of Spain, where he has been doing business for several years. One of the young staff was at the drive-in with his girlfriend and recognized the car and was surprised. Later, when they saw Papa they asked him all sorts of questions about his date at the drive-in cinema.

On my next date, I told Rani about the drive–in cinema story, and that my family would like to meet her as soon as possible. She agreed to meet my family at my home. After introducing Rani, my family fell in love with her. My Papa was extremely fond of her. He wanted to know whether she was anorexic, and suggested that he would be happy to have her become a family member. I did not take his comments seriously. I did meet Rani's family, but, sadly I was not totally accepted by them. They researched my family background, but many members of her family were of the opinion that she would have better offers from wealthier families. I disregarded their snobbery, however, and continued to date her until I left to continue my studies in Canada.

I gradually developed beautiful collegial and wholesome relationships with each of the wives of the Canadian teachers. I became attached to Nancy because of her passion for French literature, and Sandy for her great enthusiasm for English literature. With my limited knowledge I was able to participate and appreciate conversing in both French and English. Laura, the teacher-librarian always had a different perspective on any literary work being discussed, which was greatly appreciated and welcomed. Then to my surprise and delight, the wives of the three Canadian teachers took the initiative and invited our orientation team to a French morality play. Laura and Sandy had studied the play with Nancy at the Alliance Francaise. Nancy had tickets for the classic play "Tartuffe". It was to be a private presentation for members of the Alliance Francaise and their guests. We accepted the invitation but we asked for the meaning of a morality play and a synopsis of the play in English.

My Canadian teaching colleagues and their wives met us at the Kapok hotel where we were enlightened about morality plays. With my limited college French knowledge and with the preparatory notes, I realized that Tartuffe was a study of hypocrisy, and a satire with many serious undertones of human idiosyncrasies. However, it dealt with love, was very funny and very relevant to contemporary life.

After the lunch at Kapok, I went home and went to bed. While

I was asleep, the telephone rang as I wondered who would be calling me so late at night. "Awadh ! Are you ill? We have not heard from you for almost a month. Michelle and I are concerned."

"Ameer, I am busy introducing my three Canadian colleagues and their wives, who are on exchange on educational programs, to the cultural diversity, the heritage landmarks and the other things that are of special interests to the people of Trinidad and Tobago."

"I'd like to meet your Canadian colleagues and their wives. I am extending invitations to all of them to come to my home on Sunday for a barbeque with all the trimmings and full access to the pools and the bar around the pools. Michelle will be most delighted to host your friends."

"Ameer, I have four of my colleagues who are on my planning team."

"Awadh, mi casa es tu casa. Bring all of them. The more the merrier."

I kindly accepted his invitation and emphasized that first I would have to inform my planning team and our guests. After hearing their responses, I said I would get back to him. Everyone was in agreement with Ameer's invitation.

We arrived just after lunch at Ameer's residence, and I introduced each one to Ameer and his beautiful wife Michelle. Our hosts were delighted with their guests. They congratulated me for my sincere involvement with such talented and ambitious individuals. Having had a fantastic and festive time, my invited guests and I thanked our host and hostess for their generosity, kindness and friendship. In fact, Nancy, who was bilingual in French and English, spent a lot of quality time with Michelle. I would like to believe that they became good friends. As we were departing Michelle and Ameer extended open invitations to all of my friends. They kindly accepted.

After we had exposed our Canadian guests to a few flavours of the Indo-Trinidadian culture, we decided that we should focus next on the unique features of the celebrations of a Trinidadian Christmas and Trinidad Carnival.

A couple of months before Christmas, the new calypsos were gradually released in the calypso tents, record shops and over the radio stations. These calypsos were potential entries in the Carnival celebrations which would begin at Christmas and culminate at midnight Shrove Tuesday. The team decided to introduce the Canadians to steel band music, calypsos, Trinidadian comedy and the various Carnival and Christmas related activities that were performed in and around Port of Spain, before the two official of Carnival. The famous band leader, Peter Minshall, called the Trinidad Carnival pageant "theatre on the street." Since our guests resided in and around Port of Spain travelling was easy to any pan yard, theatre, play house, calypso tents and all the shows held at the grandstand in the Queen's Park Savannah.

As the Christmas season drew closer, our guests were slowly introduced to the Parang music that was prevalent at Christmas time on the air waves, television and on the streets. They loved the rhythmic beats and sounds of Parang, and inquired about its origin and the names of the musical instruments and the language of the lyrics. We informed them that genre of music was brought from Venezuela by the Amerindians and the Spanish migrants.

It was about two weeks before Christmas when Dr. Aron spoke to me privately and instructed me to invite my orientation team, the three Canadian teachers and their wives to his private Parang dance party and Trinidad style Christmas dinner at his home in St. Ann. I must confess that I had never attended a Parang party. As requested, we were all present at Dr. Aron's residence on the day before Christmas. We were cordially welcomed and cheerfully introduced first to his family and then to his other special guests. Our Canadian friends quickly struck up lively conversations in different parts of the party area with different guests who were from a wide diversity of professions. These guests were of different colour and race, and were also world travellers. Before the end of the party our Canadian friends had made many new connections. After they had narrated their reasons for their presence in Trinidad, what they had experienced, and what they had planned to do for the next few months before they return to Canada, their new connections decided to help us in our orientation program.

The aroma of the food forced our Canadian guests to make inquiries about the Christmas menu, from Naylene, Dr. Aron's wife. She was delighted to describe to them in detail how each of the foods and drinks were made and the ingredients in each. She did this as they were eating and drinking each of the following: patties, ham and hops with chow-chow, Christmas rice, sorrel, ginger beer, peanut punch, ponche de crème, rum punch, pone, black cake, and paime. They had many helpings, much to the satisfaction of Naylene. Our hosts and hostess were surprised when we presented them with gifts. Also we were surprised that they had gifts for all their guests. We all had a fabulous and memorable Trini-Christmas experience at Dr. Aron's home.

Then the unimaginable happened. I had just eaten my lunch and was relaxing at my desk in the staff room, when Charlie rushed into the staff room and shouted, "Awadh! I need your help!"

Immediately, I got up and approached him. He was flushed, sweating and appeared scared. "What's the matter Charlie?"

"They are brushing (having sex) in my math class!" I couldn't believe what I heard. "Are you serious Charlie?

"Yes! I call on you because they have great respect and admiration for you. You are the coach of their cricket team."

I hurried up to the third floor and entered the class room.

The students were noisy and milling around the room. I did not see anyone having sex. Then I questioned them about Charlie's claim. One of the students in the back row told me that the girl who sat next to him said that she was feeling horny. And that she felt like brushing. He continued that as soon as the teacher started to write on the blackboard, they did what had to be done. They assured me that they would not do it again in class. I advised them to apologize to the teacher on his return. I then departed and reported to Charlie about the situation in the classroom. Charlie returned to his classroom and continued his lesson. Charlie and I did not mention the incident to anyone. We did not want to taint the character of any student. Charlie advised the students in his class to bury the incident.

In defence of the students of the school, it is only fair that the reader be aware of the vicinity. Directly across the street was government housing for low-income families. Many students lived in those houses. Students could look down into the bedrooms of the tenants and see acts of prostitution occur. Then I learned more.

In one of my senior biology classes on the third floor, one-half of my female students were absent every Tuesday afternoon. When the absentees had returned to the next biology class, they informed me that they were absent because they had to work. I did not pry into their personal affairs, until one of my students captured my attention at the beginning of another Tuesday afternoon biology class. She led me to the opened window which looked down on the street scene. I saw the students who were usually absent from my Biology classes. They were not wearing the school's uniforms. They were dressed in colourful outfits, and they were standing at the side of the street. Being quite puzzled, I asked her to explain the picture that I was looking at. As she was about to explain, limousines pulled up and they disappeared into them. As they left, the brown-eyed student told me about the nature of the work they were doing, and why they had to do it. I kept that information to myself only for the reader's eyes and imagination and share it only now.

It was time for us to introduce our Canadian guests and their families to the various events that took place during the Trinidad carnival celebrations. The team decided it would make all pre-carnival arrangements with the assistance of the volunteers from the Parang party. Being pleased by the cooperation and collaboration of the volunteers and the orientation team, I decided to inform my special friends, Michelle and Ameer about our pre-carnival schedule. They were happy that I had considered and invited them to join in our activities. They were definitely a blessing in disguise. Ameer, who owned a travel agency, got us complimentary tickets for the shows and events that we had planned to attend. He made arrangements with the cooperation of the volunteers for the following events. The Mighty Sparrow calypso tent; the John Agitation comedy show; the visits to sites where the steel bands practised; the Panorama competition, the Calypso King competition; the Mardi Gras Queen pageant, and many other carnival related parties.

For the following five months, the volunteers from Dr. Aron's Christmas party, and those that Laura, Nancy and Sandy had recruited from colleagues at their work place, took over the responsibilities to make sure that all the items on their bucket lists, associated with the cultural, social, geographical and ecological interests, were fulfilled before they had to return to Canada. Much to our contentment and delight, the volunteers kindly included our orientation team in all their plans. This fortuitous turn of events was not anticipated by anyone of us. Although my team members and I were all Trinidadians, many of the planned activities and events were unfamiliar to me.

After the carnival celebrations, many Christians entered a 40-day period of penitence and fasting observed from Ash Wednesday to Easter. But that did not deter our volunteers from taking us on weekends to a few of the popular beaches in Trinidad and Tobago. Ameer organized a weekend trip for our Canadian colleagues to Tobago. With his connections to the travel business, we were treated royally by the people of Tobago. The warm aquamarine coloured waters of the Atlantic Ocean that washed the sandy shores soothed and refresh our guests. The blue hues of the water in the "Nylon Pool" made snorkelling a peaceable paradise. After those aquatic experiences, we were driven through the villages and small towns of the island. We stopped regularly to taste the foods and drinks the locals prepared. Finally we spent the night in the capital city, Scarborough. On the following morning we experienced the tasty and filling Tobagonian breakfast.

The volunteers were very astute planners. They decided that each weekend expedition would be a blending of the four major interests of the group: cultural, social, ecological and geographical. Consequently, our field trips became more interesting and multidimensional. Instead of driving directly to Maracas Beach, we hiked across the mountain from Santa Cruz. As we were hiking over the hills, the various flora and fauna were diligently pointed out to us by the volunteer guide. On the sandy beach, after spending lots of time swimming in the salt waters of the Atlantic Ocean, we drank fresh coconut water and ate deep-fried shark with hops bread. Hot pepper sauce was optional.

The following weekend they went to the Pitch Lake from which asphalt was extracted. On the return trip they visited the Point-a-Pierre Refineries, and the San Fernando Market. Two weeks later we were taken to the hills in the Northern Range to a Colonial–style building, which was located north of the town of Arima. Under the guidance of Dr. Kenny, we were briefed about the reptiles, birds, butterflies, and plants that inhabit the forests surrounding the building. We ended the weekend at a house on Mayaro beach.

Following a break, the festival of Phagwa or Holi, which marked the beginning of the spring in northern India, was celebrated in villages and towns in Trinidad by Hindus. This celebration is also called "Festival of Colours" and "Festival of Love." Our guest enjoyed participating in the colourful celebrations. One of them remarked that it reminded him about his childhood when he used to have water fights with his friends. Only this time the water had many different colours.

Before the end of the academic year, the Muslim population observed Ramadan, one of the five pillars of Islam. For them it was a time of self-realisation. The end of Ramadan was celebrated with the festival of Eid-al-Fitr to which we were invited. The food and sweets were mouth-watering and delicious. Then, before the end of the year, our guests were invited to Hindu, Muslim and Christian weddings. They were thrilled and amazed at the length of the Hindu weddings. After those exotic experiences, I was extremely delighted to hear them announce that the social services that we provided were far beyond their expectations.

At the end of the academic year our Canadian guests were overwhelmed by the generosity, kindness, and hospitality of their Trinidadian host and hostesses, and hoped that they would be able to reciprocate at a future date.

Then, the unexpected happened. I had just returned home from private tutoring. After having a shower, I changed into comfortable clothes and was lying on my bed relaxing, when I heard sobbing in the living room. At first, I thought I was hallucinating. I jumped out of the bed and rushed to the living room. Both my father and stepmother were sobbing .This sad scene left me completely flabbergasted.

"Papa why are both of you crying?"

There was no response from anyone of them. I called my sisters by name. But apparently, no one was at home. I repeated my

FROM EXPLORATIONS TO ENLIGHTENMENT

question.

"Papa why are both of you crying?"

There was still no response but the volume of the crying increased. I thought that an important family member had died. I stooped down to Papa and held his face and said, "Talk to me Papa." He stopped his crying, wiped his face and said, "Awadh ask your Tanty Seloni (my stepmother). She could tell you better."

Tanty Seloni stopped her crying, wiped her face, looked at me with pitiful eyes and said, "Awadh since you started to work in Port of Spain you hardly spend any time helping in the shop. On weekends you are helping your Canadian friends. Two men are taking advantage of your father and me."

"So nobody is dead!"

"No. Nobody is dead."

"Tell me what is happening."

Tanty Seloni related the following story. She reported that two young men would enter the shop during the business day and would look around the shop. When there were no other customers about, one of the men would come to the counter and order groceries and liquor from Papa. After the man had received his groceries and liquor he would refuse to pay. The other man usually stood at one of the folding iron-gates with a gun in his hand. And when Papa attempted to take back the groceries and the liquor, he would jump over the counter, and would beat him up. And when I intervened, he would also beat me up. When we could no longer withstand the beatings, we would give them whatever they had requested. On the third robbery, they started their demands for money.

"How long has this been going on?"

"About five to six weeks."

"Do they come on any particular day of the week?"

"They usually come on a Friday or a Saturday, when we have lots of money in the cash register."

"Did you call the police?"

"Yes. The policeman comes and asked a lot of questions. Then he writes a report. But before he leaves he would ask for groceries and liquor, and doesn't pay for them. So it's no use calling the police. No protection has been provided by the police."

"When were the men last in the shop?"

"Last Saturday."

"Last Saturday!"

"And the tug told us that the shop belonged to him."

I could feel the adrenalin rushing through my body as I became enraged at the behaviour of the two men and the police. I told my Papa that I'll be in the shop on weekends because other volunteers were looking after the interests of my Canadian colleagues. After that conversation, I returned to my bed, and considered possible options. All sorts of thoughts entered my mind. But they quickly dissipated. On my return to work, I contemplated discussing the issue with my trusted friend Nicholas. After self-reflection, I decided to keep my family business in the family.

I patiently waited for the weekend, hoping that they did not return when I was at work. After leaving school early on the Friday, I got home as soon as possible. They did not show as yet. Quickly, I changed into my home clothes, and after having a fast bite, I advised Papa to load the Winchester. At first, he objected. Then, I told him to take the gun and the cartridges into the shop, and to leave them behind one of the deep freezers. He did. When he was not looking, I loaded the gun with the cartridges, because Tanty Seloni stated that the man, who stood at the gate, always had a gun in his hand. Finally that the evening, the two men did not show. I unloaded the Winchester and took it upstairs.

Saturday came and this time, my Papa loaded the Winchester and placed it in an upright position behind one of the concrete pillars inside the shop. At sundown, the shop became busy. We were all occupied serving customers, when Tanty Seloni came to me and nervously whispered, "Awadh. The men are here. Jango has given your Papa his grocery and liquor list. The other man, Ranga, is leaning against the wall with his hands in his pockets. He has the gun." My Papa took the list and approached me with a terrified look. Then, as Papa was about to acquiesce to the man's demands, my adrenaline and all the biochemical reactions in my body that trigger the fight or flight response, sprang into red alert. I took the list and approached the counter, where the man was standing. I told him that he would have to pay for the groceries before I would give them to him. He looked at me angrily and barked, "Who de hell you think you talking too. I own this fukin place. I don't pay for anything dat I want! And who the fuck is yu?"

"I'm the owner. Not you. You have to pay first. Don't you see the sign?"

"What sign, I don't read sign. Look Man gimme my fuckin grocery and liquor before I kill yu ass."

At that instant, I rushed to the concrete pillar, and grabbed the Winchester. In a jiffy, I rushed back to the counter, cocked the Winchester and pointed it directly at him. I ordered him to either pay first or get lost. Then, I ordered the man at the gate to drop his gun and raise his hands above his head and not to move. Immediately, fear overcame both men. The customers ran outside. On seeing the young boy who helped us in the shop, standing on the other side of the counter, I ordered him to close the gates. I was in control of the two men with the loaded and cocked Winchester in my hands. When they realized that I was angry and would shoot, they stated loudly and clearly that they would not come back and harass my parents. I ordered them to leave the shop. As soon as they had left, we closed up the shop with the help of our assistants. We went upstairs to the dining room. No sooner we had entered the dining room three shots were fired through the windows of the upper floor. Papa got enraged, snatched the gun from me and rushed to one of the windows in the last bedroom. He told me that he could see them under the mango tree on the opposite side of the road. Then he asked me whether he should shoot them. I advised him to forget it. So he did. Naively, I thought that I had solved the problem. But according to Ajah, I should always be prepared to face and manage unexpected events.

After the three shots, Ushi called the police. The police wanted to know whether anyone was hurt. She told them that nobody was hurt. Early next day, the police arrived and asked many questions. No arrests were made and there was no follow up to our complaint. The Sunday following the shooting was rather uneventful after the police left. We had our usual lunch of boiled rice, boiled red beans, stewed chicken and staple water cress salad.

On the Monday morning, I left for work at my usual time. As I was walking past the Lum Hee's grocery and rum shop, I was startled to see Jango as he charged out of the shop, brandishing a long knife, and shouting, "Yu fucker I go kill you ass today!"

Without any hesitation, I started to run for my life. But his advance was impeded by a line of cars. Terrified at the sight of him brandishing a shining blade, I ran to the taxi stand. Fortunately, there was a taxi leaving for Port of Spain that needed one more passenger. The driver saw me running and slowed down to allow me to hop into the back seat. I got in and immediately I locked the door of the air conditioned car. Jango was now slamming the window with his fist. When the driver saw the man with a knife in his hand banging at the window of the car, he accelerated. I had to recount the entire story to the interested passengers and the taxi driver. Being completely absorbed in the story telling, I did not notice the length of the travelling time. Within days the story got embellished and was the talk of the village.

When I arrived at school, the first constructive thoughts that entered my mind were to report the gunplay at Montrose Junction to the guys that I have been paying for protection. But I had to wait until the end of the week for my monthly salary. At last, the day arrived. It was the first time that I was extremely pleased to meet and treat my security and safety team. While we were conversing, drinking and eating cutters, I interjected, "Guys! Could I please have your attention just for a few minutes?"

"Of course teach. What is the problem?"

I related the story about Jango and Ranga in vivid colour. They listened and assured me that me that they would take care of the problem faced by my parents and me. Although the shooting incident was reported to the police and my hired crime protection men in the city, I was always apprehensive. My fear for the safety and security of my family and me haunted me every moment of every day. At the end of the next month, the four men appeared for their treats. They were rather quiet and sombre. I dared not ask them to explain their disturbed looks. After we were served our drinks and cutters, two of them spoke about Jango and Ranga. They inquired whether any other person was terrorizing my family or me. With a puzzled look, I responded, "No!" I was assured that my family and I would not have any problems from them again.

The academic year was slowly coming to an end. But it was a year filled with many interesting, inspiring and enlightening activities and events. It was the time when I had to decide to which country and in which university I would select to further my post-secondary education. I had already sent applications to universities in the United Kingdom and had received admission to three universities. But owing to my financial dilemma, I was forced to earn before I could learn. But with the introduction of the three Canadian teachers into S.E. Port of Spain Secondary School, a plethora of new options became available. After informing them that I had also received letters of acceptance from the universities that I had applied to in Canada, they became extremely excited. They invited me to a meet them with their wives at Kennedy and Sandy's home to discuss my future educational plans.

I informed them that I had received letters of acceptance from Dalhousie University, University of Toronto, McMaster University, and McGill University. First they congratulated me and questioned me about my preferences. Being unsure about my final choice, I kindly sought their valued opinions and recommendations. Before they volunteered their words of wisdom, they questioned me about my application to each of the mentioned universities. Realising that I was in the presence of six highly qualified and experienced Canadian graduated educators, I had to be rational and competent in my decision-making process. I informed them that I had studied the courses of study calendars from several Canadian Universities, and had discussed them with graduates of those universities. They then inquired whether they discussed their experiences while they were in the process of studying at those institutions, and the standard of living and quality of life they enjoyed. I confessed that I did not inquire about those aspects. We all discussed the advantages and disadvantages of studying at each of the universities that had accepted me.

Although Kennedy and Sandy were graduates from the University of Toronto, they were in agreement with Bruner and Charlie that I should attend McMaster University for the following reasons: location in the Golden Horseshoe on Lake Ontario; availability of inexpensive rental properties; the greater opportunities for part-time employment; the opportunity to interact with international students with diverse cultures, customs and social activities on a smaller campus, and the natural geographical wonders of Ontario. I thanked them for all their advice and encouragement to study in Canada, and especially their views on McMaster University.

When I returned to school, I told Shane, another young teacher at my school, about my weekend with the Canadian teachers, and my decision to attend McMaster University in Hamilton, in the province of Ontario. He gave me one of his smiles and said that he had just accepted the offer to study engineering at McMaster. Then I asked him why he had selected McMaster. He proudly informed me that his brother and his wife, his sister and her husband, had all graduated from McMaster. And that they would be his guidance counsellors while he was at the university.

At the end of the academic year I tendered my resignation. I was scheduled to begin studies in September, and I was overly excited that I would be embarking on my chosen career path.

Then I received a letter from McMaster inquiring if I would like a welcoming party to meet me at the airport in Toronto. Promptly, I responded positively to the invitation. After I had informed those professionals who had graduated from McMaster that I had decided to attend McMaster and, they congratulated me. Also I informed them about the letter that I had received about a welcoming party. They told me that the welcoming party would assist me in finding a place to live. I did not want to broadcast my educational plans to the villagers or our customers in the shop until I had obtained a visa to study in Canada from the Canadian Embassy in Port of Spain. Not aware of the necessary requirements that must be fulfilled in order to obtain a student visa to Canada I made an appointment with one of the staff at the Canadian Embassy for the earliest available date. At the Canadian Embassy, the woman officer needed my letter of admission to McMaster, and any correspondence that the university had with me. Being satisfied with the documents from the university, she informed me that I had to get a medical examination from an embassy approved physician. My physical examination and biochemistry reports were accepted by the embassy. In addition, she requested a current financial statement, and a security letter from a reliable source. Having successfully fulfilled the embassy's requirements and my tax clearance from the revenue department I was granted a one-year student visa. I purchased a one-way ticket to Toronto with Air Canada. I was ready to leave for Canada.

PART THREE
FIRST YEAR IN CANADA

On the evening before my departure, we had a few friends, relatives, and my immediate family to celebrate. At the party, many surprising, humorous, and flattering comments were showered on me. But the most memorable event of the evening was the verbal exchange between Tanty Seloni and my Papa. I then had expressed my appreciation for the kind gestures of those present, and was about to conclude the celebrations, when Tanty Seloni interjected, and said to my father, "Papa, now that Awadh is going away to study, what are you going to give him! So far he has done everything on his own. You have not offered to pay for anything."

Papa got annoyed at her challenging question and answered.

"I have already given Awadh everything that he will ever need in his life. I have given him life and a brain, let him use them to either succeed or fail in his endeavours." After those remarks, the party concluded. I did not comment on what Papa had said. But I heard him clearly.

On the following morning, many friends and relatives were at the airport to bid me farewell. I looked for Rani, the beautiful young woman Papa had chosen for me to marry. But she was not at the airport. Slowly, I ascended the stairs leading to the cabin of the Air Canada aircraft, looking back for the last sight of Rani before entering the cabin. She was still not there. As the aircraft took off, I kept peering through the widow until the airport was out of sight.

It was a long but interesting flight to Montreal. Two gorgeous female tourists sat next to me on the flight. They talked about their romantic experiences that they had with the locals on the island of Tobago. I was completely entertained and enlightened while eves-dropping on the stories about their sexual adventures while they were holidaying without their husbands.

It was a long walk through the Montreal airport to the get to the aircraft bound for Toronto. It was still daylight when my plane eventually took off and headed for Toronto. As it circled around the Toronto airport and approached the landing airstrip, the landscape was significantly different from Trinidad's but welcoming. My documents were in order but immigration officials were not satisfied with them. They asked me to wait in a room for a medical examination. The temperature in the room was too cold for me. I was shivering. Fortunately, the medical officer, after looking at me, smiled and ordered me to get dressed because I looked physically fit to him.

After clearing immigration and collecting my blue suitcase, I entered the arrival area expecting to be greeted by a welcoming party from McMaster University. As I was standing looking around, Shane who was on the same flight, wished me good luck and reassured me that we would meet at the university. After approximately an hour, there was no welcoming party. And I was the only person sitting in the arrival lounge. Then, a uniformed woman came to me and inquired about my business in the country. I related my story and handed her the letter from the welcoming committee at Mc Master University. She softly and kindly asked me whether I had the name of a contact person, a telephone number, the address at which I would be staying, and with whom I would be living. I answered each of her questions in the negative. She advised me to remain in the lounge and that she would confer with her colleagues. As I was patiently waiting for something positive to happen it did.

A familiar voice heralded me, "Jags you still here! What happened?"

I related in detail to Shane what had transpired since we said goodbye to each other at the exit of the immigration area. He advised me to wait in the lounge.

"Where are you going Shane?"

"Jags relax. I'm going to tell my family and friends who are presently dining in the restaurant, about your predicament."

When he left, waves of hope and calmness washed my mind, body and spirit. The woman returned and before she conveyed her emergency plan, I informed her about my colleague who came back in search of me, and that he had gone to inform his family about my situation. I thanked her for her support and kindness. Before I was finished talking to her, Shane returned with wonderful and comforting tidings. The woman was very happy and wished me success in my studies.

Shane led me to the dining room where I was pleasantly surprised to meet Shane's brother. He was my geography teacher in college. The other adult members of Shane's family having dinner were all educators in Hamilton. I was cordially invited to dinner and being hungry, I accepted. During the discussions and cross-talking at the table, they explained the reasons for Shane returning to the arrival lounge in search of me. I learned that there was never a welcoming party at the university.

After dinner, we got into their cars and drove onto the highway. I was informed that the airport was not in Toronto but in Malton. As we entered the Queen Elizabeth Highway, they pointed in the direction of Toronto. On the highway to Hamilton there was only one lighted building visible in the forest-clad landscape. I remembered one of the adult passengers stating that if he had money he would definitely purchase as much land as he could afford. Those vacant lands were on both sides of the highway in Mississauga, Oakville and Burlington. Then we ascended a huge bridge which traversed over a large body of water. It was the largest river I had ever seen. When I inquired about the bridge, I was told it was the Burlington Skyway Bridge over the channel leading from Lake Ontario to Hamilton Bay. As we entered the City of Hamilton, the air was extremely polluted with chemicals that were not pleasant to the nostrils. I inquired about the foul scent. I was told that it was from the steel mills in Hamilton. As we ascended the mountains and drove for a few miles we arrived at the residence of my rescuers. It was a beautiful back-split home surrounded by beautiful gardens which were well lit. It was September 14, 1966. And I was freezing. The family was very compassionate and kind. Seeing that I was shivering, they turned on the heat to comfort Shane and me. Exhausted, I fell asleep quickly.

The following morning, the sun was in its full glory but I was still freezing. I went outside for fresh air and to walk in their beautifully groomed flower and vegetable gardens. Across the road was a high school with hundreds of students playing. Some students were throwing a leather ball which had a shape like a cocoa pod. These boys were shirtless and wearing shorts, showing no sign of being cold. I was fully dressed with my cardigan and English overcoat as I stood on the sideline looking at a game that I had never seen before. My curiosity compelled me to ask one of the participants, "What is the name of the game you are playing?" There was no answer. I continued watching the game attempting to understand the fundamental principles of it when one of the players shouted, "Are you sick young man?"

I didn't answer. He continued, "Are you sick? Why are you over dressed in this warm and beautiful sunshine?"

Without responding, I hurried back to the home at which I was hosted. After I had told Shane about my experience, he informed his sister. She informed me the game the boys were playing was called Canadian Football which was quite different from English football.

In the evening, Shane and I were driven to the Eaton store in downtown Hamilton to shop for winter clothes. This store was large and had a department for all sorts of clothes, shoes, coats, and other merchandise. After doing some comparative shopping on the advice of my host and hostess, I bought a brown thick Davy Crocket designed jacket, scarves, a pair of gloves and a pair of boots, which were on sale. For the next few days, Shane and I were escorted to various geographical and historical tourists' sights in the Golden Horseshoe by different members of Shane's families. We travelled through vineyards and orchards and crossed the Garden City Skyway on our way to the famous

Niagara Falls. On our return trip, we spent some time admiring the Niagara Escarpment and Lake Ontario. On another day we visited Fort George and General Brock's monument in Niagara on the Lake. Also we were driven to downtown Toronto to visit the main streets, and the old as well as the new city halls. After those hectic outings I needed a rest and a place that I could call my home.

At the end of the week, I spoke with Shane privately and told him that I would like to get a place to rent as soon as possible. And it must be as close as possible to the university campus. He expressed the same concern. After he had informed his sister and her husband about our request, they found and rented a room for us in a family bungalow on Emerson Street. Shane and I occupied one of the three bedrooms on the main floor. In my room there were two single beds with a very narrow space between them. There was one small table which we occasionally used. But we were allowed to study in the kitchen when it was unoccupied. Also there was one washroom with a hand-held shower. I was allowed to have two showers per week. I did not like the shower arrangements but being a foreign student with no other option, I had to grin and bear it until a better choice was available.

The landlady, Veronica, was a Scottish widow, whose late husband was a physician. Veronica supplemented her living with the weekly rental income from the four students who lived in her house. Her adult son, Rich, a tall blue-eyed blonde lived in the basement and shared the household chores with his mother. The two other students had already occupied the other rooms before the arrival of Shane and me. After a week, I became more acquainted with two of the other students. Joseph was a member of the Mohawk tribe. His family lived in Brantford, Ontario. He was studying sociology and politics at McMaster. Chen was a graduate student from mainland China. He was doing doctoral work in political science at McMaster. Eventually, a trusting friendship gradually developed among the three of us. Our relationships matured during our socializing and discussions with Veronica and her son, Rich, in the living room. Bonding was also encouraged during the preparation and sharing of our meals.

Veronica was not too pleased with some of the privileges granted to the First Nations People in Ontario. But whenever she expressed her displeasure with the rights of the Six Nations People living on the banks of the Grand River, Joseph would give her a big smile. Being a foreigner to Canada, I had no idea why Veronica disapproved of the privileges the aboriginal people enjoyed in Ontario. I decided that I would ask Joseph privately about the issues Veronica was inquiring and complaining about.

Fortunately, I met Joseph on my way home after classes. As we leisurely walked along the walkways on campus to our home on Emerson Street, I inquired about Veronica's peeve about the First Nations people's privileges. Since Joseph exuded friendliness, kindness, respect, and humour in every encounter with me, I seized the opportunity to ask him a series of questions concerning his culture, his family, and his personal interests. After Joseph had heard my questions, he told me that after dinner, he would enlighten me about his people in the privacy of his room. I accepted his offer.

After dinner, I joined Joseph in his room and listened attentively to the story of his people. I learned that he was a member of the Six Nations of the Grand River community of the Iroquois nation. The Iroquois nation was composed of six tribes: Mohawk, Cayuga, Seneca, Onondaga, Oneida, and Tuscarora. Joseph told me that he was from the Mohawk tribe and was one of the thousands of fortunate First Nations people to be granted 'Indian Status'. Kindly, I queried him about the significance of the 'Indian Status'. Without hesitation, Joseph informed me that the Federal Government of Canada, under the Indian act, conferred the title "Indian Status" to the Aboriginal people of the six nations, which entitled them to partial funding for post-secondary education.

Joseph informed me that he was completing a four-year degree in sociology and politics at McMaster University. He was hoping that after graduating that he would be employed by either the provincial or the federal government in the department of Indian affairs. At the Department of Indian affairs, he hoped he would be able to help his people to consider leaving the reserve by improving their education, and consequently their standard of living and life style. He strongly believed that his people and society could benefit from studying the past history of his people, and their relationships with the British, Americans, French, and other tribes of the Six Nations. He quoted the philosopher George Santayana: "Those who cannot remember the past are condemned to repeat it," and before passing judgement, people should first study the events that resulted in major wars or other important historical events. Then I inquired what the quote has to do with his people. He told me that he was disappointed in the manner new immigrants abused them. He claimed that his people have lived on this continent for thousands of years, and that they felt unappreciated by the new immigrants. His people fought side by side with the British in the war against the Americans. The First Nation people were rewarded for their participation in the war of 1812 by being granted lands on both side of the Grand River. The land was held in trust by the British sovereign. As a result they did not have to pay land tax because they were living on crown lands. Also from other taxes they were exempt. Then he brought the issue about the residential schools in Brantford. Many of his cousins and relatives were taken away from their families and were sent to residential schools against the will of both parents and the children. The residential school system was established by the Government of Canada and administered by the churches to explicitly indoctrinate the Aboriginal children in the Christian way of living, and eventually assimilate them into the mainstream Canadian society. This practice prevented the First Nations children from acknowledging their culture and heritage and from learning their native language. The children were severely punished and abused whenever they failed to follow the instructions of the residential staffs. They suffered physical, emotional, sexual and psychological damages. The children received an inferior standard of education which prepared them for mainly agricultural and simple industrial careers. At that point of our discussion, he urged me to do some research to validate his story. Later in the year, Joseph introduced me to his family in Brantford where several more sad stories were narrated.

The other student, Chen, was a graduate student in political science at McMaster University. I first met him in September 1966 when we lived in the same house on Emerson Street. He was a citizen of the People's Republic of China. Knowledgeable, but he was not too eager to answer any question about the political, social and economic issues of his country. He always wore a worried look when we were in the kitchen preparing dinner. On several occasions in the kitchen, the phone would ring, and I would have to answer it. He never answered the phone himself. Although he spoke softly, when on the phone, his polished English could clearly be heard by anyone in the kitchen. From the tone of his voice and the nature of the conversation, I surmised that there was tension in the place from where the phone call originated. It was not until the end of December 1966, that I had enough courage to initiate a question and answer session with Chen about the issues that I had overheard from his conversations over the phone. My first attempt yielded no response. Finally in March of 1967, I decided to inquire from him about the political, social and economic issues that I heard discussed on the phone.

"Chen. With all due respect, I would like to know about this Mao Zedong."

He slowly looked up from the food on his plate, and with a serious look said, "Why?"

Then, I informed him that my chemistry laboratory partner informed me about a revolution in his country, and that his parents and families were experiencing problems with the "Red Guard". I heard you talking about a Cultural Revolution to the people on the phone. I would like to be enlightened so that I could have meaningful discussions with my lab partner, Stan. When Chen learned that Stan was also from the People's Republic of China, he became relaxed and was ready to talk to me. A few days later, Chen invited me into the privacy of his room. He prefaced his socio-political and economic lectures about his homeland with a quotation from the great statesman Winston Churchill: "Every nation or group of nations has its own tale to tell. Knowledge of the trials and struggles is necessary to all who would comprehend the problems, perils, challenges, and opportunities which confront us today."

Chen forewarned me that in order for me to understand how his country was in the present state of political, social and economic chaos, I would have to answer a few simple questions. He then asked me whether I had any knowledge of the history of the dynasties of China. He was not pleased with my response and decided to spend a few evenings educating me about Chinese history and culture from a century ago. During one of his history lessons, the phone rang. Veronica answered it. She then came to Chen's door and informed him that call was for him. I went to my room and Chen went to answer the call.

On the following evening, after sharing dinner with Chen, he informed me that he had to attend important meetings and he did not know when he would be available to continue his history lessons about the "Cultural Revolution." After Chen had attended his first meeting, he stayed at the home for a few days. Then he left and did not return. After a week, Veronica informed me that Chen left to join his family without leaving a forwarding address.

During the first week on the Mc Master Campus I endured Frosh Week also called Orientation week for all first year students. It was the time when new students were invited to participate in ice-breakers as they enter into a culture which was either similar or completely different from their own. Although I had my share of culture shock in Trinidad and the other Caribbean islands where I travelled, my experience at Mac was beyond my imagination. A variety of activities, which were supposed to welcome us to our new academic home, was planned by the senior students for all the first year students. Every student that I met was a stranger to me. I had to strategically use my human capital to enter into their private spaces which in some cases was challenging. But within a short time I met few open-minded fellow frosh students. They were from different disciplines, different countries, different provinces and different colour and race. I was thrilled to interact with them. There was no language barrier because although many of them were multilingual, they all had English as their main currency of speech. Many of the adult students as well as I, who were not teenagers, were disenchanted with the stunts, pranks and activities. Besides the immaturity and degrading aspects of some of the activities, it was freezing for me.

During the orientation week, I experienced discrimination from a source that I least expected it. There were many South Asians from different parts of India who were studying for their Master of Business. They were always well-dressed. Often, I would attempt to converse with them wherever I met them. Whenever the senior students asked them whether they were a frosh, they would reply, "I'm in the MBA program."

And they were never ordered to perform any silly activity. From that moment whenever my status was questioned, I always responded that I was an MBA student. But within a few weeks, I started to experience discrimination from the many

South Asian students. They had a unique sense of pride in their citizenry. When I did meet and attempted to communicate with any South Asian student, they would ask the following question, "Bhai. Which part of India did you come from?" As soon as I responded that I was not from India, and that I was from Trinidad, they wanted to know about my heritage. After informing them about my background, their friendliness vanished. They considered me as an outcast, an untouchable. When a South Asian was aware that I was from Trinidad and Tobago, he or she would either cross the street or look away when they were in close proximity. As a result I had to change my approach in order to learn about life in India. And whenever I did encounter any unfamiliar South Asian I would be the first one to ask the question about their background. Being aware of their home town, proudly, I would give them the name of a different city in India as my birth place. After introducing that method, I was able to dialogue with them. On the other hand, I had no problem assimilating and partying with the students from any other country. Most of the students were full of life. They celebrated life at every possible opportunity.

However, I sincerely felt empathy for the female students from China and India, who were ordered to perform acts that were definitely demeaning in their culture. Many of them cried. In fact, two weeks later, during one of my tutorials, I learned from my Chinese lab partner that one of his Chinese relatives had returned to Hong Kong after a traumatic experience. Allegedly, he was blindfolded and taken into the countryside field where he was left. He was found by a farmer.

As soon as classes commenced at the university, in addition to my six courses, I learned that physical education was compulsory for all first year students.

On the first day at the gymnasium, after Shane and I had registered and were assigned our lockers, we went to find them.

Much to our amazement, we walked into a long locker room. There were of hundreds of white nude males, parading around in the locker room. I had never been exposed to so many nude white boys before. Shane looked at me and started laughing out of control. After he got his laughter under control, he looked me in the eyes and whispered, "Jags you mean we have to walk around naked with all these guys! Jags look at those big cocks! You have to watch your ass as you walk around." Soon we realized that many eyes were watching us, and maybe they were wondering what was so funny that was causing us to laugh. Quickly we joined the nude parade, and put on our trunks before entering the swimming pool area. There was nudity in the showers and the co-ed saunas. We made use of the swimming pool, saunas and the showers every day.

Each student who lived at Veronica's home bought their groceries at the corner stores and cooked their own meals. At times we shared our meals with one another and with Veronica. Every day, I walked to all of my classes. I usually came home for lunch and returned to classes. On our streets, I often met students from different faculties at the university. Also, I knew many of the students who were attending the Hamilton Teachers College located on the McMaster Campus.

By frequently sharing and bartering my cooked foods with Veronica and her son, Rich, a cordial relationship developed. Veronica taught me how to play a card game called 'crazy bridge'. Within a couple of weeks, she introduced me to her favourite couple and most trusted friends, Mary and Gregory. They were also sexagenarians. We would first converse about anything that was on the news. Then we would have dinner. After dinner we played 'crazy bridge' until late into the night. The 'crazy bridge' card game parties lasted until the end of the academic year.

One Friday evening, Veronica phoned Mary to tell her that

she would not be able to play cards because she had a fever and the flu. After complaining about her discomfort, Mary asked to speak with me. When she was finished exchanging warm salutations, she invited me to spend the weekend with them. After mentally calculating the time needed to complete my lab reports in chemistry and physics, and my mathematics assignment, I told Mary about the assignments and I assured her that I would give her my answer next morning. After dinner, I went to bed early and got up early in the morning and worked on my assignments. I had completed all my assignments and some extra reviews before eleven o'clock. I then phoned Mary and accepted the invitation. Before I left, I consulted with Veronica about what I should take to my host and hostess. She suggested a tin of British biscuits. On my way to Mary and Gregory's, I purchased the biscuits at the corner store. It was the first time that I would be spending some quality time with an elderly couple in Canada. I had neither a pre-conceived notion nor anticipation of what it would be like to be with Mary and Gregory. After I arrived at their home, they welcomed me with warm open arms and hugs. I greatly appreciated to be treated as part of their family. First we had lunch. After lunch, we retreated to the family room. On the walls were many framed photographs of young men and a young woman. Also there was a curio displaying collections of dolls from all over the world. I cautiously inquired about the people in the photographs on the walls. There was a silence. I wondered why they were reticent about answering my question. I repeated my questions. Then, with tears in her eyes, Mary responded,

"They are our children."

"I would like to meet them when they visit you."

There was a lull in the verbal exchange. Then, Gregory added, "They are our three sons and daughter. But they have not visited us for many years." I dared not ask for an explanation after witnessing how they were both pining for them. At that point in the conversation, I suggested that we start playing "crazy bridge." They both agreed and went into the kitchen where we usually played. While the game was in progress they felt more comfortable to inform me about their children and grandchildren. I learned that the three boys were engineers and that their daughter was a nurse. But they all lived with their children in the United States. They were employed and busy working and taking care of their children. On seeing how uncomfortable they were to talk about their children, I did not seek any more information. We continued playing cards before and after dinner.

On the following morning, after breakfast, I accompanied them to their place of worship, where they introduced me to a few of their friends and acquaintances. On our return, Gregory questioned whether I had relatives in Nepal. I told him that my ancestors, according to my paternal grandfather, had migrated from Tibet to Nepal where they had settled for a short period. After a couple of generations, the new generation migrated to Uttar Pradesh in northern India. Then, I asked him his reason for asking the question. Gregory informed me that he was an engineer with the British military in the sub-continent of India. He had worked with the Gurkhas in the Jagannath Battalion. He had constructed bridges and roads for the military, in the theatre of war, against the Japanese in Burma. At that point in the story telling, I realized the he had associated my surname, Jaggernath, with the name of the Nepalese, Jagannath battalion. He went on to enlighten me with many more stories about the bravery and heroism of the Gurkhas while he was with them. After lunch, I thanked them for their hospitality, kindness and entertainment. I returned to my home and continued my studies.

Veronica gradually introduced me to her family circle. I had already met her son, Rich, with whom I quickly developed an interesting and exciting relationship. Occasionally Rich would invite me to his basement apartment to listen to his music of the 60s, eat pizza and drink beer. Often he would take me either bowling, the drive-in cinema or to play billiards. She also had two beautiful, talented, kind and generous daughters. The younger daughter Jackie, a blue-eyed blonde, was married to Jimmy, a Japanese physical education teacher who was also an excellent chef. Jackie was a high school art and music teacher who played the piano. She had performed in many concerts both at her school and in public places. She would invite me to accompany her to plays, concerts and cultural events. They were diehard supporters of the Hamilton Tiger Cats football team. Through them, I was able to attend many football games. He and his wife had season's tickets for the Hamilton Tiger cats. They taught me the rules, the different roles of the players, the strategies and the language of the game. The other daughter Krystal, a blue-eyed brunette, lived with her Lebanese husband Subhi, and their two daughters in the beaches area in Hamilton. She was a librarian and an artist. Krystal invited me to their beautiful home on many occasions for exotic dinners and card games. During the early fall, she drove me along the Niagara Escarpment to see the beautiful and colourful pageant of the leaves. I was blessed to be living with this family. I would be remiss if I did not repeatedly mention the continued support of the Bhupsingh family that rescued me at the airport, and introduced me to Veronica and her compassionate family. Everything the three Canadian teachers had told me about Canadian hospitality, generosity, kindness and love was absolutely true to the core.

I was slowly but surely building friendly relationships, not only with the students that I encountered on the streets, in the laundromat and the grocery stores, the pub and also with those who were in my classes and tutorial groups.

One morning I was fast asleep when the shouts of Rich awakened me. "Awadh look through the window. It's snowing." It was daylight and I could clearly see the snow falling as I sat on my bed looking at one of the wonders of nature. Immediately I got dressed and hurried outside to enjoy my first taste of winter in Canada. I tried to catch the flakes with my mouth and eat them. Rich joined me and offered to drive me around to see the winter wonderland. We drove around to view the snow –covered fields, the mountains, the hills and the homes in Dundas and Ancaster.

My first winter was extremely cold and windy as I waded through unplowed streets and snow covered campus to get to my classes. What an exhilarating and exciting challenge I had to endure for months. The bitter coldness and the heavy snowfalls did not discourage me from enjoying the winter scenery and the winter sports that were played in the province of Ontario. Instead of worrying about the weather outside the buildings, I stayed inside and enjoyed watching competitive professional ice hockey, and the first Canada Winter Game program. Veronica and her children introduced me to the sport of ice hockey. In those days there were six hockey teams in the National Hockey League. The Toronto Maple Leafs hockey team was a household name in Ontario. I was taught the fundamentals and rules of the game by Veronica and Rich who was a good hockey player. Every Saturday night was hockey night in Canada. I watched many games but the most everlasting memory was the Stanley Cup playoffs series between the Toronto Maple Leafs and the Montreal Canadiens. In 1967, the Toronto Maple Leafs won the Stanley Cup.

The university did provide a special social service to the first year students who were from the West Indies and British Guyana. A young lawyer, Lincoln Alexander, from the City Of Hamilton, made arrangements for me, a Trinidadian, to have either dinner or lunch at the homes of prominent citizens in the community, at the different festivals and significant holidays in Ontario during the academic year. I vividly recalled having

Thanksgiving, Christmas, and Easter dinners with wealthy families in Hamilton and Burlington. For those special unearned privileges, I extend my sincerest gratitude and full respect to my counsellor and social convenor, Lincoln Alexander.

During the week of my first Christmas celebration in Canada, I was fortunate to meet a few of my college classmates from Trinidad who had migrated many years before me. They were doing their Christmas shopping with their family in the stores in Hamilton. After renewing acquaintances, I got invited to several parties within familiar bus routes. Also a few of my university classmates took me by car to see the spectrum of Christmas lights displays in Niagara, Burlington and different wealthy districts in Hamilton. While touring the Christmas scenic landscapes, all those sceneries depicted in the Christmas cards that I had seen in British and North American post cards, came alive. I am most grateful to all those people who took their precious time, energy and effort to expose me to the beautiful and spectacular world they appreciate and conserve.

My first spring was a time of serious contemplation and reflection about my state of affairs with regards to educational success, financial adequacy, marital possibilities and employment opportunities. I had joined a couple of keen students who were most willing to meet at the university to study and prepare for the coming examinations in just a few months. But one of the blessings in disguise occurred when two young men from my physics tutorial class met me at the entrance of the university bookstore. Both of them were wearing black skull caps, and were well-dressed. One of them politely addressed me. "Hello. My name is Abe and I'm pleased to make acquaintance with you."

"My name is Awadh, and it's definitely an honour to meet you."

Then, taking the initiative, I introduced myself to the other young man. In response, "My name is Josh and I'm also pleased to meet you."

At that time in my memory bank, I had no knowledge of the

significance or meaning of the black skull cap that they were wearing. They appeared very polished, astute and business-like. I wondered whether I had broken some university rule, and they were assigned to investigate me. But before that thought could be properly processed, Abe said, "Awadh. You are no "schmuck". We want you to be our friend and study with us. We have listened to you dialoguing with the physics tutorial leader and we are interested in getting to know who you are."

At that moment, I relaxed. And they asked me kindly to join them for lunch at one of the restaurants on the main street. After expressing my gratitude, I accepted the invitation, and accompanied them for lunch. During the luncheon discussions, I asked two questions. I wanted to know the meaning of the word "schmuck" and the significance of the black embroidered cap that they were each wearing. Abe started to laugh and said, "You really don't know the meaning of "schmuck"!" "Abe it's the first time I have heard the word. What does it mean?" He told me that it was a word used to insult someone whose conduct was idiotic or stupid. In other words the person was considered a prick. I felt happy that I was not a "shmuck".

Then, Josh informed me that the cap was called a kippah, and it was always worn by male Jews to honour and respect the "Divine Presence" that was always above their heads, and monitoring their behaviour. That was the beginnings of a great friendly relationship. On the following tutorial, Abe presented me with a blue silk kippah with gold-coloured embroidered lace. They both hugged me when I placed it on my head. As the academic year progressed, they introduced me to a few of their acquaintances. The yuletide season was fast approaching, and while the students in the tutorial around us were talking about what they would be doing for Christmas, naively I ask Abe about his plans for Christmas. With a big smile, he advised me to wait until after the tutorial. After class, we went to Wentworth House for coffee. There, Josh and Abe enlightened me about their important religious celebrations of which Christmas was not one. They informed me that the most important holy day for them was Yom Kippur. Then I asked why it was the most holy. Abe said that it was the Day of Atonement and Repentance. It was a time of soul-searching, reflections, fasting and praying in the synagogue. Then, another student who was on the table adjacent to us, having overheard our discussion wanted to know whether the celebration of Hanukkah was the Jewish Christmas. Josh interjected and informed her that Hanukkah was an eight-day festival of lights and exchange of gifts. It was not a Jewish Christmas. After that culturally enriching conversation, we went to our homes.

Three months after my departure from my country, I received a letter from my Papa. I was hoping that there was a money order enclosed. But much to my dismay, there was neither a money order nor a cheque; and his fatherly advice was that I should use my brains and common sense to achieve my dreams. I never received another letter from him during my studies. After the disappointing news in the letter, I clearly realized that I had embarked on a mission which I had to accomplish successfully without any support from my family in Trinidad. I telephoned Abe, and after exchanging pleasantries, I informed him about the contents of my Papa's letter. At first, there was a long pause at his end, then he encouraged me to keep on being myself, and in the end, everything would be splendid. After I had heard his encouraging words, I decided that it was time that I follow my Jewish friends, and do some atonement and self-reflection.

My finances were running low but I had sufficient to see me through the end of the academic year. At the end of the year I would attend to my financial issues. Marriage was not on my bucket list. I was not mature enough to undertake such great obligations and responsibilities at that state and stage of my life. As a result, I had to release Rani from Trinidad from my thoughts because I did not make any promises of marriage to her on my departure. In fact she was not at my departure. I wrote Rani and told her that my educational responsibilities were my paramount interest, and wished her all success in her life. Since there was no foreign aid available from Trinidad or any other country, I placed my trust completely in the "Divine Presence" to guide me successfully through any adversity on the pathways leading to my goals.

It was my first spring in Canada and the landscape came alive with a wide range of trees, shrubs, and perennials, decorated with a spectrum of colourful buds, flowers and leaves. A cornucopia of fruits came a bit later. It was quite different from the tropical landscape that I was accustomed to. The final examinations were on my radar. My health was struggling, but with the motherly care of Veronica, I successfully completed my first academic year at McMaster. On the day of my final examination, after leaving the engineering building, I went directly to the location of the chimney at the back of it. I looked up at it and uttered these words to the "Divine Presence": "Lord! Lord! Lord! I need your help. I have to attend university for three more years. I have only one hundred and twenty five dollars left. I need a job that would help me earn sufficient money to support me, not only for this summer, but also for all the expenses for my second year at university. My trust is always with you. Amen."

Slowly, I walked to my home away from home, appreciating the beautiful scenery along the streets. All the other students that had shared the house with me, had left for their families; but I had nowhere to go. I related my financial situation to Veronica. And then, she informed me that she had sold the house and had to vacate by the end of June. She said that she was extremely sad that she had to sell it. It was the first home that her husband had bought. He had lived and died in it. Also she had given birth to all her three children in the home. It meant that I would have to find another home by the end of June.

May had just started and I needed all the guidance and good luck to survive and strive in Canada. I went to Gregory and Mary, with whom I played 'crazy Bridge', and discussed my situation with them. But they could not help me.

I went to the library on campus to return a few books that I had borrowed. While there, I checked the bulletin board in search of any available jobs. The university needed students to plant flowers on the grounds of the campus, and to mow the grass on the properties that belonged to the university. I went immediately to the hiring office. I completed the job application forms in the office, and within two day, I was moving the lawns on campus. My salary was sixty -seven dollars and twenty cents per week. Realizing that with this salary, I would not be able to attend university in the fall, I returned to the chimney and repeated my prayers. Two weeks of mowing lawns on campus left me exhausted and discouraged. Then Abe phoned and wanted to know how I was doing. After relating my plight, he informed me that on the next week many businesses and companies would be on the university campus in search of students to work for the summer. He advised me to go to the library bulletin board and get the schedule for the various hiring firms. His call was the most energizing and encouraging phone call at that time of my life.

Immediately I went and got the information about the interviews. On my return home I reported my findings to Abe over the phone. He assured me that I could use his name as a reference, and that I should not hesitate to contact him in the case of any emergency. After expressing my profound gratitude to him, I returned to bed and envisioned a brighter future. On returning to work, I told my boss that I had interviews for better paying jobs. He was very understanding and cooperative.

My first interview was with a handsome, well-groomed young man with an English accent. He was most welcoming and pleasant. After giving me details of the available positions at his hotel, he questioned my ability and capability to perform as either a waiter or a bar tender. Being pleased with my responses he offered me employment at the Bigwin Island Hotel on the Lake of Bays, Muskoka. Then, he asked me for my letter of permission to work as a foreign student in Ontario. When I declared that I did not have one, he countered by saying, "I will only employ you if you have a work permit." I asked him where I would get one. He advised me to contact the immigration office in Hamilton, and as soon as I had received written permission to work in Ontario, I should immediately contact him. Mr. Lambert gave me the contact information. After thanking him for his offer, I left his office feeling exhilarated. As soon as I returned home, I contacted Abe and reported the favourable news. He was pleased with my progress. Then I informed Veronica about my interview and sought her assistance concerning the work permit. She promised to make a phone call to the immigration office and speak on my behalf. When I returned from work on the following evening, Veronica informed me that the person at the immigration office would want a transcript of my first year marks, my student visa and my passport.

On the following morning, I familiarized my employer about my search for a better work opportunity. Again, I received his approval to take the time necessary to accomplish my mission. Having collected all the requested documents, I went to the immigration office on Main Street in downtown Hamilton. I was interviewed by a gentleman, who after questioning me on several issues, and carefully reading my documents, looked at me and smiled. After making a few encouraging remarks, he presented me with the letter of permission to work in Canada during the summer of 1967. I shook his hand and thanked him for the opportunity to work my way through university. He wished me the best of luck, and hoped that I made sufficient money on my job to continue and successfully complete my studies at McMaster. Also, he advised me to return to him whenever I needed a work permit. As soon as I returned home, I shared my good news with Veronica and Abe. Then, I informed Mr. Lambert that I had received the letter of permission to work in Ontario for the current summer. He booked an appointment for us to meet in Toronto and to finalize my summer job contract. As soon as I had finished talking to Mr. Lambert, I informed my employer at McMaster about my appointment with Mr. Lambert in Toronto. He was most understanding. Without any hesitation, he granted me permission to attend the interview with Mr. Lambert in Toronto.

It would be the first time that I would be travelling to the City of Toronto by bus on my own. Veronica gave me instructions on how to get to the address on George Street in Toronto. Rich, her son, drove me to the Hamilton bus terminal where I took the bus to Toronto. At the Toronto bus station, I inquired about where and how I would get the subway to get to George Street. Carefully, I listened to the instructions from the uniformed woman at the information kiosk. She gave me a map of the subway systems and patiently marked the route on the street which led to the subway station at the corner of Dundas Street and Yonge Street. Then she marked out where I had to change the train and where to get off. I had a frightening experience at the transfer at Bloor and Yonge subway station. Being unfamiliar with the subway system, and not able to adapt quickly to the different levels of the subway station, I got on the eastbound train instead of the westbound for the George Street subway station. With advice from unknown but friendly passengers, I got off at Pape subway station, with the assistance of other travellers I was able to get on the westbound train to St. George's station. What an adventure! I walked along George Street until I found the address Mr. Lambert had given me. After the doorbell had rung twice, Mr. Lambert welcomed me. After perusing my letter of permission to work, he questioned my knowledge about various cocktails and my experiences with serving customers in a bar. Being satisfied with my responses, he re-introduced the various positions that were available at his hotel. Mr. Lambert promised that he would start me in the position of a waiter (server) in the Round Room. And based on my performance, and depending on the recommendations of my superiors, he would expose me to different jobs. He would then make the necessary alterations to my contract. I was extremely encouraged and pleased with his suggestion. With a smile, he once again reviewed the initial salary and working conditions. Mr. Lambert offered me a wage of sixty cents an hour for any task that I was assigned to perform either indoors or outdoors. On the contract, boarding and lodging were included during my work tenure. Then he introduced a concept that was completely foreign to my culture. He enlightened me about tipping. He informed me that at the Bigwin Island Hotel that I would receive tips from some of the guests who were completely satisfied with the service that I had provided. Then I ask what I had to do with the tips. Much to my delightful surprise, he said that they were all mine to keep. And I did not have to share it with anyone. Being an unemployed foreign student on a visa, and having no knowledge about working conditions and wage structure in Canada, without any hesitation, I accepted his generous offer. I was scheduled to begin my summer job at the Bigwin Island Hotel on June 1st, 1967. And my contract would terminate in the second week in September 1967.

After we had completed our business transaction, Mr. Lambert invited me to lunch in a restaurant on Bloor Street. During lunch, he informed me that I should arrive at Bigwin Island at three o'clock in the afternoon on June 1st, and wait for the arrival of a boat at the docks. I would be picked up and transported to the hotel. Before we parted, I asked him in which town the hotel was located. I learned that it was about twenty miles from Huntsville, on the Lake of Bays in Muskoka. His last words to me as I was about to leave for my train were,

"Welcome to the Bigwin family. You will have a fantastic time. Awadh"

"Thank you. Mr. Lambert.

I felt extremely happy to have secured a job for the summer. Carefully, I retraced my steps on the subway route, the streets in Toronto and took the Hamilton bound bus. Eventually, after a long tiring day, I arrived safely back at 165 Emerson Street in West Hamilton. On my return home, I told Veronica about my contract. She informed me that the major part of my income would come from tips, and if I provide excellent service to the guests at the hotel I would be rewarded handsomely. After thanking her for her honest and encouraging advice, I contacted Abe and informed him about my contract. After congratulating me, he wished me all success in my summer job. On the following day, I resigned from my lawn mowing job at McMaster and thanked my employer for the opportunity to work on the university campus grounds.

On my final night at Emerson Street, I could not sleep. Having packed my suitcase with my simple belongings, I sat silently on my bed and prayed that I would have a successful summer and hoped that I would be able to keep in touch with all the wonderful people who had taken care of me during the last nine months in Hamilton. On my final morning at Emerson Street, after having breakfast with Veronica, I hugged and thanked her for her support and advice. Sadly, I walked down those cracked concrete steps for the last time. Veronica was still standing at the open door when we exchanged good-bye waves. Slowly but courageously, I walked down Emerson street to Main street, and patiently waited for the bus destined for the Hamilton bus terminal. At the Hamilton bus station there was no one there to bid me farewell. Having bought a one-way ticket to the Toronto bus terminal, I boarded the Toronto bound bus. At the bus terminal in Toronto, I inquired at the ticket counter about the bus that would take me to Huntsville. I do not recall the cost, but as the man handed me the ticket he advised me to look for the green Northland bus with Huntsville written in its front showcase. When I boarded the bus there were puzzled looks on the faces of many of the passengers as I approached them. Finally, I found a vacant seat next to middle aged man who was extremely welcoming. Kindly, he introduced himself. I reciprocated. He was travelling to Sudbury to join his family that had migrated many years ago from Poland. His companionship for the long journey was most enlightening and encouraging. I asked him whether he was coming from Poland. He informed me that he was staying with people in Toronto who knew his family. They had made all arrangements to reunite him with his family. I asked why he was separated from his family. Then he asked me whether I had ever heard of the Holocaust. I declared my ignorance. I could not comprehend his teary eyes and saddened face. Attentively, I listened to Jacob's story about his families and friends. Not having any previous knowledge of his narrative, I was in no position to engage in any meaningful conversation with him. But after hearing his rendition of the Holocaust, he became less talkative. However, his stories were punctuated by stops at Barrie, Orillia, Gravenhurst, Bracebridge and finally Huntsville.

As I got up to leave Jacob also got up, hugged me, shook my hand and wished me all success in life. I returned the sentiment and left him with a smile. As the bus pulled away we waved farewell. Reflecting on his sad stories of survival, I watched the bus disappeared down the street. I stood on the side of the street contemplating how I would get to Bigwin.

Again, I was a stranger in a new town. The few people I encountered on my way to the nearest restaurant looked as though they had never before seen anyone with my complexion. Being confident and adventurous, I entered the first restaurant on the street. It was smoky and looked seedy. After using the washroom facilities and not pleased with the ambience, I decided to look for a cleaner dining facility. But before I could leave the premises, there were two native Indian men who were eating, drinking and smoking at the table nearest to the entrance door of the restaurant. They stopped me and questioned, "What kind of people are you?" I told them that I was an Indian. Immediately they asked, "What tribe!" At that point of the dialogue, I realized that I had given them the incorrect answer to their question. Quickly, I countered that I was not native Indian. And that I was from India. "Oh! We have never seen your tribe before!" I hurried out from the restaurant to avoid any further conversation with them. After leaving them, I found another restaurant a few blocks away. I ordered a hamburger, fries and a coke.

After I had eaten my late lunch, I inquired about getting a bus to Bigwin Island hotel. The woman proprietor laughed, and informed me that the only way I could get to the hotel would be by taxi. After listening to her advice, I went to the open yard next to the gas station and waited for the arrival of a taxi. The taxi driver and I negotiated a reasonable fee to take me to the Bigwin Island Hotel. I sat anxiously in the seat next to the driver. As the sceneries on both sides of the road slowly revealed themselves, I wondered about the location of the hotel. There were very few houses. The narrow paved road winded through dense forests mixed with both coniferous and deciduous trees. The forest attempted to conceal the rocky landscape but was not too successful. Eventually, the taxi arrived at a T-junction with a road sign. Baysville was painted on it. I asked the driver whether we were close to Bigwin. He encouraged me by always saying "not far again." As the taxi made a left turn there was a body of beautiful blackish-blue waters in which sat Martin Marina. As the taxi coursed beneath the canopy of lush vegetation, I could see a large body of water between the trees on the left side of the road. The driver pointed to the open waters and said, "There's Lake of Bays. The hotel is situated on the largest island on the lake." At last, after almost an hour, we arrived at a large open unpaved area on the left-side of the road. We entered the vacant area and stopped in front of a structure that the driver called a ferry loading dock near the edge of the beautiful lake of Bays. Looking around, there were neither people nor homes in the vicinity. Slowly, I got out the taxi. I stretched and panoramically, I scanned the scenery. I stood in amazement at the breath–taking environment that I was privileged to see and appreciate. Before paying the driver, I questioned, "Where is the Bigwin Hotel?"

"Don't you know? Have you not worked here before?"

Hesitatingly, I responded "No!"

He smiled revealing his cigarette-stained teeth and said, "Come with me."

He led me towards the edge of the lake, and over the soothing sounds of the lapping waves, patiently he instructed me to observe carefully. He pointed across the lake to a concrete tower which was partially hidden in the forest on top of a hill on the island. I informed him that I could barely see the tower but I did not see the hotel.

"Where is the hotel?" I repeated.

He told me to find the 7 o'clock position from the tower to the shoreline along the island. As I found the red-roofed buildings, I thanked him for his assistance and returned to the taxi. After fetching my suitcase, I paid him. But before he left me standing alone in the open space, he wanted to know how I was going to get across the lake to the hotel since the ferry was not in service as yet. I told him that the manager, Mr. Lambert had made arrangement for a boat to pick me up. He wished me a happy summer and drove his taxi out of sight.

Bravely, I walked along the edge of the lake looking at the picturesque island across the lake and at the surrounding forested hills on the mainland. As I walked back and forth listening to the songs of the birds, the rustling of the leaves on the trees and the waves lapping on the shore, I contemplated the following thoughts: Here I was standing on the threshold of an opportunity to earn a wage which would either keep me scurrying for survival or launch me to an acceptable success level.

After one hour, I became apprehensive and wondered whether I had the correct date. I scratched my head then I opened my note book and confirmed that the time and date were correct. My hope was reaffirmed. Eventually, in the distance a noisy tug-boat towing a metal barge approached the docks at a fast speed. As it got closer to the docks, I saw two tall handsome blonde young men and a tall alluring red-hair freckled face young woman in the tug-boat's wheel house. After they had waved to me, one of the men shouted, "Are you Awadh?" "Yes. I'm Awadh". The tug boat stopped moving with its noisy engine still running. They all came off and introduced themselves to me. After the hurried introductions, one of the men took my suitcase. As he placed it in the wheel house he instructed me and Elaine to get on the barge, and shouted, "Hurry up! I have more errands to run."

I joined Elaine on the barge and both of us held on tightly to a braided rusty cable that was fastened across it. The tug boat raced towards the island through the blue waters of the Lake of Bays in brilliant sunshine under a cloudless sky. Elaine managed to conquer the noise of the tug boat by speaking loudly. She inquired about my position at the hotel. I informed her that I was not certain whether I would be a bartender or a waiter. Elaine smiled and welcomed me to the bar crew. She would be one of the cashiers in the Round Room Bar.

The tug boat was fast approaching the island and I was most eager to get on it safely. I was extremely eager to meet Mr. Lambert and the other people with whom I would be spending my first summer in Muskoka. As the tug boat got closer to Bigwin Island, and much to my frightful surprise, the driver of the boat shouted, "Awadh. I have too many chores to complete. I'll not be going back to the main docks. You will have to jump off when the boat is closer to the shore."

"Are you serious?"

"Yes!"

I could not believe the reality of the moment. I asked Elaine whether it was one of the initiation activities that I had to experience before I would be accepted to the island community. She did not respond.

"Awadh watch where your suitcase is landing."

He took up my suitcase and hurled it into the bushes on the land and told me to jump on the count of four on the sandy shores. A tremendous fear gripped me. He started the countdown. Realizing that I was not a reality show but in reality itself, I got up. Quickly, I buttoned my jacket and looked at the moving land along the shore for a clearing to jump. Thinking that my life was in danger, I concentrated on jumping as far away from the water and making the safest fall on terra firma. As I landed on the soft muddy shore, my shoes got stuck in the mud but I was able to keep my body away from the mud and sand. When I looked back the noisy tug-boat was already out of sight. At that moment, again I realised that I had to be responsible for all my actions on the island. I was in foreign territory and should always be prepared for any challenge at any moment from these strangers. The dice was irrevocably cast and there was no turning back for me. Immediately, I put on my 'survival of the fittest' helmet and my 'struggle for existence' open-mindedness thinking cap, and commenced my self-preservation actions.

Being quite apprehensive about this unexpected scene, slowly I extricated my shoes from the muddy shore, walked to a clear grassy spot, and cleaned my shoes with whatever suitable materials were available. Then, while I was standing, I looked across the lake towards the docks on the other side, and reflected. Less than an hour ago, I was on the docks on the mainland wondering when they would come to escort me to the island so that I could start riding the summer adventure carousel. But I had never imagined that the first ride was going to be so scary.

Eventually, I became aware of the plight that I was facing. With my back to the lake, my common sense told me that my suitcase was in the bushes to the left of me and the hotel was to the right. Next, I went in search of my suitcase. Since there were neither visible trails nor tracts, I carefully and slowly fought my way through the bushes and shrubs. With every step that I took, I was always fearful of the attack of an unknown animal. Eventually, I found my suitcase. It was not damaged.

With suitcase in hand, I waded through the forested landscape in the direction of the hotel. It was not an easy trek through the bushes and brambles. At last, through an opening in the forest, I saw a part of the terracotta coloured covered walkway system which connected the main activities buildings on the campus. An intense feeling of relief flushed my entire body and mind. The magnificence of the hotel compound gradually and gracefully entertained my vision as the network of walkways came closer to me.

Much to my delight, I saw an elderly bespectacled man who was leisurely painting a Muskoka chair. As I emerged from the bushes unto the well-groomed lawns, and as I got closer to him, I hailed out to him. On hearing my exclamatory voice, he quickly looked around, and became extremely surprised on seeing me. As soon as he realized that I did not look like any of his fellow workers, he dropped his paint brush, and ran away from me in the direction of a large beautifully designed building. I ran after him as fast as my suitcase would allow me. I needed his assistance. Unfortunately, he stumbled and fell. I accelerated towards him and I could clearly discern that he was extremely scared. As I got much closer, I informed him that I was employed by Mr. Lambert to work in the bar. After regaining his composure, I introduced myself to him. He was Charlie, one of the maintenance staff. He wanted to know my reason for entering the hotel compound from the bushes and not from the main docks. After relating my story, he exclaimed, "Those bastards could have killed you! Make sure you report them to Mr. Lambert. He would definitely discipline them." I made no comments.

Charlie led me across the green manicured lawns to the concrete walkway leading to the main entrance of the large building. We walked passed the concrete shuffle board courts and slowly ascended the concrete steps in front of the main entrance of the building. We had to cross a long wide gallery before we reached the large front door. Charlie opened the door and looked inside. He remarked that the fireplaces were alive but there was no one at the registration desk. Then he instructed me to enter the building and go directly to the desk and ring the silver bell. Charlie wished me good luck and left. I followed his instructions.

At the sound of the bell, a well-groomed middle-aged gentleman emerged from an adjoining room. He looked rather surprised on seeing me. "Who are you," he asked. After identifying myself, I then informed him about the contract I had with Mr. Lambert. He became apologetic, polite and welcoming. He told me to wait. After he had left to inform Mr. Lambert about my arrival, I briefly scanned the interior decorations of the large lounge that I was privileged to experience. Within minutes, he returned with a beautiful blue-eyed blonde who, after warmly welcoming me, introduced herself as Tiffany. Afterwards, she introduced the man at the registration desk as Clive. At the brief introduction, she instructed Clive to take my suitcase to the room on the second floor to which she had already assigned to me. Tiffany cordially escorted me to Mr. Lambert.

After exchanging salutations, Mr. Lambert officially welcomed me to Bigwin Island Hotel. Tiffany was the secretary-treasurer of the hotel. He re-iterated the terms of my contract in the presence of Tiffany. He informed me that Tiffany had already taken care of my accommodations and that she would be my mentor for the summer. After hearing about my unique adventurous arrival on the island without any negative side effects, he was amazed.

Without any hesitation, she kindly asked me to follow her. Tiffany led me past two magnificently sculptured fire places across red mahogany stained floors, enriched with Persian rugs and antique furniture to a two–landing levels wide staircase to the second floor. As we walked up the stairs, Tiffany realised that I was extremely enthralled with the opulence and the grandeur of the architecture of the interior of the building. She looked at me, smiled and said, "This will be your living environment until the middle of September. I will provide you with all the pertinent information about the history, architecture and the calibre of our guests at the appropriate time. Presently I have to look after your well-being. Ok!" I shook my head in agreement with her decision.

The bedroom adjacent to the beauty salon was assigned to me. After setting me up in my room, she invited me to her room for refreshments. I thanked her for extending her hospitality to me and told her that I needed some time to change into more comfortable clothes, and freshen up before I could join her. She was most cooperative and supportive. Before she left, she gave me her room number which was on the same floor as mine. After making myself more relaxed and refreshed, I sauntered through the three hallways to her room. Tiffany was welcoming and cultured. She had classical music softly playing in the background. I had a soft drink and munched on cheese, crackers, grapes and sliced pears. After inquiring about my family background and my purpose in Canada, she promised to narrate the story of her life at a later date. She invited me to join her for dinner in the Indian Head Dining Room at six–thirty. I felt privileged to dine with her. At dinner, Mr. Lambert and Clive joined us. Lambert was humorous and jovial throughout the dinner. Clive, Tiffany and Lambert could not control their fits of laughter, when I re-narrated my tug boat ride, my experiences in the forest and my encounter with Charlie. After a very delicious dinner, Tiffany accompanied me to the main building which she called the "Rotunda". She added that the architect and the first owner decided to name the main administration building the "Rotunda" although it was not round in shape.

Tiffany informed me about the times at which breakfast, lunch and dinner were served. Also, she informed me that I would have to join the other staff members for all my meals in the large dining room adjacent to the main kitchen. After thanking her for all her support, I bid her a pleasant sleep. On the way to my room, I encountered two other summer employees who were assigned rooms adjacent to mine. I asked them to show me the location of the washroom and the showers. Without any hesitation they led me to them. After thanking them, I bid them a good night rest. After showering I returned to my room at the far end of the second floor. My single bed was most welcomed by my tired body and mind.

On the following morning, after my ablutions, I arrived too early for breakfast. Deciding once again to step beyond my comfort zone, I bravely introduced myself to the executive chef and his support staff in the largest kitchen that I had ever seen. I was amazed to learn that the executive chef and his large kitchen staff were mainly Europeans. There were sous-chefs from Italy, France, Macedonia, Germany, Poland, America, Canada and many other countries. I was given a tour of the immense kitchen facilities. Lorenzo, the Italian executive chef (chef de cuisine), on learning that I will be working in the bar, informed me that he had to work cooperatively with the maitre d' and the sommelier in the main guests' dining rooms to construct a list of the best wine match for the dinner menu. Lorenzo had to do it for each meal offered at lunch, dinner and special parties. That was an entirely new dimension of the food and wine service of which I was completely ignorant. At that moment, the thought of learning how to become a competent sommelier while working in the bar, entered my mind. When Lorenzo noticed the perplexed look on my face, he smiled. "Awadh, it seems that that you are interested in becoming a sommelier. If you are seriously interested, I will be most willing to be your teacher" he advised. In response to his offer, I told Lorenzo that I would definitely consider it, and that I would do my utmost best to see what steps that I would have to take to learn about recommending and serving wine and champagne in the Indian Head Dining Room and the Marine Dining Room.

After thanking Lorenzo, I joined the other newly arrived employees in the staff dining room. Taking the initiative, I introduced myself to the young men and women who were waiting in line with their plates to order for their breakfast. Being a neophyte at the hotel, I was exposed to a new community of people who were quite different from me. I was the only South Asian worker on the island. They were all well-dressed in the latest fashion. Although some of them were not too welcoming, I still introduced myself to as many of them as possible. I was extremely delighted to interact with these summer colleagues who were students at various universities across Ontario and Quebec. They were from a wide range of faculties and were at different stages of their study programs. I realized that I was fortunate to be working in an intellectual environment for the entire summer of '67. However, I was prepared to diversify my knowledge as much as possible.

I joined the breakfast line and continued conversing with my newly made interesting co-workers. After I got my food, I sat between a male student from Queen's University and a female student from Western University. During breakfast, I learned that the majority of student workers were from wealthy families. Many of them had vacationed at the resort with their families when they were younger. Most of them were working to escape their controlling parents or guardian so that they could grow and develop according to their dreams and aspirations. Money was not an issue with them. They craved the freedom to have a fun–filled and exciting life away from home. Quickly, I realized that my working environment would be one of enrichment and enlightenment about the lifestyles of students from different socio-economic background. I was ecstatic knowing that I would be exposed to new frontiers of education and talents.

After breakfast, I was accompanied by the two young men who were residing in the rooms adjacent to mine. On my return to my room, the sound of silence that existed yesterday was broken by the sound of music, conversations, and loud footsteps vibrating the wooden hallways. Within a few hours there were almost two hundred summer–job workers on the island. I then realized that it was an hour until the meeting with Mr. Lambert in the Indian Head Dining Room. I rested on my bed until it was about thirty minutes before the meeting.

Mr. Lambert arrived earlier than the scheduled meeting time. After he had cordially welcomed all of the summer employees to the Bigwin Island Hotel, he assured us that we would be extremely pleased with the range of exotic experiences that would inundate us during the summer. No sooner he had made that encouraging claim, Tiffany joined the meeting and apologised for her lateness. He then introduced her as the secretary-treasurer of the hotel, and added that she would be available to act as consultant for any hospitality issues that might occasionally emerge. He re-iterated that we were all employed because we had displayed the following skills most needed in the hospitality industry: Communication in all forms, verbal, written and non-verbal; teamwork with full support and integrity; excellent grooming and personal hygiene; creative problem solving; friendliness; compassion; organization and professionalism. He also reminded us about our willingness to learn new skills on the job, and to use our summer experiences as opportunities for our personal growth and development. He added that we should make lifetime learning one of our priorities if we want to be successful. The undergraduates applauded that statement.

Then he carefully detailed what the guests, visitors and strangers expect from each employee of the hotel. He said that we were employed in the hospitality business. He emphasized that the hotel has provided world class accommodation, fine dining, daily entertainment and many more services to their guests from both Europe and North America since the 1920s; all guests must always receive nothing less than premium and cordial hospitality. Mr. Lambert then instructed us about our comportment, attitude and overall behaviour in the presence of guests, visitors and anyone on the hotel's property, and in our private domains. He informed us that while we were free to do whatever we wished during our free-time, we must perform our duties effectively and efficiently. Under no circumstance were we to socialize with the guests in the privacy of their rooms.

This rule must be followed and would be enforced to avoid the creation of any scandalous event which would greatly jeopardize the reputation of the Bigwin Island hotel. Anyone caught breaching the rule would be dismissed and would immediately be transported to the mainland. In a more pleasant tone, he added that if anyone should become disenchanted with their entry position, they should not hesitate to discuss it with him. Finally he stated the following caveat: "The success of the hospitality service business is constantly impacted by new trends, the economy, weather conditions, political changes, and the taste of the potential consumers. Consequently, we have to be prepared for the unexpected."

Before the meeting concluded, Mr. Lambert gave us some rhetorical questions which he recommended that we should think about while fulfilling our employment duties: "Do you feel extremely confident and comfortable in the task that you are executing? Are you receiving compliments and reasonable compensation for the services you are providing for the guest?" Finally he invited questions from the floor. Since there was none the meeting was adjourned. It was lunch time and the employees headed for the staff dining room.

At lunch time, I seized the opportunity to make acquaintances with a few more interesting individuals. I encountered many people who were employed to work in the bar and dining rooms in different capacities. I learned about their roles, their experiences, and contents of their contract. Their basic pay was much higher than mine. I told them that mine was the same.

In the afternoon there was a special meeting in the red Round Room for all those who were assigned to provide service to the guests, visitors and strangers. The Round Room housed the main bar. It was also where all nightly dancing and comedy took place during the week evenings and night. However, the meeting was scheduled for all those who were hired to serve alcoholic and non-alcoholic beverages to the hotel's guests anywhere on the island. The bartenders, waiters, the sommelier, the maitre d', the cashiers, the manager of hotel operations, and the general manager were in attendance. After he had expressed his happiness to have us on his staff, Mr. Lambert reminded us about our responsibilities, etiquette, and general attitude and behaviour both on and off duty, whenever we were interacting with the guests.

Then, he outlined the necessary preparations that had to be completed before the bar could provide full service to its clientele. The "to do" list included painting the marine deck, repairing the Sundeck and bar furniture, general cleaning of the Round Room, the bar service areas, the wine cellars, and the storage room for supplies. In addition, we had to plant flowers along all pathways leading to the Round Room. After learning of my role, it dawned on me that I had contracted for an arduous task. But I was not dismayed. At the end of the meeting, we decided on the modus operandi for accomplishing the chores on the "to do list" on time. Having fully agreed on our decisions, we went to dinner. Immediately after dinner I retired to my room.

On the following morning, I had to get out of bed early. I got dressed and went for breakfast. It was a beautiful breezy day. A clear blue sky and brilliant sunshine bathed the Bigwin Island landscape. After exiting the colourfully painted and eclectic architecture of the Rotunda, I walked beneath the covered walkways towards the dining rooms. The blackish-blue water of Lake of Bays was a wonderful and pleasant sight to behold. It was just the beginning of my first summer job in the world-class setting of Muskoka and that was the typical summer landscape for the entire summer, except on the days it rained.

After breakfast, I quickly joined my work crew and commenced my assignment. On account of the commitment and determination of the various work teams, we fulfilled all the requirements with time to spare. Mr. Lambert was elated. And to show his appreciation for our accomplishment he treated us with steak dinners and a choice of wines.

Within a few days after all the summer employees had arrived and were ready to perform their assigned duties, the guests started pouring in by the hundreds. They were well taken care of by the staff assigned to look after their requests. The bar was opened to all who were of legal drinking age. Although I was nervously taking my first order for drinks, I confidently placed the order to any of the available bartenders. While I waited for my drink orders to be filled, I heard a voice within me say "Awadh, why don't you learn how to prepare the cocktails that you are serving? The more knowledgeable you are about what you are serving, the more impact you'll have on your customers. What do you think?" After that subliminal advice, I started to pay close attention to the process involved in the preparation of the various mixed cocktails. Within a week, I was able to describe to my customers the name of the various ingredients in their cocktail, and how it was blended. In addition, my knowledge about mixing cocktails was greatly enhanced with the aid of the cocktail books that the bartenders kindly loaned me. I made it my duty to give each customer my undivided attention when they were giving me their drink orders which I diligently wrote on my order form. I performed this ritual so that there would be no error when I delivered their requested drinks. Many of the customers would request that I run a tab for the table, and I always did my best to execute my duties professionally and proficiently. Whenever my customers were pleased with my services, they complimented and tipped me handsomely. Every time I served anyone, the little voice within me, continuously reminded me of the advice that Veronica gave me before I came to assume my duties at the hotel. I was extremely pleased with my tips after my first week as a waiter not only in the Round Room but also in the Marine Dining Room and the Indian Head Dining Room. Within three weeks on the job, I learned from the sommelier that he would need my assistance with the wine service on the long-weekend. I inquired what he meant by a long-weekend. He told me that on July 1st Canada would be celebrating one hundred years of Confederation. The Canadian government had declared it a statutory holiday for all Canadians, called Dominion Day. He informed me that there would be two large groups of over one hundred people each arriving on Friday, June 29th, and would be departing on Monday, July 1st. One group would be a combination of college, polytechnic and university graduates and professors from Toronto. The other group would be female teachers from northern Ontario. He informed me that I would be extremely busy and I would have to perform beyond my regular call of duty, but it would be financially rewarding. Not having any experience serving so many people over a long weekend I spoke to Mr. Lambert privately for some advice. He advised to continue doing my job in my own style, and under no circumstance, I should panic. Just breathe and play it cool and everything would be fine.

Our guests arrived safely and joined the guests who had already taken up residence a week ago in the hotel. The hotel lodges were filled to capacity. And after I had seen all the musical instruments that the teachers and graduates had brought, I wondered whether they were going to have a show at the Pavilion. After making inquiries, no such activity was planned by the management of the hotel. There was speculation as to what might take place during the long weekend. The dining rooms were filled to capacity and Mr. Lambert enlisted all staff members who were not on regular duty to give a helping hand as servers in the dining rooms and bar. Many of the faithful guests were completely stunned to see the invasion of the younger guests. They were not too happy with the loud talking of the teachers and graduates. The incompetence and the commotion created by the extra untrained servers also greatly annoyed them. For example, one of the servers who usually worked in the stable tried to open a bottle of Champagne. When he had experienced great difficulty to get it open, on the advice of one the jesting guests, he shook it violently. He then tried to uncork it. The cork shot out at a high velocity. After it had ricocheted from the ceiling, it struck one of the elderly female diners on her nose. This unfortunate incident was not easily handled by the manager of the Indian Head Dining Room.

Eventually, the majority of the dinner guests returned either to their rooms or the large lounge in the Rotunda. Some went to walk along the beach front to enjoy the cool breeze blowing across the lake under a romantic moonlit starry night. And some went to the Round Room to continue their drinking and dance to the lilting music of the five-piece orchestra. Although the serving of alcoholic beverages was discontinued at one o'clock in the morning the young adults did not leave the bar until after two o'clock. After the bar and the Sundeck were cleaned, I staggered to my room, and was only able to go to bed about four o'clock on the Saturday morning.

Being greatly exhausted, I awoke very late. Having missed breakfast, I went to my friends in the kitchen who took care of me. The kitchen chefs were amused about the champagne incident. Then Lorenzo, the executive chef, informed me that the Saturday night dinner would be more challenging than last night. He had learned that the teachers and the graduate students had planned to have a musical sing along in the dining room either during dinner or after dinner. If it should take place, the older folks, who have already registered their complaints, would be greatly disappointed with this crowd that was allowed to vacation in their private vacation retreat. At that point, I questioned whether Mr. Lambert was aware of the intentions of the graduates and teachers. Lorenzo didn't know. Being a young adult myself, and being extremely pleased with the compensation that I had received I was prepared for an evening and night of fun and gaiety while I performed my duties. Much to my delightful surprise and the majority of the workers, and most of the guests, the most unexpected and welcomed musical sing along took place, just after lunch, on the front lawn of the Rotunda and in the open spaces between the trees. The teachers and the graduates employed their musical talents, and sang all the top hit songs of the Beatles, Rolling Stones, Mamas and The Papas, Supremes, Bob Dylan, the Temptations and every hit song they knew from 1965-1967. Whether they were inebriated either by alcohol or drugs I could not tell. Their clothes were extremely colorful. They also wore accessories like head bands, beads, gaudy necklaces and many other colourfully designed jewels that I had never seen before. But they were quite respectful and full of joy and ecstasy.

The evening for the most part was unusually tranquil and peaceful after the fantastic party that developed between the teachers and the graduates. At dinner time, the anticipated musical show did not materialize. The teachers and graduates were formally dressed for a Saturday dinner night and were not segregated. And those elderly guests who had witnessed earlier the explosion of the talents of the teachers and the graduates, and had thoroughly enjoyed and participated with them, were enormously happy and pleased to be in their presence. In fact the young and the vivacious started to mingle with the elderly. These younger teachers and graduates revived the memories of the older guests of their days when they were young and having fun. Saturday night events were not as long as the Friday night's. On Sunday the two groups of young adults repeated their performance of musical talents at the same venues. And the reception once again was greatly appreciated by the long-term guests of the resort.

On Dominion Day, some of the merry making teachers and graduates devoted the day to playing golf, some went horseback riding in the trails in the forests and the rest of them spent the day at the beach and bar. Just before dinner on the Monday, the teachers and the graduates waved farewell to all their wellwishers.

For me, it was one of the most exciting and rewarding collection of experiences that I had had in months.

After being on duty for only four weeks, Mr. Lambert, who always seemed to be evaluating the performance of each service provider, invited me to a meeting in his office. It was scheduled for the next morning. I had a sleepless night. I wondered whether Mr. Lambert had discovered some faults in the performance of my duties. After an early breakfast I met Tiffany and informed her about my unexpected meeting with Mr. Lambert. She encouraged me to be confident and to anticipate a positive outcome from the meeting. I knocked on Mr. Lambert's office door. He invited me to enter. I sat directly in front of him, extremely apprehensive. Without delay, in a business-like tone, he uttered, "Awadh. Do you know why I have asked you to meet with me in my 'inner sanctum'? After a contemplative moment, humbly I responded,

"No Mr. Lambert!"

With a smile he informed me that he had received positive feedback, not only from guests but also from the dining room staff about the efficient services that I had provided since I started to work as a server, not only in the dining rooms, the Round Room bar, and the Sundeck, but also at the piano pre-dinner recitals. Having heard the positive feedback from the various sources, Henri, the Maitre d' and he, made their own observations to verify the reviews. Pleased with my performance, they decided to make some alterations to my contract with my approval.

I thanked him for their appreciative words, and anxiously waited to hear the consequences. On the Saturday night's grand balls, and the long weekends, I would be the assistant sommelier in the dining rooms to serve fine wines and champagne. He assured me that my new responsibilities would be less laborious than that of a waiter. If I was interested, he would make the necessary arrangements with the sommelier and the Maitre D' to spend time educating me on the secrets of recommending and serving fine wines and champagne. Also a few of my daily chores would be removed so that I would have the time available to be trained. Elated and extremely interested in acquiring and applying the new skills mentioned I snatched the golden opportunity offered with great confidence and commitment. This offer was strictly confidential and was not to be discussed with anyone except those directly involved.

On the following morning at breakfast, Mr. Lambert informed me about a meeting in his office with Henri and Maurice, the sommelier. They had all sorts of charts about the different wines they had in the cellar located beneath the Round Room; the different types of glasses; the etiquette of wine serving; a lexicon of terms commonly used by sommeliers and general cleanliness and professionalism. At the end of the meeting, I was given a black tuxedo, two black bow-ties, a cummerbund, and money to purchase a pair of black shoes. After I had thanked both of them for all their instruction on the duties of an excellent sommelier, and for their promise to help me to become competent in my added responsibilities, they led me to the wine cellars. The wines were all resting in horizontal position in small circular cribs. To the best of my recollection, there were wines from France, Germany, Italy, Portugal, and other countries. I was amazed at the size of the wine collection. Maurice and I spent many evenings tasting different wines and evaluating their properties.

They were correct when they assured me that functioning as an assistant to the sommelier during the busy business nights in the dining rooms would be more financially rewarding than running up and down the stairs to the main bar for drinks as a waiter. Daily I thanked the "Divine Presence" for His tender mercies and blessings.

After a brief rest in my room, I reported for duty in the Round Room which was located beneath the Marine Dining Room at the edge of the lake. As soon as I entered the bar, one of my regular customers hurried to me and inquired about the location of my station. I asked the reason for his inquiry. He told me that his party was sitting in the Buffalo Head fireplace area, but another waiter was serving them. And he wanted to know the reason. I informed him that the management has created several serving stations in the bar and on the Sundeck, due to the complaints of the waiters that certain waiters were serving only in certain strategic areas because they were at work very early. As a result stations were created by management so that the waiters were in a different station each day. He wanted to move his party to my station but I advised him to remain in the same serving station. Being a bit disappointed, he whispered, "I understand. Next time, I will find out where you are serving." After thanking him kindly for his support, I hastened to attend to the guests seated in my station. It was a busy business night. And as usual, Luigi and his quartet had the dance floor vibrating with the rhythmic feet of the dancers who were at different stages of inebriation enjoying his energising music.

Having shadowed the sommelier for couple of weeks, a fortuitous opportunity presented itself. At breakfast one rainy morning, Henri asked me whether I would be willing to be the acting sommelier for the dinner in the Indian Head Dining Room for the next two evenings. Maurice was under the weather. Being confident that I had adequate knowledge and skills to perform the duties of a sommelier, I eagerly accepted his offer. As soon as I got the encouraging news, I went to the kitchen to speak with Lorenzo, the executive chef. Inspiringly, he advised me to return to him before dinner time and he would have wine pairings annotated notes (cheat sheets) for me. Elated that I had his professional support, I anticipated a successful debut as acting sommelier in the main dining room. As fate would have it, my performance was highly appreciated by Henri. He informed me that he was most pleased to see me perform seamlessly from a server to a sommelier.

A few days after my role as acting sommelier, I was in the Tea House enjoying a vanilla milkshake with a few of my colleagues. Mr. Lambert approached and addressed me, "Shadow, Henri enlightened me about your successful debut as an acting sommelier. He assured me that you were efficient and effective in serving the guests. I have decided to rename you Shadow, because you know what pleases the hearts of our guests." At first, I didn't know how to respond to the name he had given me. But I thanked him, being my employer, for considering me as a crime stopper. According to my knowledge of the comic hero, Shadow, was a crime stopper because he knew what evil lurked in the hearts of men. I did not object to the nickname. In fact, my co-workers were excited to call me Shadow. By the end of the summer, almost everyone called me Shadow. Even many of the guests felt comfortable calling me Shadow. With the new name I became more popular with the staff of almost two hundred. I was invited to many more private social activities of which I was not previously aware did take place on the Bigwin Island Hotel property.

Towards the end of July 1967, my status as a simple waiter was transformed by these two unexpected events which entitled me to privileges reserved for a selected few. My role as acting sommelier, and my new name Shadow quickly promulgated through the rank and file of the entire staff.

My dating seeds, which so far had been dormant, started to germinate. One of the waitresses in the Marine Dining Room invited me to a skinny-dipping party at one of the cottages on the island. She gave me all the pertinent information about the party. Being a young adult from Trinidad, I had never heard the descriptor "skinny-dipping" for any party that I had ever attended. I was advised to bring wine and snacks.

On the eventful summer evening, being well dressed for an indoor party, I headed for the cottage. As I was making my way through the shrubs and trees along the golf course, and as I got closer to the cottage which was at the edge of the lake, I heard the voices of both males and females loudly singing along with Van Morrison's "Brown Eyed Girl", spinning on a record player. I was dressed for an indoor dance party and the high volume of the music was seducing me. I quickened my pace. But as I was on the verge of clearing the bushes, I was instantly struck by a scene similar to those on Hieronymus Bosch's paintings. The sandy beach was crowded with people dancing and cavorting in the nude. Immediately, I retreated in the bushes to convince myself that these were the same people that I worked with. While I was attempting to identify the various faces, Bianca who had invited me, having seen me peeping, ran toward me completely nude and escorted me to the cottage. Everybody was naked. She started undressing me in the presence of everyone. I completed undressing and gleefully joined the fun. I was literally in "the Garden of Earthly Delights". Debauchery was in full progress in every scene that I could remember. Bacchus had taken possession of the minds, body and spirit of these young adults. I participated fully in only some activities. The D.J. had a collection of albums from Jefferson Airplane, Jim Morrison, Van Morrison, Otis Redding, Pink Floyd and many other musical hits from that era. When the Bacchanalian celebrations started to wane, and most of the participants were either exhausted or stoned, Bianca and I relaxed in the warm waters of the Lake of Bays. My invitation and initiation to the skinny-dipping party was my passport for many more private parties during the summer of '67. On the following day, Bianca met me at lunch and requested that what we had done at the beach party must not be divulged to anyone. My discretion was rewarded by invitations to other private parties.

Soap operas were played out in many of the public buildings on the Bigwin Island, not only by the paying guests but also by visitors from other lodges and cottagers from the mainland, and also with the undergraduate students employed for the summer. The people who frequented the Island came in search of happiness, and they were daring to use any ploy to achieve joy, pleasure and well-being. I was privileged to witness several episodes of various people working diligently to ignite romantic relationships. Among the love-seekers were people of different sexual preferences: Singles, married couples, swingers, gays, bi-sexuals and many other colourful characters, some with strange fetishes.

During the summer of '67, there were visitors from both Canada and the United States. According to the registration records about forty percent of the guests were Americans. It was a beautiful sunny day and the view over the Lake of Bays was breathtaking, when four American couples from Boston arrived on the Island to spend a few days at the resort. The men, all retired professors from universities in the Boston area, told me while I was serving them cocktails on the sun deck that they had stayed at the hotel a few years ago. After I had served them their drinks and food, I was intrigued by the age difference between one of the professors and his partner. His mate had to be either his daughter or his young trophy wife. The curiosity of many of the servers on duty was also aroused. The passionate interest of Serge, who was paired with me on the lunch shift, was clearly focused on the young gorgeous woman. Serge wanted to get to know her intimately. As I continued to serve them their second round of cocktails, I learnt that they were on a golfing holiday. But only the men would be involved. The women would either be shopping in Huntsville or relaxing on the sandy beach strip. With this important information, I decided to assist Serge in his quest. Serge was a young, intelligent and a handsome third year law student. After the four couples had finished their lunch, one of the professors asked me whether there was still dancing in the Round Room. After my positive response, he smiled and said, "See you after dinner in the buffalo head area." At dinner time, I spoke privately to the sommelier about serving the professors' party. He kindly obliged. During the dinner, the young gorgeous woman from Boston excused herself to go to the powder room. Immediately, I informed Serge to meet her in the corridor leading to the ladies room and to discreetly express his interests. Serge did as instructed. After dinner, only three of the four couples reported to the tables that I had reserved for them. As soon as they were seated, the young woman asked me my name. I told her that it was Shadow. "How did you get that name?" Before I could answer, the men started to order their drinks. Luigi and his orchestra commenced the evening's entertainment with his Latin beat of "Quando caliente del sol" which brought the dance floor to life. On my return they were still dancing. Patiently, I waited for their return to serve them their drinks. Soon the Round Room got busy and, as a result I had to provide drink service to the other guests seated in my station. I hustled among the tables and provided my signature service to all my guests. But the group seated at the fireplace left before I was able to answer the young woman's question about my name.

On the following afternoon as I slowly descended the wooden stairway to the main floor of the Rotunda lounge, I noticed the young woman from Boston reading a book in one of the alcoves. Without hesitation and seeing no other guests in sight, I took the liberty to socialize and answer her question. After wishing her a pleasant day, I inquired about her evaluation of her vacation to date. Before answering my question, she closed the book, got up and after replacing it in its appropriate space, invited me for coffee in the Tea House. As we walked across the large Rotunda lounge, she introduced herself as Ruth. And with a smile she added "like in ruthless". Her bantering was most refreshing and inviting. During our coffee time, no one from her group was present. After I had related the origin of my alias Shadow, she informed me that she was the mistress of the retired professor who was a wealthy socialite in the Boston area. Then, she mentioned her brief encounter with Serge, and inquired whether I had known him. I informed her that he was one of my newly found friends. She confided that she would love to have a brief affair with him before she had to leave for Boston. I assured her that it could be arranged effortlessly and safely. Having clearly outlining my plan, she wholeheartedly agreed. After the coffee break, she left for her room in the West Lodge. Pleased with the dating arrangements that I had made for my friend, Serge, I hoped only that he would be in agreement with the plans Ruth and I had concocted. Immediately, I went in search of Serge. Within a few minutes, I saw him at the registration desk in the Rotunda. But I did not interrupt him. Instead, I sat quietly in one of the high back chairs out of his line of vision. As soon as he left the registration desk, I got up and got his attention. I asked him why he was reading the guests' registration records. In a hushed voice, he informed me that he was making inquiries about the Boston group. But he did not know under what names they had registered. I invited him to take a walk with me outside. He did not respond. Instead, he walked towards the main entrance of the Rotunda. Realizing how disappointed he was with his attempts to find Ruth, I hastened to meet him in the gallery of the Rotunda. With a big smile, I enlightened him about the ploy that Ruth and I had designed earlier. He became ecstatic. And while hugging and kissing me on my neck, he thanked me several times.

After dinner, the four couples were influenced by Ruth to seat themselves in my serving station. Serge was stationed adjacent to my station. At about eight thirty that evening, Ruth informed the group that she was feeling nauseated and was developing a headache from the loud bar noises. But she continued dancing with her partner for a about twenty minutes when she asked to be excused, and promised to return as soon as she had taken a quick hot shower and changed into more casual clothing. There was no objection from her partner who took the opportunity to dance with any available female in the Round

Room.

At exactly nine o'clock the phone rang at the bar. The cashier, Charmaine, answered the phone. O'Rourke, one of the bartenders came to my station and informed me that there was a phone for me. I told Serge to attend to my customers while I was attending to the phone call for me. It was Ruth and she requested room service. I took her order and after thanking Serge for attending to my patrons, I quietly and secretly passed the order to him. He then informed his customers that he had to meet his mother who had just arrived at the ferry docks. But Shadow, his faithful friend would cover for him. After the departure of Serge, a few of his customers started to leave. At about eleven o'clock, the Boston party decided to call it a night. Immediately, I phoned Ruth's room and informed her that her sugar daddy was coming home. Within a short time interval, Serge returned to the Round Room to continue his shift.

It was one of those sunny and beautiful Muskoka summer days when I got request from another friend in distress. I was off duty sitting in the shade of silver birch trees napping when my friend Trevor's voice awoke me. "Shadow I need your help," Trevor softly asked. Slowly I opened my eyes and looked at Trevor. He continued, "I have a date and need your help."

"How could I help Trevor." I calmly answered.

He complained that he had a date with a chamber maid, but his roommate would not allow him to use the room. He wanted to know whether it would be possible to use my room to romance his date. I then ask him when his date was. "After dinner tonight," he informed me.

I promised to loan him my room in the Rotunda and informed him that I would leave my door unlocked from seven o'clock in the evening and would return to my room at nine o'clock sharp. Trevor assured me that he would need only one hour. Being pleased, he hugged and thanked me.

The following afternoon was blessed with brilliant sunshine and a cool breeze softly blowing across the island. While sitting in a Muskoka chair in the shade of the Rotunda and drinking in the pastoral sceneries of the blackish blue water of lake of Bays, the flora and fauna on the island and the mainland, someone clasped their hands over my eyes. I had no idea who would be ambushing me. As soon as the feminine voice said, "Guess who!" Immediately, I responded, "Joanne!"

"I have been looking for you. And luckily, I met Serge who told me where you were."

"Oh! Why do you want to see me?"

Without answering, she sat next to me. Tears started to well up her green eyes. I looked at her without a comment. Then she asked, "Are you going to blackmail me?"

Being perplexed by her serious question, I exclaimed, "Blackmail! That's a serious accusation Joanne. Why would I want to blackmail you?

"About what happened last night in Trevor's room."

Pretending to be innocent about what happened last night, I inquired, "What happened in his room last night?"

She then got irritated and barked, "Shadow! Stop fucking with me. You are quite aware of what happened. Are you going to blackmail me?"

"Joanne. Why are you using the word blackmail?

"Shadow, you know that I am engaged to Darren. Since both of you are co-managers of the Piano Bar, he must have confided in you about of our engagement last Christmas and our wedding plans for Easter next year."

Joanne did not realize that her assumptions were completely incorrect. Darren never divulged any information about his engagement or marriage to me. Since she believed that I had knowledge about her engagement and wedding plans, and being conscious of the fact that I had damaging information about her, I decided to ask her a few personal questions.

"Joanne, I will decide on how I will use my knowledge about last night after you have honestly answered my question."

Having agreed to my condition for confidentiality, I asked her whether last night was the first time that she had cheated on Darren. She remained silent for a while and then responded that it was none of my damned business. I agreed with her. The following thoughts fluttered in my conscience. Would it be prudent to enlighten my trusting friend, Darren, about his fiancée's affair? Or should I just keep quiet and allow her to live her life. On realizing that I had become passive when she had told me to stay out of her personal life-style, she broke the silence, "What were you doing in Trevor's room?"

"Who told you that was Trevor's room?

"Trevor told me that everyone would be at the hotdog party and that it would be safe in his room." I then informed her that Trevor told me that he had a woman who consented to have sex with him but his room-mate would not allow him to use their room. He asked me for permission to use my single room for one hour. When I returned to my room after two hours, I discovered both of you were nude and still having intercourse. Being surprised, I apologized and left the embarrassing situation immediately. Joanne was very disappointed that Trevor had lied to her. She then said, "Please save my marriage. I truly love Darren. And I am extremely sorry for betraying his trust." Before she left, I assured her that I would keep her secret and coined the following lines for her:

"Why lose a special somebody,

By fooling around with everybody,

And gaining nobody."

After she had wiped the tears from her cheeks, we embraced and left for our daily duties.

On a typical beautiful summer day, anyone seated on the Sundeck would have a magnificent view of the boats on the lake and the trees on the mainland, and the beautiful and picturesque views of the forested hills of Bigwin Island itself. On this midweek lunch Norman, the assistant manager, Sandy the social hostess, Maurice the sommelier, Tiffany the secretary-treasurer, Henri the maitre d', and Mr. Lambert the president, were having lunch on the Sundeck . At first, it was not too busy for the two other waiters and me to serve comfortably. A convoy of boats approached the Sundeck. After the boats were moored, all the passengers hurriedly stepped on the Sundeck. Some of them ran to the washrooms. The rest of them occupied the vacant seats both on the Sundeck and in the Round Room. Without delay, the waiters took the orders from the new arrivals for their drinks. After we had taken their orders, the new arrival from the convoy went to get their lunch at the hamburger, sandwich, and hot dog stands located on the Sundeck. Definitely we needed more waiters, bartender and another person to assist the cashier. This was a situation I never anticipated. The orders were slowly filled. The service to the customers was unacceptable according to my evaluation. But we did not have any other option available. We all hustled as best as we could to serve our new customers.

Then the unexpected happened. Mr. Lambert touched me on my shoulder. "Shadow, where are the extra serving trays? We are going to rectify this situation as quickly as possible." I could not believe the metamorphosis. Tiffany started to assist the cashier, Maurice, Henri and Norman served drinks to the customers, Sandy and Mr. Lambert started mixing cocktails and filling orders. No one complained about the service they had received. Mr. Lambert and his entourage saved the day. By doing what they did, the customers and guests should look more favourably on the hospitality offered at Bigwin Island Hotel. On the following days, many of the guests who were having lunch on the Sundeck, and had witnessed the rescue mission of Mr. Lambert and his cavalry, continued to keep the story alive with those who had missed it.

After Tiffany had handed me my first pay cheque, she strongly advised that I should open a saving account at the Royal Bank in Huntsville. Since I was not scheduled to work, I decided that I would hitch hike to the bank in Huntsville, and deposit all my cash and the cheque that Tiffany had given me a few days ago. I boarded the ten o'clock ferry to the mainland. As I was making my way to highway 117, two slim, attractive, and well-dressed female guests who were on the ferry with me, inquired about my mission for the day. I informed them about my intentions. After they had a private talk, they offered me a ride to Huntsville. I accepted their kind offer. As we headed for a new yellow Mustang, they introduce themselves as Sally and Tammy. I informed them that my name was Awadh. As Sally drove out from the parking lot, again I thanked her for her kindness. I sat calmly in the back seat and appreciated the picturesque landscape as it quickly went by. Sally sported a well-groomed blonde hair style. Tammy had short black hair. Their perfumes were pleasant and refreshing. As soon as we had passed Baysville and was on the winding road to Huntsville, a question and answer session unexpectedly commenced.

Tammy questioned me about my background. I informed her that I was from Trinidad and was studying at McMaster University. She probed into my reason for working at the hotel. Having answered all of Tammy's questions, and still not hearing a word from Sally, I decided to inquire about Sally's background. I learned that her parents were from Poland and that she was born in Canada. She had graduated from Western University with a degree in sociology. She was unmarried and was employed in the department of human relations with a commercial firm. I stopped questioning Sally as soon as I had realized that she was experiencing great difficulty negotiating the corners on the winding road.

After arriving safely in Huntsville, Tammy instructed Sally to park the car as close as possible to the restaurant that they had planned to have lunch. When Sally had parked, I thanked them for the ride and as I got out, Sally wanted to know if I would like to join them for lunch after I had completed my business. Her invitation took me by surprise. I accepted. After we had departed for our individual mission, I looked up into the clear blue Muskoka sky and thanked my lucky stars for introducing me to these generous and cordial women. My transaction at the bank was brief, but I spent a lot more time in the liquor store. I carefully recorded the names of the vintage wines and their prices that we did not have in our wine cellars, later to discuss them with the sommelier with the intent of including a few of them on our wine list. I then bought two bottles of Cote de Rhone. When I eventually arrived at the restaurant Sally and Tammy were absent, but my hopes were brightened when I noticed the parked yellow Mustang. I left the restaurant and stood next to the Mustang. I was in no hurry to get anywhere. Finally, after almost thirty minutes they arrived, each bearing large shopping bags filled with merchandise in each hand. I offered to assist in stowing their bags. They politely declined.

Seated in the restaurant, the waitress brought us the lunch time special menus. I ordered a hamburger with a coke. Tammy asked for the regular menu and ordered a sumptuous meal and wine. Sally had soup and salad with a cold Heineken. During the lunch the conversation got extremely interesting and enlightening, especially for me. I did not know whether the alcohol they were imbibing had any effect on their thinking processes. I was surprised to learn about the reasons for vacationing at Bigwin Island Hotel. By the end of lunch, they informed me that this was their second vacation at the resort, and that they had come with the intention of getting a wealthy husband either from the interested men among the guests or the youthful staff. Whether they were successful or not, they were interested in having a lot of fun from any source. I paid for my lunch in spite of Tammy's insistence to pay for me. Sally asked me whether I had a friend with whom she could socialize for the rest of her vacation. I did not respond. After reflecting on the experiences that my colleagues and I had already tasted during the summer of love at the resort, Serge was the only face to appear on my radar screen as the person. As we drove into the Bigwin parking lot, Sally repeated her question. I informed her that she would have to meet me on the verandah in the front of the Rotunda before going for dinner. The ferry arrived. The captain, my humorous friend wanted to know why I was not on duty in the "Round Room." After hearing how I spent the day, he winked at me.

At the terminal on the island, I thanked Sally and Tammy for their kindness and friendship. As they walked towards their rooms in the East Lodge, Sally reminded me of our arrangement. Being aware that Serge was on duty in the "Round Room", I went directly to inform him about Sally. He was at the bar attending to a customer. Anxiously I waited. As soon as he had completed serving his customer, he came directly to me. "What is the matter Shadow?"

After I had narrated the day's events, he agreed to meet with Sally.

"What about you Shadow?"

"Serge, I would love to tango with Tammy. But she has not asked me whether I was interested or not in a date with her."

"Why don't you ask her?"

"I will inform you about Sally's plans as soon I get them."

Both Sally and Tammy met me at the Verandah. Sally gave me the key to her room in the East Lodge. Then she told me that Serge should be in her room to open the door for her. She added that he should only open the door after three knocks. I told her that she would have a great time with Serge. And I wished both of them to have an enjoyable dinner. As I turned and started to walk away, Tammy said, "Here is my key. See you later Awadh. And wait for my three knocks." After thanking her, I looked at her and smiled. I stood on the spot and admired her walking under the covered walkway to the dining room. Immediately, I hastened to meet Serge. After informing Serge about the arrangement that I had made for him, he became ecstatic and restless. In his excitement, he did not ask me whether I had a date or not. I did not venture any further information. Before he left,

I advised that he should wear his red Bigwin jacket to and from Sally's room. I then went and had a shower.

As I sat in one of the reading alcove upstairs in the Rotunda, and focused at the exit of the Indian Head dining Room, I spotted them. I put on my red Bigwin jacket. I walked bravely into the main entrance to the Tudor-designed East Lodge as though I was on an errand. As I was on the verge of stepping on the second floor, I met Lena, one of the dining room waitresses, who had just descended from the third floor. "Shadow, what you are doing here?" I told her that I was on my way to make a date with one of the girls on the third floor.

"Who are you looking for?"

"I'll tell you later Lena."

I ran up the stairs leading to the third floor where the female workers resided for the summer. I walked down the corridor of the third floor under the pretense that I was in search of a date. Gingerly, I retraced my steps to the second floor. Fortunately, there was no one in the hallway on the second floor. Without looking around, I quickly opened Tammy's door and entered the room. Having closed the door behind me, I breathed a great sigh of relief. Her room was extremely neat. Her bed was inviting. But I resisted the temptation to rest on it and slow down my pulse rate and lower my blood pressure. I went to the window facing the woods and looked at the two tennis clay courts. No one was playing tennis. No sooner I had sat on the bed three knocks on the door reached my ears. After unlocking the door, I stood behind it to allow Tammy to enter. I quickly closed the door. A feeling of comfort re-entered my mind. As soon as she entered the room she started to French kiss me and squeezed my penis which was in erection mode. She got completely naked in a flash and started undressing me. I looked at her nude body and could not resist my desire to have sex. I held her tightly and while kissing her we got in bed and started fucking. She was making loud moaning sounds which I stifled with the palm of my hand. After we had orgasmed we showered and towelled each other. On returning to the bed, she preferred to remain nude under the covers. I followed suit. We continued making love and having sex until it got pitch dark.

Then much to my frightening surprise, someone was knocking on the door. Then I heard the distinct voice of Peter O'Rourke, "Room service." Immediately I rushed into the bathroom stark-naked and closed the door. Tammy put on her robe and allowed Peter to deliver a tray of cheese, grapes, crackers, and a bottle of Asti in an ice bucket. She tipped Peter. After his departure, Tammy could not stop laughing at my terrified reaction to the unexpected room service knock. I opened the sparkling wine and celebrated our evening of love, romance and sex. I spent most of the night with Tammy. After midnight we had sex again. After showering, I got dressed and returned to my room.

On the following morning, Serge had breakfast with me. After narrating the wonderful and sensuous experience Sally and he had shared, Mr. Lambert entered the staff breakfast room. He came directly toward our table. He was enraged. A silent hush flowed through the breakfast tables. My heart started to palpitate and extreme fear raced through my veins. I felt guilty even before a charge was made against me. Then, to my unexpected relief, Mr. Lambert spoke to the chambermaid who sat next to me having breakfast. She was ordered to report to his office immediately after she had finished her breakfast. She was quite aware of her dilemma which was revealed by her tears. At that moment, no one dared to probe into her personal affairs. But human nature did not prevent the curious young adults from seeking reasons for Mr. Lambert's unexpected visit to the staff dining room so early in the morning. No sooner had the chambermaid left the gossip machine went into high gear. There were numerous allegations, speculations and assumptions which made me wonder about the maturity of my fellow workers.

Serge turned to me and said, "Shadow, I was quaking in my

boots when I saw Mr. Lambert coming directly at me. For a split second, I thought that he had seen me in Sally's room. But I was greatly relieved after he had accosted the chambermaid."

Apparently, Sally did not inform Serge about my tryst with Tammy. I decided to keep it secretly. After breakfast, Serge stated that he would not be getting involved with the guests again. He added that there were too many eyes looking at us. It was almost the end of the summer of '67, and he did not want to be dismissed. Later that morning, I learned from Tiffany, after I had sworn to secrecy, that the chambermaid was fired, because she was caught having an affair with one of the guests' husband.

In order to maintain and protect my blemish-free record, I realized that I had to meet Tammy as soon as possible. Lunch time was fast approaching, and I did not have to assume my duties until five o'clock in the afternoon. I waited patiently in the Tea Room, seated in a strategic position so that I could see her as soon as she exited the East Lodge. Fortunately, she was alone. I followed slowly behind her. When I was within earshot, I said, "Tammy, do not turn around. Slow down and listen carefully to my instructions. I have a very important message to impart privately to you. Keep on walking toward the ferry and take it to the mainland. I will meet you in the parking lot by the Mustang. Just keep calm."

As I was making my way to the ferry which was about to leave with Tammy, I was hoping that I did not meet either Sally or Serge on the ferry. Pensively, I stood at the rear of the ferry. Tammy went directly to the Mustang. As I got to the car, I told her to get inside and drive out of the parking lot. I instructed her to drive slowly toward Dorset.

As she drove out of the parking lot she questioned in a serious tone, "What is going on Awadh? Why are you so dramatic? Did you get in trouble with the manager?"

On realizing that she did not have any information about

the dismissal of the chambermaid, I told her that I needed her assistance and cooperation. Tammy stopped the car on the shoulder of the road in the shade of the trees. "Awadh, I'm a paying guest at the hotel and I am entitled to invite anyone to my room. You were my invited guest last night. So, what is the problem?"

First, I narrated the story of the chambermaid. After learning what the chambermaid had done and penalty she had to pay, Tammy displayed a puzzled countenance. And in a soft voice said, "How can I be of assistance?"

"Tammy, did you tell Sally that I was in your bedroom last night with you?"

"No!"

"So only you and I know."

"Yes"

Having received her assurance that our affair was not in the public domain, I hugged and kissed her. Kindly, I asked her not to mention it to Sally as long as they were at the resort. Tammy then added, "Since the management is keeping close surveillance on the staffs' interaction with the guests, I will not encourage you to meet me in my room at hotel. Instead, I am extending to you an open invitation to visit me at my home in St. Thomas. On your return to university, you can visit me at any of the statutory holiday: Thanksgiving, Christmas, New Year and Easter." After that encouraging speech, she gave me her address, telephone numbers and her full name. We hugged and kissed, and drove back to the parking lot. In the parking lot, I thanked her for the beautiful and wonderful experiences we had shared, and I promised to visit her during my academic year on one of the statutory holidays. After our arrival on the island, Tammy went for lunch on the Sundeck, and I went to the staff dining room for lunch.

There was another hour left for lunch. Quickly, I joined the lunch queue. Then I heard Lena's loud voice, "Shadow after you get your food come and join me. I am keeping a spot for you." I didn't expect to meet Lena at lunch. I courteously joined her for lunch to establish a sound alibi for my presence on the third floor last evening. However, that was too much tension and stress for my mind and body to manage after a one-night stand. After joining her, she immediately inquired whether I had secured a date with one of the girls on the third floor. As I had already placed food in my mouth, I hesitated to respond to her 'none-of-your-business' question. Slowly swallowing food, I informed her that there was no one to ask. Much to my surprise, she told me that she would love to be on a date with me. I looked at her and said, "Are you serious?" Lena responded, "If I wasn't serious I wouldn't have said it. Shadow the ball is in your court."

After lunch, I returned to my room to rest. At reflecting on my day's emotional rollercoaster ride, I got up. And after having a shower, dressing, I left early for my evening shift on the Sundeck. It was crowded with cottagers, visitors from other resorts, and our guests. One of the servers shouted, "Shadow we need your help. Please serve those people getting off the large mahogany boat." Fortunately, there was available seating to accommodate the new arrivals. After they were all seated, one of the servers brought me a serving tray and order forms. For the remainder of the evening until late in the night there was a steady flow of customers. The night sky was filled with stars. And the northern lights were dancing in full glory for the patrons who were drinking, snacking and conversing and who were lucky to get a seat on the open-air Sundeck.

Later that night, Sally and Tammy joined the dancing in the Round Room. They were accompanied by two handsome gentlemen. I had served these men on several occasions. They were cottagers. As the bar was about to discontinue the sale of alcohol, the two men escorted Sally and Tammy to their boat and drove away in the direction of the mainland under a starry night. After the bar was finally cleaned and closed, Serge met me in the Tea House, which was still open, to share milkshakes. Rather annoyed, he declared, "Shadow, did you notice what Sally and Tammy did?"

What did they do?"

"They left at almost midnight in a boat with two men."

"What is the problem? They are paying guests. They have the right to do whatever they want with their time."

"How could Sally sleep with me last night and go with another man tonight?" I responded that I was not a psychologist. At that stage of the conversation, I advised Serge to stop talking about last night if he wanted to keep his job. I had no idea what transpired between Sally and Serge, but he was highly emotional. After searching in his red Bigwin jacket pockets, he found some loose coins. He got up, and walked slowly towards the Juke box which was playing "Lucy in the sky with diamonds". After he had inserted a coin in the juke box, the following song started to play as soon as he had sat down opposite to me. And he sang along with Frank Sinatra:

Strangers in the night
Exchanging glances
Wondering in the night
What were the chances
We'd be sharing love
Before the night was through
Something in your eyes
Was so inviting
Something in your smile
Was so exciting
Something in my heart told me I must have you
Stranger in the night, two lonely people
We were strangers in the night
Up to the moment when we said our first hello
Little did we know
Love was just a glance away,
a warm embracing dance away

And ever since that night
We have been together
Lovers at first sight
In love forever
It turned out so right
Strangers ...

Serge replayed this song several times. Many of the staff who were in the Tea House joined in his singing. Being sleepy, I wished them a good night.

But as I was about to enter the front door of the Rotunda, one of the girls wanted to know who Serge was singing about. With a late night smile, I walked away without a response. Within two days, Serge regained his colourful personality.

On the following morning, as I was going for breakfast, I saw a collection of golf bags leaning against the wall in front of the dining room. Instantly, I remembered the promise that I had made with my friend, Michael, a few weeks ago. Michael was in charge of the golf pro shop. The shop was on the first floor of the clubhouse. We had forged a genuine friendship and he spent personal time to teach me the fundamentals of golf. Michael wanted to know what sparked my interest in golf. I told him that a few days ago, while I was serving cocktails and snacks to a group of golfers who had already played all the holes on the Bigwin Island Golf course, I overheard them analyzing and criticizing, and at the same time complimenting various players on their performance on the fairways and on the greens for every hole they had played on the Bigwin golf course. I added that my curiosity was triggered by the terminology and lingo they used to describe the culture of the game. And when the following golf terms were bantered around, I wanted to know what they meant: iron, woods, driver, putter, sand wedge, sand trap, eagle, bogey, birdie, long game, short game, front nine, back nine and a continuous usage of different golfing jargon, I became interested in not only learning the terminology but also how to play the game. When I had heard those unfamiliar golf terminologies, golf sounded like a game for only intelligent people. Being theoretically exposed to the golf culture, I decided that the only person who would be able to enlighten me would be Michael. Michael smiled. Then he placed his right arm around my shoulder and said, Awadh, "I will simplify this game for you. But you will have to come to the clubhouse where I do my teaching and manage the pro shop."

On the morning after my exposure to the golf language, I went to meet Michael at the pro shop. Since most of the golf players were already assigned their tee-off times and were already playing the course Michael, after speaking to his pro, was given some free time to enlighten me on golf lingo, the names of different golf clubs and their functions, a few basic rules of the game, and the reason people play the game. Although my brain was unable to process so much novel information in such a short time interval, I was excited to learn and to get involved in the golf culture. Then he led me out of the pro shop to the putting green which was directly in front of the pro shop. He asked me to select a putter from a bin, then he handed me two white golf balls. He instructed me to watch how he was holding the putter, where he was placing his feet and how he was striking the ball with the putter. Every time he struck the ball it went straight into the hole. He repeated the process several times. Then he asked me to hit the ball into the hole. After several unsuccessful attempts and with his advice, the balls were going into the hole. Michael advised me that the game was based on the principle of hand-eye coordination. After practising for about half an hour, Michael invited me to play the putting game. He explained and showed me how to play, and that we would be playing for money. I informed him that I did not have any money. But on another morning, I would return and play for money. "How much money are we playing for?" He informed me that, "The person who gets the ball into the hole with fewer shots wins, and receive a quarter from the loser." I promised Michael to return at a later date to play the putting game for a quarter per hole.

After reflecting on how Michael had enlightened me about the fundamentals about golf, I phoned him and inquired whether he would be willing to play the putting game for money. Eagerly, he accepted my invitation. At the clubhouse, Michael loaned me a putter and a ball. We played for about an hour. I lost eight dollars. But it was worth every penny. Because Michael took me under his wing, and slowly taught me how to use the driver, pitching wedge, putter, different iron clubs for different distances and many other skills and tactics of the game. At the end of the summer he and I were playing nine holes on both on the front nine and back nine. He was extremely pleased to be my friend. And I was most appreciative that we had bonded with me while he was not only teaching me how to play golf but also by playing together on the Bigwin Island course. At the end of our contracts in September, Michael invited me to his home in Toronto to meet his family and for dinner.

The summer of '67 was gradually coming to an end for the temporary summer employees on the Bigwin Island payroll, and I had to return to Hamilton to secure accommodation for my second academic year at McMaster. I had no forwarding information for Veronica, my first landlady. Fortunately, I had the telephone number for one of her daughters who lived in downtown Hamilton. I made a phone call to the music teacher. Her Japanese husband, Jimmy, answered. After exchanging some pleasantries, I informed him that I must return to Hamilton to find living accommodation. Jimmy informed me that I would have to call back later in the evening when Jackie would be at home. I felt confident that I would receive positive news when I called back. Later that evening, I phoned again. It was extremely refreshing and pleasant to hear Jackie's soft and musical voice. Again, after exchanging a few interesting and wonderful news about Veronica, her mother, and her brother, she invited me to stay with them during the time that I would be searching for living accommodation. Before the conclusion of our conversation, Jackie informed me that they would gather information on the availability of student rental facilities in the vicinity of the university. Being most encouraged by her interest to assist me, I thanked her for their consideration and cooperation. In addition, I informed Jackie that I would telephone them at least one week before my departure for Hamilton. Immediately, I informed Tiffany about my situation. She told me that, in the morning, she would discuss the issue with Mr. Lambert. On the following afternoon, Tiffany informed me that I was granted a leave of absence with pay for three days. After thanking her for her support, I hastened to call my friends in Hamilton. On the following Sunday morning I took the first ferry for the mainland. In my bag were two bottles of French wine, but I kept all my important documents and cash in my jacket. Waiting for me on the mainland was the taxi that I had hired to take me to the train station in Huntsville.

After arriving in Toronto, I took a taxi to the bus terminal on Bay Street. I bought my ticket to Hamilton, phoned my friends in Hamilton and informed them about the approximate time of my arrival. Jimmy and Jackie were waiting for me at the bus terminal. It was refreshing to be welcomed to their home again. After getting me organized for my stay, I presented them with the two bottles of wine. They were thankful. After sharing some cold cuts and cheese snacks, they showed me the places that were available for rent for the next academic year. Since it was almost dinner time, Jenny advised me to attend to it in the morning. We celebrated our reunion with a refreshing pre-dinner cocktail. After dinner we played a game of 'Crazy Bridge'. On seeing how sleepy I was Jimmy suggested we all go to bed and have a restful and rejuvenating sleep.

I was still lolling around in bed when I heard my friends'

voices. It was the signal to get up and prepare myself to face the world. After my morning ablutions, I went downstairs and greeted them. Jimmy had already brewed coffee and prepared breakfast. Jackie, still in her night robe, was reading the Hamilton Spectator. After breakfast, they asked me whether I needed them to take me to the areas that I had highlighted on the papers that they had collected. I thanked them for their thoughtful offer, but I declined. I wanted to re-familiarize myself with the bus routes in Hamilton. Also, I wished to walk around the university campus and the streets that I had grown accustomed to. I walked to King Street and waited for the West Hamilton bus. When the bus had arrived at the corner of Main Street and Emerson Street, I went directly to the phone booth located outside the church on Main Street. I called the first number on my list that had advertised vacancies for students, on Emerson Street. The landlady informed me that she had one room available, and that if I was interested she would reserve it for me. I told her that I would be there in less than a minute. I rang the doorbell and waited. A woman opened the door, and as soon as she saw me, stopped smiling and questioned, "Can I help you?" Then I told her that I had just spoken to her on the phone about the room that she said was available for rent. She looked me in the face and said, "All the rooms are already taken." And she closed the door while I was still looking at her. Being disappointed but not discouraged, I decided to walk along the other streets in search of vacancy signs. There were few vacancy signs but after ringing the doorbell, I was informed that they should have taken down the sign. Being a bit frustrated, I decided to have lunch at the Pancake House on Main Street. One of the waitresses was in my mathematics tutorials, remembered me.

She wanted to know whether I was returning to university. After answering in the affirmative, she inquired about my presence. Having related my summer story and my experiences for the day, she encouraged me to continue my search.

After lunch, I continued my search for vacancy signs. Finally, I saw a vacancy sign in front of a beautiful two storied house on

102 Sussex Street. As I was crossing the street, I saw a woman walking down the front steps. Thinking that she was the owner of the house, I addressed her as soon as I was within her hearing range. "Good afternoon. Are you the owner of the house?" "No! I am a foreign student looking for a room to rent. But the landlord told me that his family rents only to male students."

Having thanked her for the lead, and feeling encouraged, I rang the doorbell. A tall handsome blue eyed blonde gentleman opened the door. He was extremely welcoming. After he had heard my request, he invited me to see the room. A great feeling of bliss instantly started to invade my entire being. He led me up a flight of stairs to the second floor. Helmut informed me that only the back room was available. I looked around the room, and was greatly pleased with the ambience. Before I could inquire about the cost, Helmut invited me to meet his wife, Anna, and their two young sons. Before finalizing a rental contract, Anna invited me to share tea with the family. It was during tea time, we negotiated the rental agreement. I had to pay the first and last month rent. The cost of renting was reasonable, but although I was to take up residence in the middle of September, I had to pay for the entire month. Being pleased with their hospitality and friendliness, and understanding their point of view on the economics of the availability of rental facilities, I accepted the conditions and signed the agreement. Feeling as though I was already living at 102 Sussex Street, I waved goodbye as I walked away. I phoned my friends and informed them that I had successfully rented a room across the road from the university. They wanted to know at what time I would be returning home because they were going out to shop. I briefed them about my intention to visit the "Sunken Garden" and to stroll on the lawns that I had mowed earlier in the year.

I returned to my friends' home just before dinner. The appetizing scent of Indian food permeated the house. Jimmy had prepared my favourite foods. Also he had Kingfisher beer to complement the taste of the Indian delicacies that he had leisurely prepared. During dinner, Jackie asked whether I had any difficulty finding the room. I responded that I had a few interesting experiences after I had stepped outside my comfort zone. She probed no further. After a couple of after dinner liquors, we went to bed early. I had planned to return tomorrow to Bigwin on the first bus bound for Toronto.

After the Northland bus dropped me off in Huntsville, I taxied to the Bigwin dock. The S.S. Bigwin was about to leave for the mainland, but on seeing me running, the captain shouted, "Shadow, hurry up." I heeded his call, and was able to arrive on time for dinner. Serge saw me and wanted to know the reason for my absence. After hearing my story, he asked me whether I would be interested in replacing him in the dining room wine service. After questioning him why, he softly informed me that woman who was in charge of the stables had asked him for a date earlier in the day, but he was unable to accept because he was scheduled to work. I told him to contact her immediately, and to find out whether she would still be interested. He returned with a big smile on his face. I had less than an hour to get to my room. After dinner, I went to my room. I freshened up, got dressed and assumed Serge's duty.

Later that night in the Round Room, Mr. Lambert and Tiffany entered with a few of their friends who usually spent their summers in their cottages around the Lake of Bays. "Shadow, you're back. How did everything work out?" Pleased with my answer, he asked me to attend to his party. Mr. Lambert signaled to me to take the drink orders from his friends. Each one of them had expensive taste. They ordered Louis X111 Cognac. Before the night was over, Mr. Lambert privately told me that the drinks were on the house. On the following day, after Serge had given me some colourful details of his date, I realized that we both had a win-win evening. However, Serge continued to date the female staff interested in having some more fun before the Labour Day holiday. Two weeks before the beginning of the Labour Day weekend, and after I had co-hosted a caviar and champagne party during a piano recital given by the Austrian pianist in the Rotunda, Mr. Lambert called me into his office. He said softly, "Shadow, I did not thank you properly for the services you had provided to my personal friends when they paid a surprise visit to me. But I have some good news for you."

Before he could complete his oration I expressed my sincerest gratitude for allowing me to serve his special friends. But he barked at me, "Shadow, don't ever interrupt me again when I'm speaking." A brief silence swallowed the office as he looked at me with frustration. He continued, "Shadow, on Labour Day, one of the largest and most opulent yachts in the Muskoka region will be paying a special visit to our waterfront. There will be approximately twenty to twenty five people on board. The owner of the yacht will be celebrating an extremely significant anniversary on board with his close friends on his yacht. His personal secretary has made all the arrangements with our executive chef to prepare special seafood dinner menus for the occasion. The dinner will be served by selected members of our dining room team. And I have placed you in charge of dispensing all the cocktails, champagne, wines and all other alcoholic and non-alcoholic beverages aboard the yacht. I am confident that you will provide each guest with premium service. I am quite aware of your training and experience. What do you think Shadow?"

At first, I looked at him without saying a word, but felt privileged to be chosen to be the bottler aboard a millionaires' yacht. After a brief pause, he added with a smile and a wink, "Think about it and give me your response in twenty four hours." I thanked him for placing his faith in me. We shook hands. And I left. On the following morning, after contemplating the responsibilities with which Mr. Lambert had entrusted me, I sought the advice of Lorenzo, the executive chef. He encouraged me to accept the offer but with certain conditions. Lorenzo, always being busy, advised me to call back at the end of the day. And by that time he would have a written plan of action for me. On my return, he reassured me that if the following conditions were acceptable to Mr. Lambert then accept the offer. After studying Lorenzo's recommendations diligently, I presented them to Mr. Lambert. When he had read the prescribed conditions, he commented that I had driven a hard bargain. I did not share this private contract with the other servers.

    The hour to perform my special duties aboard the yacht was approaching. At last, the yacht appeared on the horizon at the end of the Lake of Bays. Patiently, I awaited the arrival of the yacht. It was long and beautifully finished in wood. Highly polished, it sparkled in the early evening sun under a cloudless sky. The people on board were elegantly dressed and impressive in appearance. They were waving and seemed anxious to get on the island. At first, I did not recognize anyone on board. But in my mind, I knew that by the end of the evening's celebrations on board, and after serving them their drinks, I would no longer be an unfamiliar face on the yacht. I admired the crews' prowess and finesse as they moored the yacht like a toy along the docks. Much to my surprise the gentleman dressed as the captain of the yacht called my name. At first, I did not recognise him because of his captain's outfit. But, as soon as I had recognized that it was the voice of Hahn, I felt extremely comfortable and confident. The yacht with the beautiful people was wonderful sight to behold. He invited me to come on board. When I had ascended to the main deck, he shook my hand and announced to his friends that I had been quenching his thirst since the beginning of the summer. I felt extremely privileged to serve these glamourous and exuberant people. He informed me, in private, that his best friends and immediate family were invited to celebrate his fortieth wedding anniversary. After he had introduced me to his gorgeous wife, I congratulated both of them on their silver wedding anniversary, exchanged a few pleasantries and asked to be excused. I quickly joined my support team in the private outdoor bar where the Dom Perignon and white wines were chilled for the black tie celebrations. In a jiffy the champagne was served with lobster and crab appetizers. The vintage wines and alcoholic drinks were supplied by the hotel. Mr. Lambert appeared on the yacht. After congratulating Hahn and his wife, he welcomed the guests to the Bigwin property and encouraged them to continue enjoying its hospitality. As the evening leisurely but interestingly unfolded, and I circulated among the guests serving them their drinks, many enlightening conversations ensued. Many were interested in my background and my presence at the Bigwin Island Hotel. But I was also playing an unassigned role as a human drone among the guests. I could not escape hearing the animated and juicy stories that were discussed in the different cliques, as I stood outside their private space, waiting for their alcohol requests.

In one case, there were four middle-aged women gossiping, laughing and bantering about members of their own families. One of them, named Mildred, asked to be excused to socialize with another clique in a different part of the yacht. Within a few minutes, one of three women focused her attention on the one who had just left. She was reporting to the others that Mildred's husband was having an affair with one of her friends. And, being a faithful friend, she was wondering whether she should enlighten Mildred about her husband's affair. At that point, I had to replenish the drinks of several guests. When I returned to the group with their new cocktails, Mildred had rejoined them during the time that I was preparing their martinis. I did not hear what transpired at the table, and Mildred did not express any uneasiness. Everything was flowing harmoniously in every part of the yacht.

As I continued circulating replenishing drinks, one of the female guests captured my attention. Helena called out to me by name. Promptly, I attended to her call. She informed me that she was monitoring my performance and that she was greatly impressed on how I executed my duties on board the yacht. After I had thanked her for her kind compliments, she inquired whether I did accept private bartending opportunities outside the Bigwin Island properties. Having informed her that I do accept private bartending jobs on the mainland, she offered me a job to serve the drinks from her bar to her friends at her end-of-summer garden party at her cottage.

She continued that the party would be for about thirty people in the evening on the following Saturday. I informed her that my contract with Bigwin would end on Friday, and that I have planned to leave as soon as possible to catch the early train to Toronto. Also I told her that my classes at McMaster would commence in the middle of September. Helena smiled. She then assured me that she would personally come to Norway Point on Friday morning, and wait for me. She would provide all accommodations for me on Friday, Saturday and Sunday. And she promised to take me to the Huntsville train station early Monday morning. Then I asked her what was she was willing to pay for my work. She scratched her head and made me a generous offer. I told her that I would give her my answer before the end of the party.

Unexpectedly, the chef Lorenzo appeared on deck to find out from the owner of the yacht whether the meals, presentations and services were all to his complete satisfaction. Before he got off the yacht, I told him about the offer from Helena. He advised me accept. As promised, I confirmed the oral contract that she had made with me. Late in the night, I waved goodbye to Hahn and his guests.

On the Saturday evening before Labour Day, there was a black tie dinner and dance in the Indian Head dining Room. There was a full orchestra playing swing music from the big band era. The musical arrangements of Glenn Miller were most popular with the wealthy seniors. They were all dancing and singing: In the Mood, Pennsylvania 6-5000, The Little Brown Jug, Tuxedo Junction, The Chattanooga Choo-Choo, String of Pearls, and several other favourites. By midnight, most of the guests were exhausted but happy. It was definitely a swinging dinner-dance extravaganza. Meanwhile there was another band entertaining the young and middle-aged from the surrounding cottages, residences and resorts. At 12:30 in the morning, the last call for the bar was made. Suddenly, we became increasingly busy. The liquor and wine orders were doubled. We rationalized that our guests were planning to continue dancing as long as they kept on tipping the band leader. And they did. Then the unexpected happened. Many of the guests had become hungry from the dancing and prancing. A few of them inquired about a late night snack. We informed them that the kitchen was closed for the night. While we were busy serving the drinks orders, we were not paying close attention to the various movements of the guests, whether they were going to the washrooms or going outside to get a breath of fresh air. The corridor that led to the washrooms also led to the doorway to the kitchen. Since both the kitchen and the washroom entrances were not visible from the Indian Head Dining Room, and not expecting any pranks from the venerable guests, I did not see the activities in the corridors outside the dining room. On learning that the guests who had requested late night snacks were eating sandwiches, and being aware that the kitchen was closed for the night, I decided to investigate the source of the sandwiches. As I walked towards the entrance of the kitchen, I saw more guests exiting the kitchen with sandwiches. For a moment, I thought that the chefs were preparing them complimentary sandwiches. However, I beheld a sight disgusting to relate. I was not prepared for such human 'racoon' behaviour. There were scores of guests who were having a self-serving sandwich party with whatever edibles that they could scavenge. They had already raided the open refrigerators and the pantry. After they had used up all of the packaged food, they decided to capsize the garbage containers in the kitchen and salvage any material that was reasonably edible. I stood speechless looking at what hungry people, under the influence of alcohol, would do to satisfy their hunger,

FROM EXPLORATIONS TO ENLIGHTENMENT

regardless of their socio-economic status.

What I had observed in the kitchen reminded me of a famous quotation:

"To a hungry person, every bitter food is sweet.
When the preferable is not available,
Then the available becomes preferable."

After returning to the dining room, I informed the social hostess and the sommelier about what was taking place in the kitchen. They went to verify my story. On their return, they decided to inform the chef and the manager immediately. Gradually the crowd dwindled and we started to clean the tables and collect and dispose the garbage left behind by our guests. Before we had finished cleaning up the dining room, Mr. Lambert and the kitchen staff came directly to me." Shadow, what happened in the kitchen?" Mr. Lambert, after scratching his head, advised that we help the kitchen staff clean up the mess left behind. Before the night was over we were advised that what happened in the kitchen must remain in the kitchen.

By the end of Labour Day all the guests had checked out from the Bigwin Island Hotel. It was the responsibility of the general staff to clean and pack away all the furniture, tools, and equipment for the fall and winter. Likewise, the bar staff had to attend to the storage of the unsold liquor and the glass wares. The kitchen staff managed the storage of non-perishables and the wares. After all these chores were completed, the summer student employees gradually left the premises to return to their universities. As I was returning to my room, and having completed my to-do-list, Mr. Lambert met me as I had ascended the front steps of the Rotunda. After placing his right hand on my left shoulder, he instructed me to meet him in his office before I leave for the S.S. Bigwin. I continued to the second floor of the Rotunda to my room. Before arriving at my room, I had to bid farewell to many of my colleagues. There were several bittersweet partings. But we had to continue on our journey of life.

After collecting my belongings and packing my suitcase, I walked through all the corridors on both the second and first floor, mentally reliving the wonderful activities that I had experienced during the summer of '67. Before reporting to Mr. Lambert's office, I had to say good bye to Tiffany. She was not only my social, spiritual and financial advisor but also my trusted friend. I went to her room and knocked gently on it. There was no response. Hurriedly, I descended the wooden stair case in search of Tiffany. She was relaxing in one of the leather recliners. As soon as she saw me she got up. I dropped my suitcase and hastened towards her. We locked our arms around each other and kissed cheek to cheek. Then she said, "Awadh, it was definitely a delightful pleasure to meet you, and getting to know you. I do hope that we do meet again. Good luck in your studies." After our final hugs, I looked at her, and expressed my sincerest gratitude for all the support she had given me during the loving summer of '67. Also I wished her all success in all her future endeavours.

Mr. Lambert's office door was wide open, but I still knocked. He was not in his office. I stood outside the door for a few minutes and was just about to leave, when he appeared. After inviting me inside, he asked me to sit. "Shadow, was it a good summer for you? Did you make sufficient money to cover all your university expenses for the coming year?"

In response to his first question, I informed him that I was deeply indebted to him for giving me the opportunity to work at such a world renowned hotel and to meet and interact with people from all strata of socio-economic backgrounds. I had a marvellous summer learning many new skills, performing several novel tasks, and experiencing and sharing the lifestyles of the wealthy, highly educated, and cultured people of the American continent. Before I could attempt to answer his second question, he interjected, and said that he was extremely pleased and happy to know that he had given me such an enlightening opportunity to experience a different and exciting social ecosystem.

I continued by carefully answering his second question. "Mr. Lambert, I will always be grateful to you for giving me every opportunity to earn extra money in various capacities. I know that I have saved sufficient funds to cover all my expenses for my entire year at university. I wish you excellent health, prosperity, peace, love and happiness."

Then, he asked me whether I would be interested in returning to Bigwin next summer. Without any hesitation, I responded in the affirmative. "Well Shadow, complete the application form before you go. If you should change your mind, please contact me as soon as possible." We shook hands and with a smile, I left for the Bigwin ferry. Slowly I walked under the covered walkway to the S.S. Bigwin ferry. As the S.S. Bigwin crossed the Lake of Bays to Norway Point on the mainland, I kept looking at the beautiful buildings and the picturesque landscape as they slowly receded from my sight.

On my arrival at Norway Point, Helena was waiting on the docks. She greeted me with a big smile and a strong hug. Her cottage was located on the shores of Lake of Bays, in close proximity to Dorset. A paved curved driveway led us under a canopy of trees to the cottage front door. It was large, exquisitely designed and rested on a handsome property. "Welcome Awadh to my cottage, my home away from home."

"I thank you Helena for inviting me to your sanctuary of peace and happiness." The property was a gorgeously landscaped, with tall evergreen trees giving it complete privacy from the neighbouring cottages. Taking a panoramic look at the gardens and the landscape stretching towards the lake, and greatly appreciating the idyllic setting, I entered the foyer of her countryside mansion. While I was observing the beauty of nature that surrounded her home, Helena went inside to prepare lunch for us. She came out from the kitchen, and said that she would show me to my private room. I followed her upstairs to the room. From the windows, I could see a swimming pool surrounded by shrubs. After making myself comfortable, I joined her in the kitchen. We had a delicious soup and salad for lunch. Helena drank wine with her lunch. I drank orange juice and water.

After lunch, she told me that we had to go to the liquor store in Dorset to purchase the liquor that she needed for the garden party. Helena requested that I accompany her to purchase the drinks for her party. She bought a variety of alcohol for the party. On our return she showed me the outdoor bar. After setting up the bar, I started to wonder whether she lived alone, but on the walls in the living room and family rooms there were pictures of her families and friends. I bravely asked Helena if she lived alone. She curtly responded that she lived with her business partner. I was asleep in my room when Helena's business partner returned home. When I awoke, I decided to seek out Helena. As I opened the door and was about to step out of my room, I startled a woman who was standing nude in her room with the door wide open. As soon as we locked eyes, she screamed, and rushed to close the door. I became extremely frightened. Her loud scream brought Helena charging upstairs to investigate the reason for the loud scream. She saw me standing at the open door to my room completely terrified. "What happened?" Helena questioned. After I told her what had happened, she became very annoyed. She advised me to go downstairs. The reason for such an awful embarrassing incident to occur had to be either a misunderstanding or a miscommunication on the part of either Helena or her business partner. In the living room, I patiently waited to see Helena's reaction. Several unpalatable scenarios resonated through my mind, but I preferred to wait and learn what action they had decided to pursue. Just for a few more dollars in my pocket, I had inadvertently placed myself in an unexpected predicament.

About thirty minutes later, Helena joined me in the living room. She was pensive and kept looking at the oak floor.

Then, she declared that it was her fault that the unexpected embarrassing situation occurred. I made no comment. Being hungry, I inquired whether we would be having dinner. She confirmed that we would have dinner as soon as Hazel came down. Momentarily, a great weight was lifted off my shoulders. No sooner Helena had spoken Hazel joined us in the living room. She sat next to Helena. She was beautiful. After I was formally introduced to Hazel, I apologized for my unintended invasion of her privacy. Having accepted my apology, we moved into the dining room. The conversation during dinner was about the real estate businesses that they had owned.

After dinner, we returned to the elegantly furnished living room. Helena inquired about my family background and my reasons for selecting Canada to continue my university studies. Intermittently, Hazel would interject with her questions. The relationship became more pleasant and interesting as I learned a bit about their families' stories. During the conversation, both of them sipped cognac. I preferred to sip my coffee with rum. Being tired from the day's events, I asked to be excused. The coffee spiked with rum sent me to dream land without delay.

On Saturday morning, I awoke early. After getting dressed, I went downstairs. Much to my surprise, both of them were drinking coffee and discussing business. As soon as I had entered the kitchen, they both said, "Good morning Awadh. Did you sleep well?" "Thank you for asking. I had a peaceful sleep." Helena outlined what she had planned for breakfast. After the delicious pancake breakfast, Helena informed me that we had to do some last minute shopping for the garden party, and that we would have to travel to Huntsville. On our drive to Huntsville, Hazel pointed out the church that she would be attending on Sunday morning. I heard her clearly, but made no comment. After shopping we returned to their magnificent home. On our arrival, there a few vehicles and many people setting up furniture, potted flowers, special lightings, sound equipment, decorations and many other garden party paraphernalia. The workers greeted Helena and Hazel as though they were friends, having catered this social gathering for many years.

After lunch, I organized the bar and confirmed that I had everything that I would need to perform my duties. From Bigwin I had retained my sommelier outfit. I told Hazel that I would like to borrow an electric steam iron to remove the wrinkles from my tuxedo. Much to my delight, she volunteered to do it for me. As I was waited, the food cater arrived and took over the kitchen. All preparations for the garden were smoothly executed by specialized professionals.

An hour before the garden soiree commenced, the elegantly dressed and charming guests started to arrive. They all drove expensive automobiles. I had never anticipated that I would be bartending in a garden party for the wealthy denizens from the Muskoka and Lake of Bays' regions. By five o'clock the hors d'oeuvres were in motion among the guests, the D.J. was already taking the guests down the memory lanes of their era, and I was busy popping champagne corks, serving cocktails, wine, and an assortment of liquor at the stand-up bar. The bar occupied a romantic spot. It was located between stone statues by Rodin and of the first kiss of Cupid and Psyche. These garden sculptures, strategically placed in the picturesque garden landscape, sparked enlightening discussions which brought back colourful memories to the global travellers. A few of the guests, after recalling seeing me bartending on the yacht on Labour Day at Bigwin, wanted to know whether I was a professional bartender. Quickly, I erased that mental picture. It was definitely a fun-filled garden party. It officially ended at eleven o'clock. But a few of the guests were in no hurry to leave the party, and were invited by the hostesses to continue partying in the house. After midnight, they were still drinking, snacking, singing, and reminiscing about the wonderful memories they had formed with one another over many years. As soon as I had completed cleaning up the bar and putting away all the unused alcohol, I quietly retired to my bed room. I felt greatly blessed to be working and interacting with the privileged people of the earth.

It was still dark when I opened my eyes. Lazily, I waited for the sun to show its first rays. I arose, shaved, showered, and dressed. Helena and Hazel were already in the kitchen having their first cup of coffee and listening to the news from the radio. After exchanging morning salutations, we had breakfast. As soon as Hazel had finished her breakfast, she invited me to accompany her to church. Eagerly, I accepted her offer. Then, Helena rather surprised at Hazels' decision to take me to church, questioned her motive. Hazel did not answer and went upstairs. Sensing that Helena did not fully accept Hazels' offer to take me to church, I told her that I had not attended a Christian service since the end of May, and I greatly appreciated the opportunity to attend church. Helena then suggested that Hazel could drive me to the train station in Huntsville after church service. Her suggestion was most welcomed by me. Without much delay, she went upstairs and presented me with a sealed envelope for my bartending duties. I did not open it. I thanked her for the unique opportunity that she had given me, not only to work for her but also to witness the lifestyles of the wealthy and educated. I hastened to my room and got my belongings as quickly as possible. When I returned downstairs I hugged and kissed Helena on her cheek and expressed my sincerest gratitude to her.

On our way to church, Hazel questioned me about my decision to leave after the church service. I informed her that I had felt that I had overstayed my welcome, after I had startled her in her bedroom. Hazel remained silent until she had parked the car in the church yard. She turned to me and said that Helena did not inform her about me. As a result, not expecting to see a stranger looking at her nude body from across the corridor absolutely scared the shit out of her. She added that Helena was more annoyed because a complete stranger had seen her partner in the nude. I apologized again as we exited the car. She just smiled.

The pastor of the church delivered an interesting homily about the virtues of generosity. He lectured that whatever we have learned and earned must be shared with the less fortunate in society. It was imperative that we should not only help but also share our wealth whenever possible. He alluded to one of Einstein's quotations: "We live for other people." And he added that we must seriously think about the legacy that we want to leave with our families, friends and the world. We have to give a reason for living. After the long church service, Hazel invited me for a coffee. But I had to decline because I had a long journey to complete before arrival at my new home. Hazel drove directly to the Huntsville train station. After thanking her for her kindness and generosity, I kissed her on the cheek and wished her continued success and happiness. At the Huntsville train station there was a large gathering of university students who had completed their summer jobs, and were waiting for the train to take them to Toronto. These young adults were overflowing with enthusiasm, joy and hope for a prosperous and successful future. They had all made sufficient funds to return to their respective universities, colleges, and their families. I deduced these sentiments while I communicated with them in the ticket lounge. Once again I was in the company of complete strangers just as I was on the first day at Bigwin. But at Bigwin, I had three months to bond with my new colleagues. However, when the Northland train bound for Toronto arrived, I was extremely pleased to be homeward bound.

PART FOUR

MY SECOND YEAR IN CANADA

After my arrival at the Hamilton bus terminal, I hustled to King Street for the West Hamilton bus. At last, I entered the front door of the house on 102 Sussex Street.

As I entered, my landlady Anna greeted me with a big hug, and said, "Welcome home!" Being aware that I had a long day travelling from Huntsville, she excused me without delay. I hauled myself upstairs. As soon as I entered my room, I quickly got naked and went into the bathroom. After a long warm shower, I got into my pyjamas, and ate my dinner on the table in the corner of the kitchen. After brushing my teeth, I returned to my bed, and immediately fell asleep.

When I awoke the following morning, I felt as though I had entered a new world. I was in no hurry to get out of bed. Then, I heard male voices in the kitchen. The sounds of knives and forks striking dishes aroused my curiosity. The distinct flushing sound of the toilet and the gurgling of running water compelled me to investigate my new environment. I rushed into the vacant washroom and prepared myself to meet my house mates. As I entered the kitchen, two young adults welcomed me. After we had introduced ourselves, they offered me coffee and breakfast. I accepted their kind offer. After breakfast, I returned to bed and slept. I got up at lunch time. Having not bought any groceries as yet, I went shopping at the grocery store with which I was familiar. When I returned home, I put away my groceries, ate lunch, and went back to bed. Later that evening, I joined my house-mates in the kitchen. Eddie was from Mauritius. He was a doctoral student at McMaster in the Faculty of Chemistry. Stan was from Windsor, in southern Ontario. He was in his fourth year at McMaster completing his honours degree in mathematics. After learning about their special interests, I realized that I would be in the company of two interesting students.

Next morning I went to the Bank of Montreal on Main Street

and deposited my summer earnings. Then I went to the university. After visiting the book store, I went to the library, and made copies of the past examination questions in each of the courses for which I had registered. Although there were hundreds of students milling around the campus, I did not encounter a familiar face. "Where did all my friends and acquaintances go?" I pondered. While wandering on campus, finally I met a few familiar faces and exchanged a few stories. On my return home, Eddie and Stan were in their rooms. After a big lunch, I returned to my room to carefully read the detailed outlines for my courses. I immediately recognized the academic challenges that I had to encounter and overcome.

One week later my courses commenced. By the end of the first week of lectures, I had purchased the recommended textbooks. During that weekend, I correlated the course outline with the prescribed textbook material and the corresponding past examinations questions. I did this for the first chapter of each of my six courses. The voice of my father continuously reminded me to always read and make notes on the next topic before it was taught.

Due to the various locations of my lectures, I had to use different walking routes. I had to walk across the Hamilton Teachers' College campus to get to the Natural Sciences and Engineering buildings for a few courses. My other courses were on the other side of library, in the Hamilton Hall. For those courses, I walked along Broadway Street which led directly to Hamilton Hall. The undergraduate nursing students also had their lectures and laboratories in Hamilton Hall.

On a few occasions, I had the opportunity to stop and converse with several of the future teachers in the parking lots. Many of them were interesting and friendly. After inquiring about their studies and their teaching goals after their graduation, a few of them told me that they would be most willing to discuss it over a coffee. Courteously I accepted their offer. But only one of them was able to keep her promise. Silvana took out her daily agenda and quickly leafed through it. With a smile, she offered me two options. We could meet either Thursday or Friday at 4 o'clock at the Pancake House on Main Street for coffee and something to eat. She accepted my preference for the Friday. Excitement raced throughout my neural and hormonal systems, knowing that it would be the first time that I would be privileged to experience a coffee date with a future young Canadian female teacher.

It was a brilliant sunny afternoon when I left my home to meet Silvana at the Pancake House restaurant. I scouted the tables, but she was not there. By four thirty, I decided to return home. As I was about to leave, she appeared and apologised for her lateness. After we were seated, she informed me that at the end of her presentation, the questions and answers session was exhaustively long. She remarked that she was extremely happy that she had successfully completed her most difficult assignment. Silvana, full of gaiety and joy, asked for the dinner menu. During the dinner, I learned that she lived with her parents and siblings in Hagersville. After their arrival In Canada from Poland, her parents continued to be farmers. But her father was self-educated, and he encouraged her after she had completed high school to go to university and pursue a degree in English. Having obtained her degree, he further advised her to get into education. After listening and hearing her proudly spoke about her father, I saluted her for following her father's advice.

She wanted to know about my background. I told her that I would enlighten her about my background at another time. After sharing the cost for our dinner, she offered to drive me home. I told her that that was not necessary. She insisted. On arrival at my home, she wanted to meet my house mates. I told her that my landlord did not permit us to have female visitors. Silvana did not comment. But before we departed, we exchanged telephone numbers. Through the open–window of her car, I kissed her cheek. She smiled and drove down Sussex Street.

Every week we would converse on the phone about school and social activities. Then Silvana inquired whether I like to go dancing with her. Surprised by the request, I questioned, "Why do you ask me Silvana?" Timidly, she informed me that her teachers' college would be having their first dance at the beginning of October, and she would love to attend, but no one had invited her to it. After listening to the sweet and inviting tone of her voice, I responded that it would be a great honour and privilege to escort her to her formal dance. She added that the dinner and dance would be held in a banquet hall in downtown Hamilton. In one of her phone calls she informed me that she would like to invite me to the room that she had rented. But her landlady does not allow any male visitors in the house. In response, I told her that if she wanted male visitors that she should find another place where male visitors were welcomed. She said that it was too late to make any changes to her living facilities. Then, she suggested visiting me at my place. I then told her that my landlord also does not permit female visitors in his house. Being mindful of my academic mission, I did not think that it would be prudent to have her visiting me. Eddie spent his private time with his girlfriend either at her family home or in his office at the university. Meanwhile Stan's girlfriend, Camille had an apartment in Beverly Hills Apartments on Main Street.

Then the day for the formal dinner and dance arrived. Silvana came to my place earlier than I expected. She waited for me in her car. After she had approved my outfit, she drove to the banquet hall in downtown Hamilton. It was a gala affair. Everyone was splendidly dressed for the formal event. Silvana joined her cherished friends at an assigned table. After officially introducing me to her friends, she asked me to accompany her to the bar. She ordered for a glass of sherry and I had rum and coke with two dashes of Angostura bitters. We sat down at the circular table which comfortably seated ten. Next to me was seated, an immaculately groomed and dressed young woman. She was the attractive potential teacher whom I had seen on many occasions in the teachers' parking lot, but was not fortunate to meet. Already introduced to her, I took the opportunity to strike up a conversation. I learned that the young man seated next to her was her husband, and that they were both studying at the Hamilton Teachers College. After answering her probing questions, there was an announcement. A woman at the head table blessed the meals. And after she had extended her sincerest gratitude to all those who organized the gala event, dinner was slowly served. During the dinner process, lively conversations continued around the table. The orchestra played soft romantic music during the serving of the different courses. But before the dessert and coffee were served, the dancing music started. It was the era of the hippies. And the musicians played all the top hits of the British, American and Canadian music world. The young adults made the dance floor vibrate with their wild and wonderful footsteps. Without any hesitation, Silvana and I joined the energetic and happy dancers. By looking at the future teachers and their dance partners, gyrating, swinging, singing and romancing energetically on the dance floor, their limbic system had to be operating at maximum efficiency and effectiveness. Silvia and I were definitely a part of that vibrant culture. We were both soaking with perspiration. But we were joyfully dancing and singing the hours away. We drank water for the last few hours of the dance party. According to the ticket, the dance was scheduled to conclude at 1 o'clock. At 12:30.a.m. Silvana told me in my ear that she wanted to leave. Since she had invited me, and she was the driver, I acceded to her wish. After I had said goodbyes to those I had met I accompanied Silvana to her car. As she drove along King Street, she informed me that there was a secret to defeating the traffic lights. She said that if she got to the traffic light as soon as it had turned green and if she drove at a certain speed she would get all green lights to McMaster University. Convincingly, she proved her claim.

When we arrived at my home, she said that she urgently needed to use the bathroom. I was quite aware that I was not to have any female visitor in the house, but I thought that after midnight my landlord and his family would be asleep and Silvana cold pee without their knowledge. She accompanied me upstairs to the bathroom. But before entering the bathroom, she wanted to know whether Eddie and Stan were at home. Having confirmed that they were both away, Silvana hurried to the bathroom. To allow her some privacy, I quickly went in my room. Lazily, I changed into my night clothes. I was tired and sleepy. Then, much to my amazement, I heard the shower. It was after 1 o'clock in the morning. I remained resting on my bed, patiently waiting for her to leave. The shower stopped. I waited to see what would happen. Silvana entered my room wet and naked, and asked for a towel. Before I could give her a clean one, she took the towel from the back of my chair and proceeded to towel herself dry. Immediately, I got off the bed and closed the door. Then I inquired about the reason for showering. Standing completely nude next to me, she said that she had an accident and had soiled herself. I desisted from any further interrogation. Without complaining, I looked on as she displayed herself. She had a beautiful and erotic figure. Not knowing her intentions, I kept on smiling and admiring her body. But I could not stifle my erection. She was a sexy teacher. We had a fabulous time. But she claimed that she was a virgin, and that her virginity would be surrendered only to her husband. I respected her request and acted according to the script that she had prepared without my knowledge. I said that it was time to leave. And I bid her goodnight. I stood on the landing of the staircase and watch her descend to the front door. The front door slammed shut behind her. The front lights were switched on. Immediately, I realized that my landlord was disturbed from his sleep.

On the following day, Helmut came upstairs and inquired about who had a shower at 1:25 o'clock in the morning. I informed him that my dance partner had an accident and had soiled herself. He complained that the shower had awakened the entire family. I apologised for my guest's actions, but he was not pleased with the excuse. Before leaving, he advised that I should be more considerate. Being aware that Helmut was not happy with my dance partner's actions, I feared that he might evict me. I realized that I had to inform Silvana about my landlord's complaints. From that day, I always had an excuse to refuse her request to visit.

Then one evening, I met her at the McMaster bookstore and she suggested that we go for a coffee at the Maple Leaf Pancake House. While we were having coffee, Silvana became annoyed at me and demanded to know the reason for not communicating with her. I remained silent, in the hope that she would calm down and become a bit more rational. She continued, "Is it because I would not have sex with you?" After she had calmed down, I praised her for her high moral standard and assured her that I had no intention of hurting her. "Then why aren't you contacting me?"

I told her that that my landlord was extremely annoyed that I had allowed you into the house to shower after midnight. Early next morning, he spoke to me and gave me a letter stating that he would evict me if I continue to disrespect the rules of his home. After I reported the admonition I had received from my landlord she said that she was sorry. After thanking her for the wonderful time at the dance, I told her that it would be in my best interest to end the relationship. She made no comment. After coffee, I kissed her on her cheeks and left. I felt extremely relieved that I would not have to worry about Silvana and the dreaded issue of eviction.

As I exited the Hudson Bay store in downtown Hamilton, I encountered one of my former lecturers, Harold, from the Donaldson Polytechnic Institute in Trinidad and Tobago. I was excited to meet and greet him. He wanted to know what I was doing in Hamilton. Before I could reply, Harold invited me to lunch in a down town restaurant where I learned that he was a lecturer in a College in Hamilton and he was married to a Canadian nurse employed at the Hamilton General Hospital. He then invited me to a Halloween party at his home in Stoney Creek.

At the party, Harold introduced me to his beautiful and cordial wife Claudia. Both of them then introduced me to their friends. The setting was similar to a typical Trinidadian party. There was a smorgasbord of Trinidadian delicacies, curried and stewed meats and vegetables. The bar was stocked with alcoholic and non –alcoholic drinks and was self-served. Harold played his private collection of calypso and Latin selection continuously. I felt as though I was back in Trinidad. I danced with every female who were available, but I spend most of the night dancing with Pauline, a brown-eyed blonde. She was rhythmic, smooth, energetic and romantic. She definitely enjoyed dancing as much as I did. We spend the latter half of the party eating, drinking, singing and dancing as though we were old lovers. Towards the end of the party, I asked Harold about Pauline. He told me to talk to Claudia. I learned that Pauline had to complete some practical training at the Hamilton General Hospital for the nursing degree she was reading at McMaster. Before Pauline left the party, I told her that I greatly enjoyed dancing and spending the night with her, and if she should need a dance partner I would be available. After I had given her my phone number, I wished her a good night and save driving. With a smile she thanked me for the offer and the fun we shared during the party. I spent the rest of night with Harold and Claudia. I thanked them for inviting me to their home and promised to keep in touch.

For the next week I could distinctly smell Pauline's erotic perfume, clearly see her happy smiling face and definitely experience the rhythmic motion of our body on the dance floor. She was the missing person that I needed to complement my studies. Anxiously I waited for her phone call. A week later, Pauline phoned and invited me to go dancing. When I accepted she said she would fetch me at the address I had given on the phone. At the rendezvous I was introduce to one of her classmates and her fiancé. First we had dinner followed by dancing. The rhythmic Latin music of the live band made dancing with Pauline euphoric and magical. In the dimly lit dance floor I caressed, kissed her neck, cheeks and French kissed her. Our chemistry was definitely reacting harmoniously. I was continuously staving off erections. The urge to ravish her alluring body was flooding my body mind and spirit, but I was mindful of the people around me. Pauline looked at me and whispered, "I am aware that you want to have sex. The feeling is mutual but not tonight." Her whisper assured me of the possibility of sex in the future. We continue to drink, munch, dance and laugh until it was midnight. On our way home she parked on Leland Street where we kissed and caressed. She then gave me her phone number and before she drove away, she said, "Awadh. I feel that our friendship will develop into a fantastic loving relationship." Not knowing an appropriate response at that moment, I thanked her for a happy, humorous and fun-filled evening. I could not fall asleep because my mind was vividly replaying the euphoric memories of the evening with Pauline.

A few days later, we arranged to meet for lunch at Wentworth House. After lunch Pauline introduced me to few of her beautiful classmates. She then asked me if I was free on the weekend. I told her that I would call her when I returned home. After she learned that I was available after lunch on Saturday, she gave me her address and told me to take the bus to Camelot Towers on Main Street.

When I entered her apartment she was alone. Pauline had prepared lunch for us. After lunch she wanted to know about my background and how I ended up studying at McMaster. After listening to my life's story, she told me about hers. She lived with her parents and two younger brothers in St. Catharines, Ontario. Her parents were employees of the Federal Government and her brothers were in high school. After our conversation, she said that she felt like having a drink and dancing. She poured a glass of red wine for each of us and then turned on her record player. On the turntable was long play record of Sergio Mendes and on the record stand were many records with Latin music. Since it was brilliant sunshine outside, Pauline closed the curtains to simulate the dim lighting of the dance floor. The wine was beginning to take effect on me and the music was irresistible. Pauline took off her shoes and I did likewise. As soon as I embraced her and started to dance the happiness hormones accelerated through my body. We kissed and caressed as we danced. I could not resist the temptation of her sensuous body, her sweet body scent and her soft body. She held my erection and kept on massaging it. In response, I managed to get my right hand into her underwear. Pauline then stopped dancing and ordered me to get naked. Before I could finish she was stark naked. We continued dancing in the nude with my erection rubbing against her crotch. We managed to achieve penetration while dancing and caressing. We both had an orgasm. She said it was the first orgasm she has had while dancing. I did not respond. We stopped dancing and went into the shower. After the shower we went in her bedroom and had sex. I cautiously after we had sex whether she was on the birth control pill. She said that she was a nursing student and does not have to worry about getting pregnant. Then the phone rang while we were in bed. One of her friends was coming over. We decided to end our tryst before the arrival of her friend. While walking back along Main Street to my home on Sussex Street, I thanked my lucky star for finding Pauline. She had her own apartment, loved to dance and enjoyed having sex. I returned home and went to bed.

On the following day Pauline phoned me and told me she definitely enjoyed dancing with me and having sex at the same time, and we should do it frequently. On hearing her sweet voice utter those sensuous confession, I thanked her for her honesty. Then she told me that she would contact me as soon as her time-consuming and strenuous assignment at the hospital was completed. I wished the best of luck.

It was the middle of November when Pauline and I met for lunch at the Tally Ho restaurant on Main Street. After lunch she told me on the way to her car that she had a couple of free hours before returning to the hospital and she would like to spend it with me at her apartment. I had no objection to her suggestion. At her apartment, during our long warm shower we had sex which I had experienced and enjoyed at Bigwin. But Pauline was not in the mood to do the standing doggy style position. After the delightful sex in the shower we went in the bed and continued with oral sex. It was time for her to go to the hospital. She left and I slowly walked home.

A few days later as I approached my home, there was a car parked in front of our building. There was a beautiful woman seated behind the steering wheel. As I was about to ascend the stairs, Eddie, well dressed, was about to descend the stairs. I waited for him to come down and asked "Eddie where are you going looking so dapper!" Without answering he led me to the parked car and introduced Francesca, a gorgeous beauty queen. Her green eyes fascinated me. She was glamorously dressed. Definitely, I would love to befriend a woman as outstandingly attractive as Francesca.

"Where did you meet her?" I questioned.

Eddie told me that he met Francesca in the McMaster bookstore. Instantly, he was attracted and mesmerized by her charming beauty. As a result, he showed a keen interest in her studies. She was in her final year honours psychology programme. Francesca, on learning that Eddie was in a doctoral programme, did not refuse his invitation for coffee at Wentworth House. At that point, I stopped asking questions. Eddie then told me that they were going dining and dancing and wished me a good evening and left. On the same evening while doing my reading assignment, Stan came home. He knocked on my door. He inquired whether I had dinner. I told him not as yet. He had bought Chinese food and invited me to share it with him. While we were eating, he wanted to know whether I had any plans for the Thanksgiving Day celebrations. I revealed that I did not make any arrangements, but I had friends in St. Thomas, who had given me an open invitation to visit them during the holiday. Stan then stated that if I didn't have a place to go that he would have taken me to his family's home in Windsor. Having courteously thanked him for his invitation, I told him that I would give him my decision as soon I have contacted my friends. He was most understanding.

Without any delay, I phoned Tammy. After the third ring she answered. I could feel the excitement and joy in her voice. After some motherly advice about my studies, and having assured her that I would have all my assignments and lab reports completed, Tammy invited me for the Thanksgiving. I then informed Stan that my friend in St. Thomas invited me to celebrate Thanksgiving with her. He was pleased. The day after I had accepted Tammy's invitation, Pauline phoned to invite me to celebrate Thanksgiving with her family in St. Catharines. I told her that I would love to meet her family and celebrate with them, but I had already accepted an invitation from another friend. She was disappointed but did not complain. She then wished me a happy Thanksgiving. I reciprocated.

A few days before Thanksgiving, I left from Hamilton by bus for St. Thomas. After a tiring trip, I arrived in the rural town of St. Thomas. Following Tammy's instructions, and with the help of a pedestrian, I finally arrived safely at her office. She welcomed me and then introduced me to her co-workers and a few close friends. Tammy was allowed by her female supervisor to leave a few minutes early.

The small town was not densely populated. And it seemed that everyone knew Tammy. Not realizing that my south Asian brown complexion was attracting attention, I walked innocently and bravely with her to her home in the residential area of the town. At last, we arrived at her beautiful bungalow. As soon as I entered her home, I heard the voices of children rushing towards the door to meet Tammy and me. The little boy hugged me and so did her daughter. I was absolutely startled. Before Tammy could attempt to explain anything, the little boy looked at me with happy face and said, "Are you our new daddy?" I did not know how to respond. I felt extremely emotional and helpless. Then Tammy introduced me to her daughter Natalie and her son Nathan. The young children were happy to see me and they kept hugging me. Then, I told them that I was not their new daddy but their friend. And that I had come from school to spend the Thanksgiving with them. I felt awful that I had brought a gift for only Tammy. I asked Tammy whether I could take the children to the store to buy them gifts for the Thanksgiving. She told me that would be a great gesture, but it would not be prudent to take the kids. I went to the stores that I had seen on my walk to Tammy's home and bought them a few things that I thought would be appropriate. The children were most appreciative. Tammy was also delighted with her gift. While I was helping Tammy prepare dinner, I questioned her about the children's father. She informed me that she was divorced for about five years, and that I had nothing to fear. Although she assured me that I was in neutral territory, I did not feel comfortable. After dinner, we left her daughter to baby sit her brother, and went grocery shopping. While we were shopping, Tammy introduced me to a few of her friends, who were also shopping. After the children went to bed, I showered. Then, I changed into my night clothes and went to my assigned room.

On the following morning, the children were in the kitchen with Tammy having breakfast. Realizing that I had overslept, I hurriedly got dressed and joined them at the breakfast table. After breakfast, one of Tammy's friends came over to invite her to an afternoon party at a dance club and bar. Tammy introduced me to her. Then she informed her friend that she had met me at Bigwin Island Hotel in Muskoka during her summer. After she had received a full account of my summer job and my reason for being present at Tammy's home, she smiled and extended an invitation to me. At that moment, the perplexed look on Tammy's face made me think that she had given her friend too much information. To my surprise, Tammy told her friend that she would not be able to go to the dance party at the pub because she had to spend some quality time with her children and me. Natalie having heard what excuse her mother contrived for not going to the party told her mother that she would take Nathan to play with the neighbours' children. Tammy inquired whether I would like to stay at home with her and the children or go to the dance party. I had never gone dancing at a pub. Consequently, I chose to go dancing. Tammy told her friend that we would meet her at the pub. Tammy called the neighbours and told them about her plans to go to the dance, and that her children would be coming over to play for the afternoon. Having received the approval of her neighbours, we left for the dance party.

At the pub a live band performed on a stage. There were singers with beautifully tuned voices accompanied by enthralling music. The tune that I remembered distinctly was "A Lighter Shade of Pale" and "If You're Going to San Francisco…" We ate, drank and danced. Her friend who invited me to the dance took every available opportunity to dance with me. During the few dances that we had, I learned that she was divorced and lived alone in an apartment. She invited me to come to her apartment for a thanksgiving drink. After about three hours of dancing and prancing, on the wooden floor of the pub, Tammy hinted that it was time to return home.

Then I informed Tammy about the invitation of her friend. She advised me to decline her invitation. Her friend was disappointed. But I was not. I had an extremely fantastic and fantastic at the pub dance.

It was still daylight when we returned home. The children were at home anxiously waiting for our return. As soon as we returned, I ordered pizza, chicken wings and soft drinks. Within an hour the food and drinks arrived. The children thoroughly enjoyed the meal. After the feast, we played a board game with them. Then Tammy instructed them to get cleaned up for bed. After the children went to bed, we showered and went to bed. We had sex and fell asleep. Before we got out of bed on the following morning Tammy wanted to know the reason for her friend inviting me for a thanksgiving drink at her apartment. I told Tammy what her friend had related to me about her marital status. Then she invited me for a drink at her place. Then Tammy under her breath, said, "I will handle that slut." I remained silent.

On Sunday morning, after breakfast, we all got dressed and walked to neighbourhood church. Before the service, the pastor welcomed all new visitors. He delivered a powerful sermon on the attitude of gratitude. He emphasized that the secret to health, happiness and inner-peace was to be grateful for all the things that we had accumulated and achieved in our lives.

After the religious services, Tammy took us for a drive to another rural town. We enjoyed tasty and delicious hamburgers at a fast-food restaurant. We drove around for a bit on the county roads. The country side displayed a wide range of autumn colours. After we returned home, her energetic children were allowed to join their friends who were playing in the small park across the street. Just after the children had left to play with their friends, another one of Tammy's friends paid her an unexpected visit. From Tammy's reactions to her unsolicited visit, I surmised that she did not appreciate the presence of the woman. After the friend had left, I asked Tammy for her uneasiness with her friend. She told me that the two visits that she had had so far, were great surprises. She had not seen or spoken to them in months, and she did not know how to interpret them. I told her that I was a bit exhausted from all the activities and would like to nap. She also decided to take a nap until the children returned from their friends. After our naps, we got refreshed, and prepared a simple dinner. For dessert, we had made milk shakes and carrot cake.

The exhausted children took their baths and went to bed early. Soon afterwards, I had a warm bath. I read until I felt sleepy. Then I joined Tammy in bed. While we were in bed having sex, the telephoned rang just after 9 o'clock. Tammy answered the phone. As soon as she heard the voice, she hung up the receiver. The phone continued to ring. Tammy did not answer it. Then I asked her who was continuously telephoning. She told me that it was her ex-husband, and I should not worry.

But I was extremely scared, even fearing the safety of my life. After the telephone stopped ringing, Tammy took the phone off the hook and dialed her own number and left the receiver on the side table. We went back to bed. I was restless. My sixth sense told me that her ex would be coming to the house. In less than half an hour, I heard the screeching of the brakes of a vehicle outside her house. Then, there was loud banging on the front door. A man's voice shouted, "I know that you have a black man in the room. I will break down this door, if you don't open it." We both sat on the bed. Soon we were joined by the children who were definitely frightened. I looked at Tammy. She looked confused. The banging and shouting continued until the voices of the neighbours intervened. The banging stopped. We heard the car drove away. But I had to evacuate Tammy's home as soon as possible. Boldly and bravely, as she got up from the bed, she said, "Awadh, I will make sure that you don't get hurt." I kept quiet. But I wanted to know her action plan. She took the children back to their beds and told them that their daddy would not hurt them. As I sat in this strange bedroom, I realized the grave danger that I was facing. Tammy became business like. She called the police. And she informed them about the actions of her ex-husband.

Then, she made a phone call to Sally. She enlightened Sally about my presence and the reactions of her ex-husband. Without any delay, Sally ordered Tammy to leave at once and come to her home. She lived in another rural town not far away from St. Thomas. Quickly, we got dressed. I helped Tammy to load the trunk of her car with all that she had prepared to celebrate Thanksgiving Day at her home. It was dark. The children were half asleep in the back seat, as Tammy drove away from her home. My entire being was filled with fear, traumatized by uncertainties. I dared not ask Tammy any inappropriate question. The car sped through the unlit country road. Quietly, I sat in the front seat, bracing myself as she took dangerous curves and making unexpected stops. In her anxiety, Tammy had made an incorrect turn so it took much longer to get to Sally's home.

On our arrival, Sally welcomed us with cordial arms. First, she offered us food and beverages. After the children had drunk their warm milk, Sally told them to sleep in the middle room. Meanwhile, Sally and Tammy hugged and kissed. Tammy was crying hysterically. Sally tried her best to comfort her. But I, realizing that I never in my wildest nightmare had envisioned such a dramatic scenario, just remained flabbergasted. Sally, seeing that I was yawning, showed me to my room. I had no idea what had happened. Extremely exhausted and stressed, I fell asleep.

On Thanksgiving morning, we all slept in. It was almost 9 o'clock when we had a nourishing farmers' breakfast. After breakfast, I informed Tammy that I would greatly appreciate her taking me as soon as possible to the nearest bus depot. "Aren't you staying for the Thanksgiving dinner?" "I do not feel safe. And I have lost my appetite for celebrating anything. Please take me to the bus or drive me to Hamilton." Sally interjected and volunteered to drive me to the bus stop where I would be able to get the Hamilton–bound bus. Tammy apologised for not revealing to me that she had been divorced and had two children. After I had extended my warmest farewell to the children, Sally and Tammy gave me a bag with a complete country style Thanksgiving dinner. They waited with me until the Hamilton Bus arrived. From my window seat I waved goodbye as they watched the bus drove away.

As the full-to-capacity bus drove through the countryside, making frequent stops, I contemplated the unexpected and uncomfortable experiences that I had at Tammy's home. At that moment, I decided that I had to be more careful and selective with whom I associated. On my arrival at home, both Stan and Eddie had gone away for the Thanksgiving celebrations. I was most happy to be back in my own room. After a warm shower I dressed slowly in my best clothes. Afterwards I went into the kitchen. I set the table and slowly enjoyed my delicious Thanksgiving dinner. Whenever anyone inquired about how I had spent the Thanksgiving, I painted a sumptuous dinner with Tammy, Sally and the two beautiful children in the town of St. Thomas. On my return to classes, I listened to the Thanksgiving stories of my classmates, lab–partners, and their friends about the wonderful time they had with their families and friends, keeping my embarrassing and depressing experiences to myself. When Pauline inquired about my Thanksgiving experience, I painted her the most peaceful scene imaginable.

After Thanksgiving, I visited my friends in downtown Hamilton. Jimmy and Jackie had cooked a salubrious Japanese dinner. After dinner we played a game of "crazy bridge". During our card game, they invited me to celebrate my birthday at the end of November. I gratefully accepted. On the morning of my birthday, November 27, Eddie and Stan made me breakfast and each of them gave me a gift from the McMaster book store. I thanked them for their kindness and best wishes for many more happy birthdays. On my arrival at Jimmy's, I was surprised to see Veronica and Rich, my first land lady and her son. We had an enjoyable reunion. We spent the evening doing the things we had done one year ago at Veronica's home on Emerson Street. Furthermore, as I was about to depart for home, Jimmy and Jackie invited me to see the Grey Cup game with them. They were Tiger Cats supporters. And after witnessing how diehard Tiger Cat supporters celebrated when their team was victorious, I joined the fan club. On December 2, 1967, I sat with a house full of Tiger Cats supporters. They were fully garbed in Tiger Cats jersey to watch the Grey Cup game televised live from Landsdowne Park in Ottawa. The Tiger Cats mauled the Saskatchewan Rough Riders. The final score was 24 to 1 for the "Cats". After the game the partying continued, but I had to leave. When I arrived at my room, both Eddie and Stan had gone to sleep.

Quietly, I prepared for bed. The following morning, I got up early and did some studies. At breakfast, my house mates inquired about how I had spent my Sunday. I told them about the exciting and happy afternoon I had experienced with my friends eating, drinking and looking at the Grey Cup game on television. In response they related their wonderful and enchanting adventures with their female partners. They then asked about the woman I was having lunch with at Tally Ho restaurant a few weeks ago. I told them that she was studying nursing at McMaster and I met her at Wentworth House in October. They wanted to know whether I was dating her. I told them that we meet sometimes for lunch and sometimes we go dancing with her friends. They did not ask any more questions. Since I was only interested in having fun with Pauline, and was not interested in marriage, I did not wish to disclose the intimate relationship that existed between Pauline and me to anyone. We continued enjoying and celebrating our friendship at every possible opportunity. On Fridays we would order either for Chinese food, Italian meat balls, lasagna or pizza and drank red wine. After eating, we dance to the rhythm of the Latin beat, have sex and then sleep. Early next day we would have a light breakfast and continue our studies. In early December, Pauline drove me to St. Catharines to meet her family. Her family was most welcoming, kind and generous. Their bungalow was warm and cozy. I spent a night at her parents' home. Pauline slept in her bedroom and I slept in the spare room in the basement. I felt comfortable and appreciated. Her mother then invited me to spend Christmas with them. Before I could express my gratitude for the invitation, Pauline told her mother she would have me in the house on the day before Christmas so that I would be able to attend Saint Patrick Roman Catholic Church with the family. I then thanked her mother for the invitation. On my return from St. Catharines, I told Eddie and Stan about the hospitality and friendship that Pauline's family extended to me, and that I was invited to accompany them to church on the evening before Christmas. I asked them for their advice on purchasing gifts for the family member. I took their suggestions and bought the gifts. The day before Christmas, I had already bought gifts and wrapped them for each member of Pauline's family. Stan, Eddie and I also exchanged gifts.

At Saint Patrick Roman Catholic Church the parish priest was warm and welcoming. The mass service was similar to the ones I had attended as a student at the College of St. Philip and St. James in Chaguanas and it brought back vivid memories of my college days. I definitely had a wonderful time on Christmas day with Pauline's family. In January 1968, Pauline and I continued our regular relationship.

Her birthday was 14th January which we celebrated with her family. A week after her birthday at her apartment Pauline shocked me with the following statement: "Awadh. I'm pregnant." Instantly, a lightning bolt of shock struck me.

I looked at Pauline in disbelief and softly said, "Pauline. Are you positive that you are pregnant?"

Pauline closed her eyes and remained quiet for a long time. I also remained silent.

She then said, "I'm one month pregnant, and I have to decide whether to keep the unborn baby or abort it. I'm a good Catholic woman, and my family is highly respected in the community and in the church. I cannot afford to be an unmarried pregnant woman."

Then her tears started to flow down her beautiful face. I hugged her and rubbed her neck and shoulders gently. Holding back my tears, I whispered, "Where did we go wrong Pauline?" For several minutes there was silence. But I could feel and hear her heart pounding. Her tears had morphed into cries and sobs. I stopped hugging her and wiped her tears with my clean handkerchief. While I was looking in her brown eyes, she said, "Awadh. There is no need to be worried. I have no intention of getting married before I graduate as a nurse. Presently, you cannot support a family. I must protect the respect and integrity not only of my family but also myself. I did miscalculate my ovulation period. You did promote safe sex from the onset of our relationship. But I declined your offer for personal reasons."

"What are your options Pauline?" "I will speak to my friends at the hospital and decide on a potentially safe solution."

I listened attentively and clearly heard Pauline say that she would solve her pregnancy issue without my opinion. Although I did not feel comfortable with her decision, I had to only listen because I had no bargaining leverage. After two weeks, Pauline informed me that she was no longer pregnant. I felt relieved.

However, I had doubts about her pregnancy claim. Was she really pregnant? Or did she fabricate the pregnancy story just to get rid of me? I would never know the truth. Pauline never contacted me again. I never mentioned the pregnancy to anyone.

At the end of February, 1968, I received an unexpected phone call from Silvana. She inquired about my plans for the weekend. I told her that I had to prepare for my tests and must complete my lab reports. She inquired whether I could spare either a Saturday or a Sunday with her. She would like to introduce me to her family in Hagersville. I told her that I would have to check my study schedule and get back to her. She was comfortable with my request. After carefully analyzing her wish, I realized that she had given me an opportunity to experience a different part of Ontario, and to meet and learn about her Polish family and its lifestyle. On the following day, I phoned Silvana. I told her that I looked forward to meeting her family and her on Sunday. And she should meet me at approximately ten o'clock at the corner of Main Street and Leland Street.

The drive to her home took about an hour. I thoroughly enjoyed the scenic countryside. On our arrival at her parents' home, I was warmly welcomed by her mother, father and sister. Her elderly father, a colourful and intelligent gentleman, educated me about his early life in Poland and his rationale for leaving his country in search of more opportunities for a better lifestyle. As he narrated, his wife continuously added sauce to her husband's stories. In addition to his homeland stories, her father, Benji, informed me that the sidekick of "The Lone Ranger" from the television show was one of their local heroes. Jay Silverheels, better known as "Tonto" was a native of Hagersville. During the narration session, Lucy and Silvana also embellished their parents' stories.

Lucy, her elder sister eventually managed to steal me away from her parents and Silvana. She wanted to know about my background and how I got involved with Silvana. Then she asked an extremely personal question. She wanted to know whether I was sleeping with Silvana. Being surprised and a bit embarrassed by the question, I questioned her motive for posing the question. Lucy smiled, and replied, "I wanted to know whether you were lucky."

I told Lucy that I would not refuse the opportunity to sleep with Silvana, but from my first date that I had with her last September, she had informed me that she was still a virgin, and that she has vowed to save herself for her husband. "Are you serious? Silvana told you that she is a virgin." "Yes." There was a puzzled silent and a smirk on Lucy's face. Then she whispered in my ear, "She is a liar. She is no virgin. The next time you are alone with her, be brave and get some." That was the end of my conversation with Lucy. As though Silvana had overheard what her sister had revealed, she briskly entered the room and wanted to know whether we were discussing her. I told her that Lucy wanted to learn about my family, and why I had decided to come to Canada and study at McMaster University. After being educated about Silvana's family life and a bit more enlightened about her, I became concerned about the women that I had chosen to socialize with.

Her mother had prepared her favourite Polish recipes for dinner. Her two daughters helped with both the preparation and serving of the meal. The family was most hospitable and generous in the manner they accommodated me in their country home. I thanked them for their kindness and friendliness. After dinner, Silvana drove cautiously along the country roads of

Haldeman County.

On our way home, Silvana kept on asking me what information Lucy had given to me about her private life. Being discreet, I did not share the new confidential information that Lucy shared with me. It was my secret. When we re-entered Main Street in Hamilton, I asked Silvana to drop me off on Broadway Avenue and Sussex Street corner. After I had expressed my profound gratitude for the new enlightening experiences that I shared with her family, she wanted to know whether I would still be interested in going out with her for dinner and dance. Being encouraged by her sister's advice, I responded positively. Then, she invited me to have dinner with her at her new apartment. I told her before getting out of her car that I would be able to give her my answer after my examinations. But once again she wanted to know what information her sister had shared with me about her. I smiled and gave her no answer. After seriously reflecting on the problem that Silvana had created for me with my landlord, and the shocking conclusion of my relationship with Pauline, I wondered whether I should accept a dinner invitation from Silvana at her apartment. Many factors had to be analyzed and evaluated before making any commitment for dinner with Silvana. My studies were my first priority. Secondly, I was a foreign student on a student visa with limited finances. I had recently escaped from a possible marriage, and spared an out-of-wedlock fatherhood. My conundrum was "To accept or not to accept her dinner invitation?" After one week, Silvana phoned to finalize dinner arrangement. We did.

I vividly recall that it was an evening after one of my examinations. As I left my room, Eddie wanted to know where I was going. I informed him that I had a dinner date with a teacher in her apartment on Hess Street. "Awadh be extremely careful in that hippy area." I thanked him for the warning, and left. When I arrived at her studio apartment, she had already closed the drapes and turned on the lights. She greeted me with a tight hug and a long kiss. I did not resist her advances. She was overly romantic and cheerful. First we sat on her sofa bed and behaved like teenagers in love. Within a few minutes, she left for the bathroom. A little tired, I closed my eyes and relaxed. My stomach started to growl. I was hungry. On the side table, I helped myself with a few candies. Then she came out from the bathroom, she was wearing a translucent pink negligee. And she resumed the same sexual behaviour that she had displayed in my room several months ago. While we were intimately engaged in romantic activities, her sister's advice was paramount on my mind. But, I had decided that Silvana must decide voluntarily on what she wanted to do. After our love–making session which concluded without any sexual intercourse, she returned to the bathroom. After she had dressed for dinner, and was in the kitchen, I refreshed myself. She served Polish meals that were similar to her mother's.

Toward the end of dinner, someone was whistling a special tune beneath her window. It sounded to me either like a love call or a signal to do something. Clearly, I heard it at least three times. Silvana looked at me and told me to remain quiet. And I should not get up from the dinner table. At that moment, I became concerned. She looked worried. The whistling stopped. Then, she slid down from her chair and crawled to the window and peeped from behind the closed curtain to look outside. On observing her unexpected behavior, I slid down my chair and sat on the floor. I had no idea what game she was playing, and with whom. I became scared. I wondered about the whistler. I sat on the floor waiting to see what was transpiring. She did not turn off the lights. It became eerily silent in the bachelor apartment. Then, I whispered to Silvana, "What is going on? Am I in trouble?" Her frightened voice whispered to be as silent as possible. Then, I heard heavy footsteps ascending the wooden stairs. They stopped. Then they continued and stopped in front of her apartment door. At that point, I became extremely terrified. But my only option was to stay on the floor and be as quiet as a mouse. Then, there was a knocking on the door. The door knob was turned but the door did not open. Silvana held on to me terrified. The knocking resumed. A male voice shouted, "I know that you are at home. I will come back later." Not getting any response, the knocker retraced his heavy footsteps along the corridor, down the stairs. He slammed the door shut on his way out. Silvana rushed to the window and peered through the side of the curtain to see whether he had left the building or he had pretended to have left. With a terrified look, she apologized for the interruption. Then, she instructed me to get ready to move as quickly as possible as soon as he had exited the building. In my fear, I told her that I would leave her apartment only after she had enlightened me about the precarious situation that she had choreographed. She remained silent for a moment. Then, she confessed that the man at the door was her lover. She did not expect him to show up that evening. He was supposed to be out of town on business. Feeling somewhat relieved, after thanking her for an extremely interesting but intriguing evening, bade her farewell and left. She walked with me down the corridor. After I had opened the front door, I looked up, and waved to her on the upper floor. Quickly I hurried down Hess Street to King Street for the westbound bus to my home.

Eddie inquired about my dinner. After narrating my narrow escape, he advised again that I should be more careful with whom I associate. I had a sleepless night. While I tossed and turned restlessly in my bed, frightening thoughts roamed in my mind. Silvana and I did not keep in touch after that memorable evening at her apartment.

By chance, I managed to escape from the perils of my female associations. My final examinations were around the corner. Adopting the scholarly advice of Eddie, I re-copied the notes for each of my course a few days before either a test or an examination. After the completion of my examinations, I telephoned Mr. Lambert. I learned that I had to be in his office on the last day of May. As soon as I had completed my conversation with Mr. Lambert, I phoned my contact person in the immigration office in Hamilton. He was most pleasant. I informed him that I had written all my examinations and as soon as I have received the final marks, I would make an appointment for a work permit. He agreed with my proposal. I informed my landlord that I would terminate my accommodation contract at the end of May instead of the end of June. He decided to refund me my last month rent because he had several applicants who need living facilities from the beginning of June. For the next two weeks, I visited my friends in Stoney Creek, downtown Hamilton, and in the vicinity. With their assistance, I rented a room from an Italian landlord on Broadway Street for my next academic year at McMaster. After I had paid the first and last month's rent, my landlord offered to keep my books and clothes that I would not need during my summer job in the Lake of Bays. Having obtained my final marks by visiting the various professors, I went to the immigration office and got the mandatory working permit and renewed my student visa.

PART FIVE

MY THIRD YEAR IN CANADA

On the morning of May 31st, 1968, Suzanne and her parents arrived at my home on Sussex Street. They had promised to take Suzanne and me to Barrie to fetch the Northland train to Huntsville. Suzanne was my physics laboratory partner during my second academic year. During classes and during our laboratory experiments, I had related many of my Bigwin experiences to her. Having heard about the splendour and glamour of the Bigwin, she asked me whether I would recommend her for employment at Bigwin Island Hotel. I informed her that she should check the employment bulletin board for the date and time when the Bigwin would be conducting their interviews. Suzanne did. And on the day Mr. Lambert was on McMaster Campus, I accompanied and introduced her to him. I waited for her in the foyer of Wentworth House where the interviews were held. She was employed as a waitress and was advised to be at the hotel at the end of May.

Her parents were extremely cordial, and with great care drove us to Barrie. But during the first leg of our journey, her parents inquired about my background and what were my duties at the hotel. Being satisfied that I had answered their questions, I told Suzanne that I was hungry. She informed me that we would have breakfast in Barrie. Her parents treated me to breakfast. I thanked them for their kind consideration, and promised to work closely with their daughter, Suzanne. Her parents waited with us until the train had arrived. We waved goodbye to then from the moving train. It was my first train experience to Huntsville. The scenes were refreshing and interesting as the train passed through the forested landscape to the Washago station. The Northland also made briefs stops at Gravenhurst and Bracebridge before it arrived at Huntsville station.

Suzanne and I walked to Main Street in search of a taxi. Before hiring a taxi, we decided to use the facilities in one of the restaurants. We bought a couple of sandwiches and took a taxi to Bigwin Island Hotel. Having arrived at Norway Point, I was extremely happy to be greeted by familiar faces. It felt like a family reunion. After introducing Suzanne to my colleagues, I made a few new acquaintances. Since the Bigwin ferry was not in service as yet for the summer of '68, we had to wait for motor boats to transport us across the Lake of Bays to the idyllic island. It felt like the first day at a new university. There were so many new beautiful and friendly people from different towns and cities in Ontario. Being familiar with the protocol, I headed for the covered walkway that led to the Rotunda - the main administration building. As I entered the grand Rotunda, feelings of ecstasy completely enshrouded my being. It was wonderful to return to such inspirational surroundings. After greeting the familiar face at the front desk, I joined the newbies who were waiting to meet with Mr. Lambert. A few of them inquired about my memories and experiences that I had collected during the summer of '67. Meanwhile, Suzanne got acquainted with her future colleagues. Then I saw Tiffany. As soon as our eyes made contact, we hastened to embrace and greet each other. After trading pleasantries, I introduced Suzanne to her. As our turn to meet with Mr. Lambert arrived, I instructed Suzanne to meet with him before me.

As soon as I entered his office, he got up and said, "Shadow, welcome to your summer home!" After we had greeted each other, he informed me that he was encouraged that most of his dedicated staff had returned. Not long after, Tiffany entered. She finalized my new contract. She asked me about my accommodation preferences. I informed her that I would prefer to remain on the second floor of the Rotunda, but I would like to share a room for the '68 summer. Without any hesitation, we walked up the stairs to the second floor of the Rotunda. It was busy in the corridors. Tiffany led me to the double-occupancy room at the end of the south wing of the Rotunda. I loved her selection. The window in the room opened unto the roof of the first floor gallery. Also the branches of one of the oak trees rested on the roof. The branches could serve either as a lover's nest or an escape route. After thanking Tiffany for her thoughtful choice, I unpacked and went to sleep on the bed nearest to the window.

When I had awoken, my roommate had not checked into our room. After a quick shower, I got dressed and visited my friends in the kitchen. Most of my friends and acquaintances had returned. I renewed our trust and friendship for the summer of '68. Lorenzo, the executive chef, and my reliable friend from last summer, told me that it was dinner time. The staff dining room was alive with sounds of voices renewing old friendships and creating new ones. Then I saw Suzanne. She had already cultivated a cell of friends. She signaled me to join her at her dinner table. A few of her new friends were my old friends. After dinner, Suzanne told me that she had settled with her roommate in a room on the third floor of the East lodge. I informed her of my double room located on the second floor of the Rotunda. She wanted to see it, and I obliged. We returned to the Tea House to listen to the Juke box music. Most of the staff had gathered there to relax and talk. The women were beautiful and the young men were physically fit and handsome.

When I started to yawn, I bid farewell to my friends and went to my room. My roommate had arrived and was lying in his bed reading. On my entry, he got out of bed, shook my hand and finally embraced me. He introduced himself as Eli. I told him that my name was Awadh. He was not much taller than me. But he was handsome, humorous and well-spoken. He had just completed his first year at Osgoode Law School at York University.

During our conversation I learned that we would be working in the Round Room bar and the Indian Head Dining Room and Marine Dining Rooms in the Samara building. Then Eli inquired about the meeting with the maitre'd and the sommelier. I informed him that it would be held in the Round Room at ten o'clock. After that clarification we went to bed.

At the meeting the next day, I was most excited to learn that my responsibilities were the same as the summer of '67. By the conclusion of the meeting, I learned that the hotel would officially open for business on the 10th June for the summer of '68. That date meant that the staff had to work around the clock to ensure that all facilities and services were at optimum operation for the arrival of our guests. Unfortunately, the assassination of Senator Robert Kennedy on Wednesday, June 5th, greatly affected the mood of the Bigwin Staff. But with courage and determination all preparations were successfully completed in time to welcome the guests. Some of the American guests and Canadian guests were emotionally upset about the assassination. Many conspiracy theories surrounding the assassination were disseminated and discussed throughout the buildings on the Bigwin Island. In the privacy of our room, Eli informed me that he had learned that Senator Robert Kennedy was assassinated because of his support for Israel in the six-day Arab-Israeli war in 1967. Not being familiar with the details of the six-day war, I encouraged him to enlighten me. After Eli had given me only a sliver of the history of the war, I recalled and related the military comic relief show that had taken place in the Round Room at the end of June in 1967. It was a Saturday night when dozens of guests dressed as Arabs ran wildly into the Round Room, howling and brandishing life-size plastic rifles. As they were prancing around the dance floor, Luigi and his orchestra started to play "Hava Nagila". No sooner the Israeli folk song had caught everyone by surprise, a band of guests dressed as Israeli soldiers rushed into the Round Room waving their life-size plastic guns. They chased the Arabs around the room like little children on a school's playground. Both cohorts sang "Hava Nagila" as they ran around the centre post of the dance floor. That celebratory scene was greatly appreciated by the other guests as they enjoyed every moment of the show. Eli knew the folk song. He informed me that it was an Israeli folk song traditionally sung at Jewish weddings and bar/bat mitzvah. "What is the meaning of the song?" I inquired. Eli decided to impress me with his melodious voice and sang the entire song:

Hava Nagila (Let us rejoice, let us rejoice)
Hava nagila, hava nagila (Let us rejoice, Let us rejoice)
Hava nagila ve-nis'mecha (let us rejoice and be glad)
Hava neranena, hava naranea (Let us sing, let us sing)
Hava neranea venis'mecha (Let us sing and be glad)
Uru, uru achim (Awaken, awaken brethren)
Uru achim belev same'ach (Awaken brethren with a cheerful heart)

The morning arrived when the S.S. Bigwin ferry brought the first load of guests to the Bigwin shores. By mid-afternoon, hundreds of guests had already checked in. And the Bigwin Staff was executing their duties efficiently and effectively. In order to serve the guests with peak performance, I continuously honed my bartending skills and increased my knowledge of the responsibilities of a sommelier.

Within two weeks of the opening of the hotel to the public, Mr. Lambert asked me to meet him in his office. Being concerned, I decided to consult with my mentor, Tiffany, before I attended the meeting. I informed her about the meeting. She confided that there were a group of investors who have decided to invest large sums of money to improve not only the image of the hotel but also its accessibility. Mr. Lambert might want either to enlighten you about the investors' plans or about new responsibilities that he might want to harness on you. She advised me to listen carefully and analyse his information before making any commitments.

After thanking her for her words of wisdom, I went to the meeting. He welcomed me and told me to have a seat in front of his desk.

"Shadow, last August you informed me about the first Caribbean Carnival Celebrations in Toronto. Being unfamiliar with the concept of a Caribbean Carnival, you enlightened me about the origin and evolution of the celebrations in Trinidad and Tobago. Then you advised me to hire one of the calypso bands in Toronto to perform for our guests on one of the Saturday evening dinner and dance party. I listened and heard your message loud and clear. But I did not think that our North American guests and visitors were ready for Caribbean culture. However, after I had witnessed and experienced the magical influence Harry Belafonte's calypsos had on the tourists in Barbados, I have seriously re-considered your recommendation. I have hired Dick Smith to perform at the Bigwin Island Hotel in July this summer. You had also suggested that the Fireplace Lounge bar in the Rotunda should be converted into a discotheque. If this was done professionally and tastefully, it would be a magnet for fun-seeking guests from other resorts around the Lake of Bays, and the fun-loving cottagers and residents of the region of Muskoka." Then he paused to have a drink of water. Being surprised that he had remembered my suggestions and had decided to take some action greatly boosted my confidence and my mood. Since he had alluded to my discotheque idea, I felt that he would adopt it. Mr. Lambert continued. He informed me that he would like me to operate the discotheque as soon as the redesigning of the Fireplace Lounge had completed with the most modern sound system, and New York style lighting arrangements. Being overly excited and pleased with the encouraging news, I thanked him for entrusting me with the operation of the first discotheque in a Muskoka hotel.

After the meeting, I went directly to Tiffany. I then narrated the fantastic news that I had received from Mr. Lambert, she was extremely happy that a new dimension was added to my already interesting and fulfilling responsibilities. In her excitement, she inquired whether Mr. Lambert had divulged any other important information about the improvements the new investors had planned for the property. In my glee, I questioned, "What other important improvements will be taking place Tiffany?" Before responding to my question, she said we should get a coffee or milkshake in the Tea House. After we had ordered and got our drinks, we walked to the front gallery of the Rotunda which overlooked the beaches on the Lake of Bays. As we sipped our drinks she revealed that the new investors have decided to construct two swimming pools in the front lawn of the Rotunda. There would be a larger pool for the adults, with a built-in-bar, and a smaller pool for the children. The construction of a landing airstrip on the island for small aircrafts had already commenced. Several of the fairways of the golf course would be re-designed, and the greens would be re-sodded with more exotic grass. The stables would be renovated and there would be an increase in the number of horses, and the Boathouse and many other structures would be refurbished. Her positive information made me feel confident that the summer of '68 at Bigwin would be more exciting, more interesting and more fulfilling than the summer of '67. I returned to my room and related the good news to Eli. After congratulating me on my added responsibilities, he volunteered to assist me, with the music selections for the discotheque. Eli had brought with him his expensive stereo sound system. He also had a large collection of records and albums of the greatest rock and roll hits of the 60s in the room. He was not the only one who had brought their stereo equipment and their record collections. There were music lovers in every room on the second floor of the Rotunda. I was fortunate to be surrounded by young male and female adults who had interests in a wide range of music genres-Classical, Jazz, Rock & Roll, Latin–American, and many other exotic music genres.

It did not take much time to re-model the Fireplace Lounge Bar into a modern discotheque. It was located at the left back corner of the main floor of the Rotunda. However, it was directly beneath our bedroom on the second floor. When the other staff members learned about the story about the discotheque they inundated me with a wide range of suggestions. Lorraine, the hostess in the Main dining room had a few excellent ideas on how to use the proposed discotheque efficiently and effectively. She was studying business management at the University of Western Ontario in London. Lorraine suggested that the discotheque should only be operated three days a week. Then she suggested other potential activities for the other four days.

I thanked her for her suggestions and promised to inform her about Mr. Lambert's responses to her ideas.

After I had presented and discussed Lorraine's suggestions with Mr. Lambert, he decided to adopt them. Immediately, fliers, advertising the opening night of the discotheque and the proposed programs, were designed and printed. Within a few days, the fliers were delivered to the holiday resorts in the area, the cottagers, and residents of Lake of Bays. Elated, I met Lorraine in the main dining room. I told her that Mr. Lambert had accepted her proposals and have decided to implement them without delay. She was extremely pleased with the news.

On the first Thursday of July'68, the discotheque was formally opened. Only customers, twenty-one years and over were admitted. A strict dress code was in effect. The bouncers were given discretionary powers as to what was acceptable. Also each customer had to pay a cover charge. The two bouncers were responsible for screening the clients and admitted an equitable number of males and females into the disco room. In the bar, the cashier took the liquor orders and payments. Serge and I filled the drink orders. One of the female dining room servers volunteered to look after the dirty glasses and other incidentals. Mr. Lambert welcomed the customers as they entered. They were greeted by the Doors rendition of "Come on baby light my fire". Jim Morrison's haunting rhythmic tune was the first selection on the opening night of the disco. The sound system acoustics were pure delight for the auditory senses of the customers. The rotating silver globe at one corner of the room had a psychedelic effect on the dancers. The spectrum of coloured lights, synchronized with the frequencies of the music, danced continuously on the white corrugated satin curtains at the back mirrored-wall of the disco room. Another set of flashing coloured lights reflected on the other partially mirrored walls of the room. This ambience created a dynamic romantic setting for rock and roll music lovers. As soon as all the seats in the disco room were occupied, Mr. Lambert came to me and said, "Shadow please remind the customers that there would be a hamburger service offered on the back porch. And that it would be in operation from ten o'clock to twelve o'clock. I'll talk with you tomorrow about the results of the first disco night at Bigwin." Before I could respond he left. Immediately, I told Eli, the resident DJ to inform the customers about our food services.

The disco scenario was pure human energy in motion. The loud rhythm of the rock and roll musical hits of the '60s had mesmerized not only the dancers but also the onlookers. Eli was feeding the dancers and the listeners the top hits of: Steppenwolf, Bob Dillon, Joe Cocker, Herb Alpert and the Tijuana Brass, Marvin Gaye, Gary Puckett & the Union Gap, Elvis Presley, The Beatles, The Mamas and The Papas, The Young Rascals, The Fifth Dimension, The Rolling Stones, Jimmy Hendrix, and the best hits from 1960 to 1968. Eli also took personal requests from the dancers and listeners. The disco floor was crowded and alive with gyrating bodies. In the dim lighting, softcore porno was happening. The scene reminded me of a night club that I had visited only once with my girlfriend in Port –of- Spain, Trinidad. The night club was called the "Crab Hole". The dancers did anything sexually imaginable while dancing to the romantic selections of "Silver Strings" and "Esquires" orchestras of Trinidad, in the solid darkness. Those who did not gain admission to the disco room danced in the immense lounge of the Rotunda. They bought and brought their alcoholic beverages from the Round Room Bar. Regardless of the time, as soon as one customer left, another paying guest entered. There was a steady flow between the Rotunda lounge and the disco room. Two of us were preparing the cocktails and we were hard pressed to fill the orders but, with the patience of the customers, we managed to satisfy each one. None of the customers complained about the exorbitant prices of the drinks, since they were having a rollicking euphoric time and price did not matter. The love hormones were in full circulation in the hot perspiring bodies of the funlovers. As the alcohol consumption increased among the female and male dancers, they became less inhibited in their wild behaviour. There was much wooing taking place both on the disco dance floor and on many of the side-tables in the dim but provocative light. The young- at- heart clients were extremely cool and cooperative. There were no overt obscenities and fighting but, mind and mood altering drugs were in usage in the disco room. The first night was extremely successful. At one o'clock in the morning, the bar service was terminated, but Eli patronised the late comers with a few more selections. By two o'clock, Serge and I, with the help of the bouncers, had cleaned the disco room. The Fireplace Discotheque was ready for the Friday patrons. After locking up, we went upstairs to our room. Exhausted from the unexpected demand for bar-service and the loud vibrating music, I quickly fell asleep. Eli did likewise.

On the following day after breakfast I met Tiffany on the front steps of the Rotunda. Wearing a big charming smile, she hugged me and said, "Awadh! The rumour at the breakfast table in the Marine Dining Room was the disco was a fantastic hit. The guests loved the musical selections, the ambience, the younger crowd, the food and the bar services."

After I had heard Tiffany's report, I went to Mr. Lambert office. I re-iterated Tiffany's comments. After congratulating me on the successful opening of the discotheque, he inquired whether I would need additional support in the bar and with the music. I told him that I had already had a few "music gurus" assisting me with the musical selections. However, I suggested that a temporary bar should be located next to the hamburger station for the guests who could not get in the discotheque. He assured me that he would make the necessary arrangements for a temporary bar. Again, I thanked him for the opportunity to be responsible for the operation of the first discotheque in Muskoka hotel. As soon as I left Mr. Lambert's office, I saw Lorraine. She was rather romantic; she hugged me and kissed me. "Awadh, you have done me a great favour by presenting my ideas and having them accepted by the president of the hotel. Now I have concrete great evidence that I will be a successful business manager." Our casual platonic relationship gradually morphed into a summer love affair. She was a caring and intelligent human being. I returned to my room to relax and to reflect on the discotheque experience and my new relationship with Lorraine. Eli was in his bed reading. As soon as I had entered, he stopped reading. He got out of bed, and declared that the discotheque would be the main attraction at the hotel for the summer of '68. I had to remind him that it was only our first night of business. He smiled, and said, "I know success when I see it. And I have seen it." Extremely tired, I went to bed. Eli continued with his reading.

Friday night at the disco, a new wave of beautiful faces flowed onto the dance floor. Eli cranked up the music a few more decibels. I found it difficult to hear the customers at the bar. Then the familiar scent of cigarette smoke slowly permeated the room. Immediately, I instructed the bouncers to keep the front doors open. Eli had a wonderful musical selection that kept the dance floor vibrating continuously. The rhythm made Serge and me dancing bartenders for the night. We were having a fantastic time humming and bouncing around behind the bar. Everyone was in a loving mood. It was another successful night. On the Saturday night, the entire discotheque and the Rotunda lounge were crowded with happy dancing and either inebriated or stoned customers. People of all ages were mingling, dancing, and romancing, not only in the discotheque but anywhere the sounds of the disco music travelled. Mr. Lambert and I agreed that the discotheque would operate only on Thursdays, Fridays and Saturdays. On Sundays, the Austrian pianist, Hans, entertained the guests in the Rotunda lounge. Other bartenders and servers supplied the cultured listening audience at the piano recital with cocktails prepared in the discotheque bar. Bar tabs were settled either with cash or charged to the guests' rooms. Although it was summer the beautifully designed fireplaces were lit. The combination of the melodious classical music from the piano and the sound and scent of the crackling fires created a heavenly ambience for the high society crowd.

On Mondays, Tuesdays and Wednesdays, after the early piano

recitals, the discotheque was used to host either an evening of smooth jazz, easy listening or Latin music. The social hostess for the Rotunda, Elaine, selected the music with the assistance of different members of the staff who had special interests in such music.

Elaine engaged both male and female members of the staff to play the music on the discotheque sound system. Only the coloured lights that were synchronized with the frequencies of the music were used on those evenings. Elaine invited me to be the bartender on the Latin evenings. I thoroughly enjoyed those special evenings, admiring and appreciation the dancing talents of the guests.

The countercultural revolution that had started in San Francisco in July 1967 only came ashore on Bigwin Island during the second week of operation of the Bigwin discotheque. Before the introduction of the Bigwin discotheque, Bigwin Island Hotel was renowned for the big band sounds and the dancing music of the Round Room Orchestra. It had catered to the more mature and sophisticated wealthy guests, cottagers and the fun-loving wealthy businessmen and women. The marvellous and wonderful experiences that the paying and non-paying customers had had during the first week at the Bigwin discotheque were quickly communicated to their families, friends and acquaintances. Although the Bigwin discotheque opened for business at 9:00 p.m. the island was unusually crowded before opening time. The demographics of the newcomers were significantly different from those who had patronised the discotheque. The "flower child" generation had landed on Bigwin Island. I felt privileged to be serving those beautiful and fun-loving people. As I made my way to the front door of the disco room, proudly wearing my red Bigwin jacket, I greatly envied them. It was definitely surrealistic to be in the midst of a live hippy gathering. As I scanned the crowd waiting impatiently in the din of their own conversations for the doors to open, I observed some of them had beautifully designed headbands in a spectrum of technicolour. Some had painted the peace symbols on their cheeks, others had flowers in their hair and some had painted flowers on the cheeks on other parts of their bodies. They wore clothes that had every imaginable colour and pattern. The bell-bottoms were in vogue. With those vivid images, I entered the discotheque accompanied by the other support staff. Eli opened the dancing with the hit tune, "If you're going to San Francisco...".The lyrics of the song was written by John Philips from "The Mamas and The Papas" and sung by Scott McKenzie. It was a light and sound show that I would never forget. What a spectacular experience to witness a disco room crowded with the hippies singing and dancing to the lyrics of "San Francisco" while they were toking marijuana. Although I was not dressed like a flower child, I was a part of them in spirit. When The Mamas and The Papas sang "California Dreamin'", it was a heart-throbbing experience for me. Behind the bar, Serge and I danced and sang along with the ecstatic and free-loving hippies while mixing drinks. Later in the night, most of them were stoned. Then, Frank Sinatra's rendition of "Strangers in the night exchanging glances ..." triggered a wild love-in. Finally the DJ closed the celebrations with "Born to be Wild" by Steppenwolf. What a night! The second weekend at the disco was the most memorable and most exciting for me.

After the second disco weekend, two policemen arrived by boat on the island. They inquired about the smoking of marijuana in the discotheque. Receiving no positive feedback from the staff, the police paid unexpected visits to Bigwin Island.

On the third weekend, there were fewer hippies at the disco. From my observations, the customers, regardless of age and looking for fun, romance and companionship, fulfilled their needs.

During the fourth weekend, a fight occurred between two men. According to the rumour that quickly travelled through the room, the wife of one of the combatants was sexually harassed by the other man, while she was on her way to the ladies room. On her return, she reported the incident to her husband. After she had pointed out the culprit to her husband, the fight ensued in the middle of the dance floor. The bouncers quickly intervened. After a little struggle, they stopped the fight, and ejected the offender. At the end of the fourth week of operating the discotheque, I realised that the loudness of the music, the flashing strobe lights, the second-hand marijuana smoke and the late hours had greatly affected my health and my wellbeing. I discussed my wellbeing with Lorraine. She advised me to inform Mr. Lambert. I took her caring advice. After I met with Mr. Lambert and discussed my issues with the operation of the discotheque, he was most understanding and cooperative, and asked if I had a reliable replacement. I informed him that I have spoken with Serge about my health issues, and he said he would be would be happy to be manager of the discotheque if it was offered. At the end of July of '68, I resumed duties on the Sundeck, the Round Room, and the Indian Head dining Room and Marine Dining Room.

When rain was not in the weather forecast for the Lake of Bays, the kitchen staff during the lunch hours would barbecue hamburgers and hot dogs on the Sundeck for the guests, cottagers and visitors. More often than not, the Sundeck would be crowded. The bar servers were busy taking cocktail orders. Peter, Mike and Elaine would prepare the cocktails on the order slips. Those customers who did not enjoy the hot sun retreated to the cooler and quieter Round Room. Luigi and his talented orchestra did not perform during the lunches. However, Luigi would dance around on the Sundeck playing the favourite love tunes of the time on his accordion. "Cuando Calienta el sol" and "Al-Di –La" were the tunes most requested. The Italian maestro, not only played melodiously his accordion, but also charmed the customers with his lilting Italian rendition of the Italian songs.

Sometimes, when it was not too busy, I would serve the customers who were seated in the Round Room. On one occasion, I had the privilege to serve a gorgeous young woman who was having lunch and cocktails with a female companion. I observed that she had charged the total bill to her room. But she had signed it with her first name and the last name of one of the prominent business men who was a regular guest at the hotel. The businessman, in question, had a line of credit with the hotel. I knew him and his family. Since the summer of '67, I have served wines to him, his family and his friends in the Indian Head Dining Room, but I had not seen that stunning woman at his table at any time. Realizing that I had to be discreet about this discovery, I did not mention my findings to anyone. I decided to wait until he was in the hotel.

Much to my surprise, at the end of the week, I encountered him seated on the Sundeck alone. He was looking at the calm waters of the lake and relaxing with a double martini. With a smile, I told him that a few days ago I had served one of his beautiful daughters, cocktails at lunch. At first, he displayed a blank look. Then he exclaimed, "My daughter!" After I had given him the name she had written on the bill, he gulped down his martini and stood up. Then he placed his right arm on my shoulder and he told me that the information that I had given him must not be divulged to anyone. I kept silent. After a pause, he advised that I should continue to serve her whatever she wanted to eat and drink, but I must never tell her that I had spoken to her father. No one should know about her. He said his family would later be joining him for dinner in the Indian Head Dining Room. He instructed me to keep the young woman far away from his family table.

At dinner time, I followed his instruction and seated her in the Marine Dining Room on a table for two. Soon she was joined by another female friend.

Although the business man had solicited my secrecy, I needed to understand the nature of his relationship with the young gorgeous woman. Was she the love child from an extra-marital affair, I mused.

I decided to discretely consult with my McMaster University

friend, Suzanne. After lunch on the following day, I went in search of Suzanne in the dining rooms. One of the servers informed me that she had the day off. I went to her room and the door was closed, but there was a key in the lock. I knocked on the door there was no response.

I called Suzanne's name and I got no answer. I then called her roommate's name, Sharon and still no answer. I turned the door knob and pushed open the door. Sharon and her male companion looked at me startled from under covers in the bed. I apologised, threw the key on the bed, closed the door and left. I returned to my room and rested for my evening shift. Later that evening Sharon met me at dinner and whispered in my ear, "Shadow I owe you one." I smiled and softly said, "I will wait for your call."

It was not until the following morning that I connected with Suzanne. "Awadh, what do you want to talk to me about?" Since she was not on duty, I asked her to accompany me to my room. Eli was at work. She sat on his bed while I narrated the story about the beautiful young blonde and the middle-aged businessman. First, I mentioned the name the young woman had signed on the bill. She responded that the name did not ring a bell. Since Suzanne could not help and in order to protect the anonymity of both the businessman and the young beauty I decided to discontinue my private investigation.

A couple of days later, Suzanne met me in my room and told me that she had met one of her friends from McMaster University, and she would like to introduce her to me. "What a small world we live in!" She remarked. In the 60s the term "Six degrees of separation" was not coined as yet. Being curious, I accepted her offer. At dinner in the Marine Dining Room, Suzanne led me to the table where her friend was seated. As I approached the table, I realized that I had served these two charming women several times within the past few days. Both of them smiled when they saw me, and requested the wine list. Suzanne interjected and introduced her friend. The name she gave me was different from the name on the bills that she had signed for me. I smiled and acknowledged the introductions. At the conclusion of dinner services, Suzanne wanted to know the reason for my puzzled look after she had introduced her friend, Anita. I did not comment. And I returned to the Round Room for the late night shift.

On the following day, Suzanne met me at breakfast. She sought a reason for not responding to her question last night. Discreetly, I advised her to wait. She wanted to know my reason for the waiting period. I informed her that it was a delicate and sensitive issue, and that we have to be alone. In the privacy of my room, I enlightened her that her friend, Anita, was the woman in the story that I had narrated to her a few days ago. "Are you absolutely sure?" She questioned. "Yes. I am not mistaken." We remained in deep silence for a few minutes. Then she spoke "Now I know the reason for her elegant lifestyle at university. Anita is a sugar babe!" I dared not make any comment.

With the assistance of the bar staff and the dining room staff, a wine and cheese party was organized. It was planned to take place in the lookout tower in the forest. Lorraine and her planning team collected the required funds from the interested staff and bought all that was needed to host a wonderful and successful wine and cheese party. The news of the party was divulged to two young couples who were on their honeymoon, who wished to be invited to the party. After obtaining clearance from Mr. Lambert, Lorraine accepted their fees, and welcomed them to the final wine and cheese for the summer of '68. On the evening of the party, the young honeymooners brought vintage wine and gourmet cheese to share with the staff. The wives brought a supply of marijuana. This was a hippy like party. The Boathouse guys brought their latest 'flower child' music and their hippy friends from the mainland.

Towards the end of the party, most of the people at the party were either drunk on wine or stoned on marijuana. The love-in participants were spent. A few minutes after midnight, one of the husbands of the married couple vomited. He was extremely drunk. If there was a law against drunk walking in the forest, he would not be allowed to leave the tower. Although the other husband was also quite drunk, he was not vomiting. Their wives were high on marijuana. A few of the Bigwin male staff who still had their senses decided to take the honeymoon couples back to their hotel rooms. One of the wives resisted. She wanted to stay with the staff and continue to party. She stayed, despite her husband's protestations. At the end of the party, one of the guys volunteered to take her back to her room. She willingly agreed. After she had left with one of the staff from the Boathouse, Lorraine and I went to our respective rooms.

The next morning, I learned from one of the bellhops who lived in the Boathouse that one of the husbands on honeymoon was inquiring at the front desk about his wife. Allegedly, one of the Boathouse guys had taken her to his room. The front desk manager had no information about the missing wife. Being extremely distraught, the husband and the other couple went back to the tower in search of her. The bellhop told me that he immediately phoned the Boathouse and informed his roommate. While the search party was on their way to the tower, the wife, having sobered and thinking clearly returned to her room. She cleaned up, got dressed and went in search of her husband and the other couple.

At dinner, it was rumoured that the lost wife was so high on marijuana that on her way down from the tower, she fell into the bushes and slept there until morning. Her husband seemed to be happy with her alibi. There were so many versions of the alibi entertaining the guests, but the errant wife knew what dark secrets lurked in her conscience.

It was the day after Labour Day in 1968, when my second summer employment at Bigwin Island Hotel ended. Lorraine and I spent the last night making love and having sex. She promised to keep in touch with me on her return to university. We exchanged telephone numbers and home addresses.

I had an interview with Mr. Lambert in his office the next day. Since it was the conclusion of my second summer at the hotel with Mr. Lambert as my employer, with cautious interest, I inquired about the success of the business. Mildly surprised at my frank question, he removed his pipe from his mouth. He looked at me with a smile and said, "Shadow I'm pleased that you are interested in the performance of the business. So far no staff member has inquired about the state of the Bigwin Island Hotel economic health." I was most encouraged by his response. I learned that there was an increase in the business revenues since he became President of the Baysville Limited and Bayswin Limited Investment conglomerate in June 1967. He informed me that the guests, the cottagers and the visitors were greatly satisfied with the services of his eclectic selection of staff, the wide range of novel activities for both adults and children, and the introduction of the first discotheque in a Muskoka hotel. They also greatly appreciated the manner in which the dance evenings at the disco were structured. He added a note of cautious optimism, and said that Tiffany, the accountant, would have the balance sheet completed in a few weeks. But he did not know whether the resort would be in operation next summer. He took my new contact information and promised to keep in touch. We bade each other farewell and hoped for the best.

Then I went to say goodbye to Tiffany. I told her that I would like to keep in contact with her. We exchanged our information, hugged and I then departed for the S.S. Bigwin. Lorraine and I took the ferry to Norway point. At Norway point, the taxi that I had requested drove us to the Huntsville train station. Lorraine and I travelled together to Toronto. At union Station we went our separate ways.

On my arrival at my new home in Hamilton, my new house mates cordially welcomed me. After I had a shower and was about to take a nap, one of my house mates, Ruddy, invited me to have dinner with him. Doug, Omar and Richard joined us with their dinners, and shared their dinners with me. We exchanged information about our studies and country of origin. They wanted to know where I had spent the summer. I told them that I was too tired to narrate my story, but I promised to give them a full account of my summer at a later date. I thanked them for their hospitality and generosity. After dinner, I excused myself and went to bed.

The following morning, I purchased some groceries. On the Monday, I went to the bank, and then to the registrar office at the university to enrol in my courses, that would commence in two weeks. With that knowledge, I decided to make a visit to my family and friends in Trinidad. I did not inform anyone in Trinidad that I would be visiting. Without any delay, I went to the travel agent on Main Street and bought a return airline ticket. On my return to the new home on Broadway, I informed my house mates about my decision to visit my parents. They promised to protect my belongings in my room. Omar volunteered to take me to the airport. Ruddy pledged to fetch me on my return from Trinidad.

On my arrival in Trinidad, I took a taxi destined for Montrose Junction. The taxi driver, instead of travelling on the fastest route to my destination had decided to take the milk-run route. I complained. He informed me that the fast route was closed for repairs. I did not buy his story. I sat quietly and enjoyed the tour of the country side. On my arrival, he asked for an exorbitant fare. Since I had no local currency, I told him to wait. No one expected to hear my voice as I shouted from the road, "Papa! Papa! Papa!" Papa appeared at the upstairs veranda. "Awadh! How did you get here?" "Papa, I need some money to pay the taxi." In the meantime my sisters and grandfather had gathered to welcome me home. Papa came downstairs and hugged me tightly. I told Papa that he had to pay the taxi driver. As soon as Papa approached the taxi, the driver immediately recognized Papa as a former taxi driver. They shook hands. Papa did not have to pay.

The family was pleased to see me. They asked many questions about my experiences in Canada. I answered all their questions over several days. The main focus of my Papa was my marital status. When he learned that I was not married, he was happy. Much to my surprise, he instructed that I should get married and take my bride with me to Canada. I had no plan to get married to anyone as yet. I told him that my first priority was to successfully complete my degree and find a job. Besides, I had no woman on my mind that I would want to marry.

Then he gave me the telephone number of one of the young women I used to court when I was teaching in Port of Spain. Rani was the young woman I had introduced to my parents before I had left to further my studies. The rest of my family wanted me to marry her. They loved her. I informed him that I had terminated my interest in Rani a few months after I had started my studies at McMaster. He asked me to explain. I told him that the harsh winter weather in Hamilton, daylight saving time, the intense demands of my course work, and my initiation to the Canadian lifestyle, dampened my spirits for corresponding with her. Also, I could not afford to make overseas telephone calls. My funds were limited.

Papa did not accept any of my excuses, and he commanded that I call Rani right away. Papa was serious about my marriage to Rani. Following my father's order, I phoned her. Not recognizing my voice, she asked me to identify myself. Playfully, I encouraged her to guess. She called out at least four different male names. But mine was not mentioned. Then I identified myself. "Where are you calling from?" I told her that I was visiting my family for the next ten days. And I would like to take her to the movies. She informed me that she already had a date for the movies. Although I was a bit disappointed, I thanked her for taking my call. Later, Papa inquired about her response. He was also disappointed.

On the following morning, Papa asked me to accompany him to Port of Spain to shop for the business. It was an opportunity to rekindle my memories of shopping with him when I was in the business. After we had completed the shopping, he asked me to walk with him on Frederick Street to observe the new sights and sounds of the capital city. When we were in front of one of the large shopping malls he suddenly stopped. Then he pointed to the upper floor of the office building across the road, and said, "Rani is working in that building. You go upstairs and take her for lunch. Find out about her future plans." Then he gave me money for lunch and left. Apprehensively, I walked up the concrete stairs to her office. I asked the woman at the counter for Rani. She went to the back office. Rani appeared. I could not believe that she had morphed into such a gorgeous, charming and beautiful young woman. She looked exotic, mysterious and classy. Without any hesitation, I invited her to lunch. She accepted. I asked her to decide where we should go for lunch.

At the 'Up and Down' restaurant, after we had ordered for our lunches, my eyes were totally fixed on her beauty and charming smile. My happiness hormones were exploding throughout my body. I felt absolutely in love with her. After I had posed a few personal questions, she informed me that she was neither married nor committed to anyone. But she would be going in two weeks to New York City to start a new job. After learning about her future plans, I gave her my Canadian home address, and encouraged her to write me after she had settled in her job in New York City. I returned to Canada with the expectations that she would write. After my return to Canada, I did not mention the renaissance of my love for Rani.

While socializing with my new house mates, I realized that

they had a wide range of interests and talents. The house was dubbed the 'International House of the Rising Sun' by the Japanese student who was one of the five students renting the basement rooms. Also there were five students living upstairs. In total the house on 96 Broadway Avenue accommodated ten students from different countries, who were studying a degree in different disciplines. The upstairs rooms were occupied by Ruddy from the Philippines, Richard from the United Kingdom, Doug from Yugoslavia, Omar from Lebanon and me from Trinidad and Tobago. The basement rooms accommodated Norman from Australia, Boris from the U.S.S.R., David from Japan, Peter from Hong Kong, and Denim from U.S.A. It was great to interact with so many different cultures. We shared our different food and drinks, listened to exotic music and stories. Also, I was greatly enlightened by the account of the history, geography, and politics of these various countries of my housemates.

Towards the end of October, the weather was still fine. Unexpectedly, I received a phone call from Lorraine. She invited me to spend a weekend with her family and her at their home in Dresden in Southern Ontario. My weekend with Lorraine and her family would prove to be extraordinarily enlightening. Her parents were most welcoming and hospitable, and were interested in my family background, my studies and my plans for the future. They were both university graduates. Her father worked for a legal firm in Chatham, and her mother was a history teacher in one of the schools. On learning that my grandparents had been indentured workers in Trinidad, after the abolition of slavery in Trinidad, her mother took the opportunity to educate me about the importance of the little town of Dresden in the abolition of slavery in the United States.

Although I had read "Uncle Tom's Cabin" in college, I had no idea of its significance until Lorraine's family had narrated the following stories. I learned that the author of the book, Harriet

Beecher Stowe had used the life story of a freed slave, Josiah Henson (1789-1883) who had lived in Dresden, Ontario, as the plot for her novel. The small town of Dresden had served as an important terminus of the Underground Railroad for slaves entering Ontario via overland and marine routes from the United States before and after the American Civil War.

Before the end of the weekend, Lorraine had taken me around the historical sites of the Dawn Settlement which was the site of one of the many Underground Railroads. Also I visited the cemetery of the Henson's family and Uncle Tom's wooden cabin. Before I left for the train, I thanked her family for accommodating, entertaining and educating me during my weekend stay. Lorraine drove me to the train station. We communicated intermittently for the rest of the academic year.

In November of 1968 Rani visited me in Hamilton to spend some private time with me. In addition, she wanted to witness and to experience the living conditions and lifestyles of university students. During her brief stay, we visited Niagara Falls, the City of Toronto and McMaster University. On her departure, she invited me to spend Christmas and New Year's with her in New York City. I was most excited to be with her in the Big Apple during the season to be jolly. After completing all my academic obligations, I informed my housemates about my plans for the Christmas holidays. In turn, they informed me about theirs. At the Hamilton bus terminal, I boarded the Greyhound bus for New York City. The bus had a difficult time driving on the snow-covered highways in the cold winter landscape.

At Grand Central Terminal in New York City, Rani greeted me. We had breakfast in a nearby restaurant. The city was crowded and noisy. Almost everyone was in a hurry. After a long subway ride, we arrived at the station where Rani usually alighted. We walked a few long blocks between large old buildings to the house where Rani lived. Her landlady, Miss Mapp, was most welcoming. After accepting her warm drink, she told me that she had decided that I could spend my holidays in one of her apartments at no cost. After thanking Miss Mapp for her consideration and generosity, Rani accompanied me to the apartment a few blocks away. It was not in the best of neighbourhoods, and the living facilities were not the best, but it was definitely acceptable for the price. Rani, with the help of her uncle and her friends, introduced me to many of the famous tourist attractions in New York City. Furthermore, we had many opportunities to spend quality private time together.

Then one night when I was asleep the unforeseen happened. Someone switched on the ceiling light. On awakening, I was accosted by a woman, "Who are you? What the fuck are you doing in my bed?" I was stunned. She was accompanied by a man, who stood at the doorway. I sat up in the bed and gave them the reasons for my presence in their rented apartment. In response, the woman became polite and looked at the man and said, "Lover, Miss Mapp had permitted this young man to stay in our room because she knows that we are always doing business in New Jersey and almost never use the apartment." They inquired about my departure date. Before leaving, they wished me a merry Christmas and a happy New Year.

On the following day, I reported to Rani and her landlady of my frightening experience. Miss Mapp laughed and made no comments. Rani and I were at Time Square to witness the 'Falling ball' which welcomed 1969. Before returning to Canada, I privately gave her my McMaster pin, which I affixed on her blouse.

Just before my third academic year ended, I received a phone call from Mr. Lambert. He inquired whether the Shadow would be interested to return for another summer at Bigwin. My positive response was pleasantly received. The immigration officer needed only my university transcript to issue me a letter of permission to work. At the same time he renewed my Student Visa. Surprisingly, he inquired whether I needed anything else. I told him that my girlfriend would like to immigrate to Canada. He became interested. After requesting more information, I informed him that she had an American green card and was working in New York City. Immediately, he excused himself. And he went to another desk and spoke with one of his colleagues. After a brief discussion, his colleague came over and introduced himself. Then he asked me to join him at his desk. After asking many questions about my finances and my girlfriend's motives for immigrating to Canada, he told me that it would be advantageous to get her in this office as soon as possible so that all her documents would be quickly processed.

I informed him that my girlfriend's name was Rani and she was presently visiting with me, and was waiting for me in the reception lobby. On meeting my girlfriend, he was most welcoming. After asking a few questions, she showed him her green card. Immediately the process for landed immigrant status commenced.

On my last day at the 'International House of the Rising Sun' I bid farewell to those present. Rani and I went to stay with my sister, Ushi, on Broadway Avenue in Toronto. At the end of May, I left for my summer job at Bigwin Island Hotel. Rani, having obtained her landed immigrant status within seven weeks and started to work at Simpson-Sears in downtown Toronto.

On my arrival at Norway Point, there were no familiar faces, but I did not hesitate to introduce myself to those who were waiting for transport across the Lake of Bays to the Bigwin Island. As soon as I had stepped ashore, a feeling of ecstasy and belonging instantly flowed through my mind, body and spirit. I was back for a third summer at Bigwin Island Hotel on the Lake of Bays, in Muskoka. What an exotic and enchanting privilege! Immediately I headed for Mr. Lambert's office, and waited in line behind the lovely, youthful and energetic new employees.

During my wait, I went in search of Tiffany. She welcomed me with a big hug and a kiss on each cheek. I reciprocated. She inquired about my studies, my marital status and my expectations for the summer. After answering her questions, she wanted to know whether I would want to live in the Rotunda again. I told her that I would prefer to live in the Boathouse. She questioned "Why do you prefer the Boathouse?" "Tiffany. I prefer to live in the Boathouse because it's cooler, quieter and far away from the loud discotheque. Also the smoke from the discotheque seeps through the floor boards to the bed rooms above." She smiled and assigned me a room with a good view of the lake.

Eventually, I entered the inner sanctum of Mr. Lambert. As soon as he saw me walking through the doorway, he got up from his leather high-back chair and exclaimed "Shadow! Welcome back to your summer resort." We embraced and exchanged a few pleasantries. Then he told me that he had some great encouraging information which he would share with me later." Are you staying in the Rotunda?" "No. Mr. Lambert. With the approval of Tiffany, I shall be living in the Boathouse for the summer." He did not comment. And I left for my room.

On the following day, while sitting on the docks in front of the Boathouse looking at the brilliant sunshine reflecting off the placid waters of the lake, clearly I heard the voice of Mr. Lambert. "Shadow I need to talk with you. Let's go to my boat." I accompanied him to his mahogany launch which was moored in one of the slips beneath the Pavilion. After we were seated in his boat, he asked my opinion of the boat. I told him that it was beautiful and well maintained. As soon as I mentioned the word maintained, he immediately snatched the opportunity to inform me that he would like me to take care of his boat for the summer of '69. Extremely surprised that he would trust me with his valuable toy, I was speechless for a moment. We sealed the agreement with a handshake. He left me standing on the dock and drove away for a business meeting with the management at Port Cunnington Resort.

After his departure, I went to the kitchen to renew my friendship with Lorenzo, the executive chef. With the exception of a few, the rest of the culinary team were replacements. From Lorenzo I learned that the business was sold. And that Bigwin Island Hotel was owned by a new group of businessmen. I wondered why Mr. Lambert did not mention the new owners to me. Being puzzled, I went to Tiffany's office. I apologized for my rude interruption of her daily programme. She kindly welcomed me and inquired about the urgency of my call. After relating the story that I had heard from Lorenzo, she put down her pen and closed the files that she was working on.

"Awadh the news that Lorenzo gave you is true."

"What happened? And who are the new investors Tiffany?"

Tiffany opened a drawer and took out a file which she used as the source for the following information that she shared confidentially with me. She informed me that at the end of September 1968, after she had done the accounting for the 1968 summer season, she had discovered that revenues collected from all sources were less than the capital expenditures for the same period. The huge financial shortfall disappointed the owners of the Baysville Investment Limited and Baywin investments Limited. Due to the lack of sufficient available capital to continue the proposed renovations, it was decided to discontinue the operation of the hotel. Decisions were made to sell the buildings and its contents. However, the owners felt that the cottagers from around the Lake of Bays should be the first to learn about the sale of the property. And they should be given the first opportunity to purchase the resort. At that stage, Mr. Lambert resigned as president of the investment companies.

The suggested sale price was $200,000. It was hoped that a syndicate of cottagers would be interested in purchasing the resort. If they did, they could ensure the continued operation of

Bigwin for the residents of the lake of Bays, the Lake of Bays Association, and the lake of Bays Yacht Club. Since no one offered to purchase the resort, the ownership of Bigwin was transferred to Pontercove Realty. Finally Bigisle Enterprises Limited, a conglomerate, took possession of the Bigwin Island properties. The ambitious investors had decided to invest one million dollars to convert and promote Bigwin as a year-round vacation paradise. Within a short time the resort name was changed to "Bigwin Estates".

Completely amazed at the startling change of fortune of the "Bigwin Island Hotel" within such a short time, I hoped that the business would thrive, and be a financial success under the new management team. I thanked Tiffany for the insider information.

On my way to the Boathouse, I vividly recalled that I had met many of the new investors. I had served them and their families in the Indian Head Dining Room last summer. They were generous, respectful and friendly individuals. On a few occasions during the summer of '69, Aldo Lorenzetti, on his return trip to his business, had driven me to Toronto where I visited my sister and girlfriend. With those positive and kind experiences with Mr. Lorenzetti, I eagerly looked forward to working with the new investors. It was during one of those visits in early July, I engaged Rani in the presence of my sister. I promised Rani at that time, we would get married before the end of the year.

On the following weekend, the hotel was officially opened for the summer to the public. I was exposed to a completely different management style. There were not many familiar faces working with me. However, a new breed of customers invaded the resort. The landing airstrip was busy. Businessmen and businesswomen were flying in from Toronto for working luncheon meetings. The newly renovated waterfront was busy with float planes that brought Muskoka's wealthy cottagers to experience the culinary delights and the total ambience of the wilderness of the "Bigwin Estates". There were conventions from different provinces and from the neighbouring states. The summer of 1969 introduced me to a wide range of lifestyles that I had not experienced in either the summer of 1967 or the summer of 1968.

There was a convention of yacht clubs up from the United States. There were about sixty elderly men in attendance. They were having their dinner in the Marine Dining Room. However, the sailors had no female companions at their dining tables. Meanwhile, in the Indian Head Dining Room there were ten beautifully dressed gorgeous younger women having dinner seated at tables for two. At first my colleagues thought that they were partners, but as the evening passed, I noticed that the yacht men slowly made their way one by one to the various tables where the women were seated. And after a brief chat each yacht man escorted one of the women out of the dining room. Two days later, I learned that the yacht clubs had brought their own escort services!

After the departure of the convention, my friend at the concierge desk informed me that he had received phone calls from one of the local escort services. They complained about the American escorts at the hotel. After those complaints, two of the local escorts booked rooms in the hotel for the rest of the summer of 1969. They presented themselves in the most alluring outfits that would mesmerize any breathing man and maybe woman. I was certainly not surprised at the business they regularly contracted and conducted.

Over the summer there were a few customer complaints that had to be re solved either immediately by a staff member or by management. After providing personal service to guests for almost three summers at the Bigwin property, and working with a range of servers from different cultural backgrounds, I learned that servers have self-worth and self–respect. The paying customers should not consider them as mere servants. Your attitude to your server should dictate the quality of service you would receive. I can describe a few cases in which customers were extremely impolite to the servers. It was a busy crowded dining room. Most of the guests had already started eating. One of the diners started to scream at the waitress about the toughness of his steak and threw it on the floor. He ordered her to get him a different well done steak. I assisted the waitress in cleaning up the mess and took the steak to the chef. We related what had happened and the demands of the irate guest. The chef smiled. He took the steak that the guest had thrown on the floor. He threw the steak on the kitchen floor and jumped over it several times. He turned it over and jumped on it. Then he smeared it with some marinade and threw on the grill. The waitress returned the same steak with some fresh vegetables to the guest. After taking a few mouthful he smiled, and said, "That is what I call a well-done premium steak". At the end of the dinner, he personally congratulated the chef. Also, he tipped both the waitress and the chef. What you don't know may or may not hurt you, but always be courteous.

Towards the end of July 1969, room service was requested by a guest in the West Lodge. Since it was not too busy in the Round Room, I did not mind getting some fresh air. Also the tips are generally substantial. I knocked on the door. A female voice from in the room invited me to come in. I entered the room, and left the door open for my safety. But there was no one to receive or sign the bill. Before putting down the drinks on the table, I shouted, "Hello!" But there was no answer. Then the door was closed by a naked woman. She walked directly to me and told me to put down the drinks on the table. She requested that I make love to her. I was terrified by her advances and managed to escape her clutching and squeezing. I fought my way to the door and finally got away. That was the last time that I went on a room service mission.

Under the new management, business was booming as far as I was concerned. Then, Tiffany informed me that Mr. Lambert was no longer a part of the business. I did not make any inquiries about his departure. There were many rumours among the staff about Mr. Lambert's departure. In August 1969, I was bookended in the urinal by two members of the conglomerate. While we were busy relieving our bladders, one of them turned to me and said, "We have been looking at your performance for the past few weeks, and we think that you are the only one we can trust with our business." I remained silent. Then the other one turned to me and said, "We are having a meeting tomorrow at 10 o'clock in the morning in the first condominium in the East Lodge. A few of the investors will be there to talk with you." I thanked them for the information, and told them that I would be there. I didn't tell anyone at the Boathouse about the meeting. I had a sleepless night.

At the appointed time I was at the meeting. Coffee and muffins were served by gorgeous young ladies. I was informed that they would like me to take over the operation of the business for the rest of the year. They mentioned a salary and a condominium as part of the package they were offering. I told them that I would need some time to think about the offer. They expected an answer within forty eight hours. I slowly returned to my room rather confused. I rested on my bed until lunch time.

After lunch, I visited Tiffany. I told her about my meetings with the new owners in the washroom, and at the condominium. Then she said, "Awadh I do not want you to be disillusioned like Mr. Lambert. He had given his blood, sweat and tears to this resort since the days of Lobraico, and he left quietly. My advice is to work the evening shift. After breakfast tomorrow, take the ferry to Norway Point. And go home to your fiancé.

This business would not survive. You go back to university and complete your studies." She then advised me to write a letter stating my reasons for not accepting the offer and give it to her as soon as possible. She would then deliver it to the appropriate person after I had left the island. We hugged and bid each other farewell. I walked upstairs to pay my final visit to the rooms that I had occupied for the summers of 1967 and 1968. Then slowly, I looked around at the large lounge on the main floor. I had served innumerable guests during piano recitals and cocktail parties in the huge Rotunda Lounge. Tears forming in my eyes, I walked to the discotheque and bid it farewell. Finally, I took my last steps on the highly polished wooden floors of the Rotunda. I returned to my room in the Boathouse. To the few guys who were present, I related the new management's offer. They strongly advised that I should decline the offer because they did not believe in the new management. With that supportive negative feedback from my colleagues, I wrote the letter and asked my roommate to take it to Tiffany. Throughout the night, I tossed from side to side on my bed, recalling the wonderful and enlightening experiences I had at the resort. I felt like an adolescent who was going to run away from his controlling parents. On the following morning, after breakfast, stealthily, I took my belongings, and left with the S.S. Bigwin for Norway Point. I kept looking back at the beautiful landscape and the magnificent buildings as they gradually diminished in my view. Before I had alighted the S.S. Bigwin, my friend, the captain, reminded me that the successful completion my degree should be the paramount interest at that stage of my life and I should not rush into marriage.

Bigwin had been a paradise island for me. It was not only the place where I earned the funds necessary to complete my first degree, but also it was the place where I was given countless opportunities to live vicariously among the wealthy and famous visitors, cottagers and residents of Muskoka. Some of the elites that I had privileged opportunities to serve were the Bassetts, Blacks, Fords, Gardiners, Jarvises, Rogers, Neilsons, Taylors and the Westons.

I stood alone at the end of the dock, and waved to the captain as he was about to navigate the S.S. Bigwin back to the island. The boat sailed away slowly. I reflected on my first arrival. Three summers ago, I was standing at the same dock waiting anxiously for a boat to take me to Bigwin Island. And today, I watched the S.S. Bigwin leave me standing alone looking at the place that had given me a chance for a better future. I wondered whether I would ever return to Bigwin Island. While waiting for the Huntsville taxi I contemplated possible career pathways.

For many days after my unplanned departure from Bigwin, I reflected on my inner life and my colourful experiences not only in Canada but also in Trinidad. Since I had experienced the wonderful beauty and charm of education both as a student and a teacher, I look forward to a career that would allow me the flexibility to explore all possibilities for enrichment and advancement at my workplace. With the security of an excellent educational background, a responsible and respectable job, and my daring spirit, I look forward to an enriched future.

ACKNOWLEDGEMENTS

My first and everlasting gratitude is offered to the divine forces that were always presents during the writing process. I was inspired and energized to keep on recalling and writing my memoir from moment to moment.

My trustworthy colleagues, friends and associates were more than kind to volunteer their precious time and literary experience to read, analyse, interpret and evaluate the language, themes and characters of my unpolished draft. My sincerest appreciation is extended to: Kevin Aver, Catherine Abbott, Maria Bautista, Myra Brezden, Gary Hardcastle and David Poprocki.

After the final draft was partly edited by Howard Aster (Mosaic Press in Oakville), the final editing was diligently completed by the following writers and literary critics: Roy Harold, Carolyn Hilton, Sean Michael Kennedy, Bill Langdon, Susan McEwen and Sharon Wong.

Special thanks must be extended to John Siddall, the manager of the renovated Bigwin Inn facilities in the Lake of Bays, Muskoka. He provided me with important historical documents which made my Bigwin memories more vivid and fascinating. He advised me to get a copy of "Bigwin Inn" written by Douglas Mc Taggart and published by Boston Mills Press Book in 1992. The book was well written.

My sincerest gratitude is extended to Emma Hardcastle, a student at Abbey Park High School in Oakville. Emma's creative painting of the Marine Dining Room and the Indian Head Dining Room at Bigwin Inn, adorns the front cover.

I would be remiss to omit the congenial librarians in the public libraries in Baysville, Huntsville, Bracebridge, Gravenhurst, Oakville and Dresden, who were most informative and interested in my memoir.

Finally, I am indebted to Sharaz Hossein, who professionally formatted both the paperback and kindle manuscripts so that it would be published by Amazon.

DISCLAIMER

From Explorations to Enlightenment is a continuation of my memoir. It is a recollection of my ventures and adventures during the 1960s in Trinidad and Tobago and in Canada. All characters, institutions, locations are real but a few names were modified to maintain their anonymity. This was intentionally done to avoid litigation from them and from me. However, any resemblance of any actual person, either alive or deceased, is entirely coincidental.

REFERENCES

McTaggart, Douglas, 1992. Bigwin Inn.
A Boston Mills Press Book.

Awadh N. Jaggernath is a naturalized Canadian citizen. He came in 1966 from Trinidad and Tobago to further his studies at Mc Master University. He has studied, worked and is presently retired. In retrospect, Awadh spent almost four decades in education in various interesting, challenging and rewarding capacities.

He represented the East York Board of Education on the Learning Partnership, a Canadian charity that prepares students to thrive in a diverse, connected and changing world. While on the partnership, he designed a mathematics program which was accepted and implemented.

After his successful role as chairperson for professional development for metropolitan Toronto public secondary schools, he was placed on the Ontario Secondary School Teachers provincial professional development team. He was one of the teachers sent to the University of Oxford on a special project on "The Relevance of Students' Testing and Evaluation."

As master coach for the East York Collegiate Institute, the Reach for the Top team, four consecutive metropolitan Toronto championships and an Ontario championship were won; and was runner-up in the national championship when the world renowned Alex Trebek, host of TV show Jeopardy, was then the quiz master for Reach for the Top at CBC in Toronto.

Awadh N Jaggernath's revised edition of his first publication, "From Innocence to Impudence" is presently on Amazon in many formats.

Made in the USA
Middletown, DE
20 January 2020